Constitutional Rights

MYTHS AND REALITIES

CHRISTOPHER E. SMITH
Michigan State University

WADSWORTH
CENGAGE Learning·

Australia · Brazil · Japan · Korea · Mexico · Singapore · Spain · United Kingdom · United States

WADSWORTH
CENGAGE Learning™

Constitutional Rights: Myths and Realities
Christopher E. Smith

Criminal Justice Editor:
Sabra Horne

Editorial Assistant:
Paul Massicotte

Marketing Manager:
Dory Schaeffer

Marketing Assistant:
Allana Kelly

Advertising Project Manager:
Stacey Purviance

Project Manager, Editorial
Production: Emily Smith

Print/Media Buyer: Karen Hunt

Permission Editor: Sommy Ko

Production Service:
Shepherd, Inc.

Copy Editor: Jeanne Patterson

Compositor: Shepherd, Inc.

Cover Designer: Yvo Riezebos

Cover Image: © Massimo
Mastrorillo/CORBIS

For product information and
technology assistance, contact us at **Cengage Learning
Customer & Sales Support, 1-800-354-9706**

For permission to use material from this text or product,
submit all requests online at **cengage.com/permissions**
Further permissions questions can be emailed to
permissionrequest@cengage.com

Library of Congress Control Number: 2003096165

ISBN-13: 978-0-534-63965-5

ISBN-10: 0-534-63965-8

Wadsworth
10 Davis Drive
Belmont, CA 94002-3098
USA

Cengage Learning is a leading provider of customized learning solutions with office locations around the globe, including Singapore, the United Kingdom, Australia, Mexico, Brazil, and Japan. Locate your local office at: **international.cengage.com/region**

Cengage Learning products are represented in Canada by Nelson Education, Ltd.

For your course and learning solutions, visit
academic.cengage.com

Purchase any of our products at your local college store or at our preferred online store **www.ichapters.com**

Printed in the United States of America
2 3 4 5 6   13 12 11 10 09

ED344

Contents

Preface

Legal rights are important elements of Americans' beliefs about their society and governing system. When Americans feel treated unjustly, they are quick to say, "That violates my rights." In schools throughout the United States, children are taught that their country's governing system is special and praiseworthy because, unlike people in many other countries, Americans have protected rights, such as freedom of speech and religion. The U.S. government criticizes countries around the world for failing to protect citizens' rights. In sum, rights are a central element in Americans' conceptions about their country's core values and their beliefs about how other countries ought to operate as democracies.

The aim of this book is to help people understand the details of the legal protections purportedly provided for them by the Bill of Rights. Our laws are misunderstood, despite the centrality of rights to Americans' descriptions of their country and other countries that qualify for the admirable label of "democracy." The precise nature of rights is defined by decisions of judges, especially the nine judicial officers who serve on the U.S. Supreme Court. Few Americans recognize the ways in which the criminal justice system and other aspects of society operate to nullify the fulfillment of the rights promised by the Constitution. Some constitutional rights are ultimately merely symbolic because the words of the Bill of Rights and the judicial interpretations of those words are not effectively translated into genuine legal protections for individuals. This book attempts to look behind the words of the Constitution in order to shed light on the actual effectiveness, or lack thereof, of legal rights for individuals within the United States. As you will see, the book is structured to contrast common beliefs about constitutional protections with factors that may leave public expectations about rights unfulfilled. You will find several features to aid your exploration:

- "Conventional Wisdom" propositions, which examine commonly held beliefs about rights

- Summaries following an analysis of the "Conventional Wisdom" statements
- Bolded terms, which may be unfamiliar and are defined in the glossary

This text was written to be used in a wide range of criminal justice and political science courses, including introduction to criminal justice, introduction to political science, constitutional law, introduction to legal issues, philosophy of law, sociology of law, and those courses in which legal concepts are discussed. This is an important subject for both criminal justice professionals and regular citizens. People who work within the justice system cannot fully understand the extent of their authority and their potential impact on the lives of their fellow citizens unless they recognize the ways in which their decisions and actions determine whether the Constitution's principles are fulfilled. Citizens need to recognize the same factors so that they know when their rights are being infringed. They must be knowledgeable and aware in order to urge their elected officials, including state judges and prosecutors, to ensure that rights are protected in the operation of the governing system.

Because this book reveals what many people will regard as flaws in the justice system, it may be easy to misread the examples presented as conveying a pessimistic view about the possibilities for protecting Americans' constitutional rights. In fact, the book has a fundamentally optimistic outlook and purpose. One can only design and implement corrective measures for a flawed process after that process has been thoroughly examined and analyzed with a critical eye. The weaknesses in the criminal justice system and other aspects of American government must be recognized and clearly understood before efforts can be undertaken to remedy deficiencies. This is not to say that a perfect system is possible. The justice system and other aspects of government are inevitably flawed because they are run by human beings who necessarily rely on mistaken judgments and inadequate information in taking actions that affect the lives of their fellow citizens. However, improvements are possible when people fully recognize how the justice system actually operates and use that recognition to develop workable improvements. Reforms need not cure all of the system's ills in order to produce improvements. Instead, they may be as modest as the simple step of providing improved training for police officers, prosecutors, and judges or devoting additional resources to the provision of defense attorneys for indigent defendants. If Americans truly wish to treat constitutional rights as being as important in reality as they are in the pervasive patriotic rhetoric about liberty and democracy, then they cannot avoid taking a close look at how law and the justice system actually affect their lives and those of their fellow human beings.

This book is the product of what I learned from my formal coursework, many informal discussions, numerous collaborative writing projects, and nearly twenty years of interactions with my students in courses about the nature of constitutional rights. I am indebted to many friends, colleagues, teachers, and mentors. None of them share my precise viewpoints, and they bear no responsibility for my analysis or errors. I wish to acknowledge and express gratitude for the beneficial influence and contributions of: George F. Cole, University of Connecticut; Joyce A. Baugh, Central Michigan University; Thomas R. Hensley, Kent State University; David A. Schultz, Hamline University; Steven B. Dow, Michigan State University; Scott P. Johnson, Frostburg State University; Madhavi McCall, San Diego State University; Archibald Cox, Harvard University; Barry Matsumoto, University of Iowa; Abraham V. Hutt; Christopher S. Auguste; Donald R. Vereen Jr.; Wayne M. Conner; Pamela S. Horowitz; Melissa Fitzsimons Kean; Thao Tiedt; Julia Hale-Harbaugh; Rebecca L. Ford; Elizabeth S. Wilkerson; Keri Middleditch; the Hon. Richard Enslen; the Hon. James Carr; Kathy Miller; Jeffrey D. Peterson; Paul Hummer; Annette Carnegie; Linda Thurston; Kathryn Zoglin; Joyce Cunha; Tony Brutus; and Andrew Olal.

I am eternally grateful for the unwavering support and encouragement of my editors at Wadsworth, Sabra Horne and Shelley Murphy. I owe special recognition to Samuel Walker of the University of Nebraska because of the inspiration provided by both the form and substance of his books. My deepest debts are to my parents, Robert and Carol Smith, for their roles in shaping my understanding of constitutional rights, and to my wife Charlotte for our continuing conversations about the interactions of individuals with government and, more importantly, for her infinite patience. My children, Alicia and Eric, deserve medals for enduring not-always-welcome lecture-ish conversations about the importance of constitutional rights. Finally, as an expression of admiration and gratitude, this book is dedicated to my good friends among classmates in the Harvard College Class of 1980 who have directed their energy and professional skill to the protection of legal rights for individuals.

REVIEWERS

Morris Jenkins—University of Toledo
Charles Chastain—University of Arkansas Little Rock
Ron Server—Prairie View A&M
Tina Fryling—Mercyhurst College
Gayle Carper—University of Western Illinois
Brad Chilton—University of North Texas
Craig Hemmens—Boise State University

THE IMAGE OF RIGHTS

News stories about criminal justice regularly raise questions about the nature and effect of "rights."[1] Sometimes the existence of rights keeps guilty people from going to prison even though it is obvious that they have broken the law. In June 2001, for example, the U.S. Supreme Court announced its decision in a case called *Kyllo v. United States*. Federal law enforcement agents suspected that Mr. Kyllo was growing marijuana inside his home. From the outside, they scanned his house with a thermal-imaging device designed to detect where heat sources exist inside buildings. The device indicated that there were "hot spots" within the house, and the agents believed that these locations contained high-intensity lamps being used to grow marijuana plants. Relying on their findings from the thermal detector, the police obtained a search warrant, searched the house, and found marijuana growing there, just as they had suspected. In court, Mr. Kyllo challenged the agents' actions by claiming that they violated his rights when they examined his house from the outside with the thermal-imaging device. The U.S. Supreme Court agreed and said that the search conducted by the agents was invalid. Thus, without additional separate evidence to support the search, the marijuana would be excluded from evidence and Mr. Kyllo would avoid going to prison, despite the fact that everyone now knows that he violated federal drug laws by growing marijuana. Cases such as Mr. Kyllo's often lead critics of the criminal justice system to claim that criminals have *too many* rights and that the existence of these rights prevents police officers from fighting crime effectively.

By contrast, other news reports seem to support a different set of critics who claim that rights do not provide enough protections for people who come into contact with the criminal justice system. The existence of these examples does not imply that police officers and other officials are typically dishonest or prone to undertake abusive actions. All evidence indicates that the vast majority of police officers are dedicated public servants who make good-faith efforts to fulfill their duties properly. However, police officers, like

1

prosecutors, corrections officers, and other criminal justice officials, are fallible human beings. Every year evidence emerges about specific officials around the country who have acted inappropriately and violated the rights of people with whom they came into contact. In the short span of three months in 2001, for example, several prominent newspapers published the results of investigations of abusive actions by criminal justice officials. In May, the *Boston Globe* reported on the sexual abuse of female prisoners and beatings of male prisoners by corrections officers in Boston's Suffolk County House of Correction.[2] In June, the *Washington Post* reported that police officers in Maryland had extracted false murder confessions from a number of innocent suspects by questioning them in interrogation rooms for time periods of up to thirty-eight consecutive hours without permitting them to see their attorneys.[3] During the same month, the *New York Times* reported on a retired police detective in Brooklyn whose voluntary investigations of old cases had freed five innocent men from prison after they had served up to fourteen years for murders that they did not commit.[4] In July, the *Washington Post* revealed that officers from one Maryland police department had shot and killed many unarmed people who had committed no crime, yet the department always supported their actions in the shootings and did not punish them in any way.[5] The *New York Times* reported that there was a nationwide shortage of lawyers willing to handle appeals for death row prisoners, even though such appeals often demonstrate that there were serious errors in death penalty trials.[6] Thus many condemned prisoners faced a serious risk that they would be executed despite the existence of rights violations or new evidence of innocence in their cases.

What do these examples demonstrate about the nature and existence of rights in criminal justice? Although reasonable people may disagree about whether there are *too many* rights or *too few* protections for individuals, news stories demonstrate that the American criminal justice system regularly fails to fulfill its objective of investigating, prosecuting, and punishing lawbreakers while simultaneously ensuring that people's rights are protected.

Do you believe that there are too many rights for criminals? You might have already formed an opinion about that question. Alternatively, this may be a question that you find difficult to answer. Before clinging too strongly to any specific conclusions about that question, you may need to ask yourself how much you really know about the nature and effect of rights in criminal justice. Do Americans have all of the rights that they believe they should possess? Do existing rights protect individuals within the criminal justice system in the manner in which the public believes that they should? Are any rights so fundamental and enduring that we can count on them always being there for us, or can all of our rights change and disappear at a moment's notice? These are important questions that can affect people's views about the effectiveness of the criminal justice system and about the need (or lack thereof) for changes in the way that the system operates.

Constitutional rights concern more than Americans' perceptions about the legal protections to which they are entitled. Rights define the limits of governmental officials' authority and the extent of people's freedom. The United States claims to distinguish itself from countries that lack liberty by the fact that American governmental officials possess only limited power and authority over citizens. Citizens enjoy significant liberty to make their own choices and, in many ways, live their lives according to their own decisions without governmental interference. Rights also help to ensure the fairness of governmental processes, especially the criminal justice process that threatens to deprive individuals of their freedom and punish them for extended periods of time. Due process rights in the justice system are intended to protect the innocent against improper conviction and punishment, promote the equal and fair treatment of all people, and prevent governmental officials from employing abusive methods in their efforts to stop crime and punish lawbreakers. Constitutional rights play an essential role in making the United States a democratic country that pursues idealistic values of freedom and equality. When rights promised by the Constitution remain unfulfilled, the goals and values of a democratic nation suffer as a result.

The purpose of this book is to look closely at rights, especially those in the criminal justice process. One of the book's themes is that the actual definition of rights often differs from commonly held beliefs about the nature and effect of legal protections for individuals. Moreover, the book also illustrates how the existence of a right in the law does not necessarily mean that individuals enjoy the protection of that right when they are drawn into the criminal justice system. Thus, some rights can be "hollow" or "symbolic" and lacking in the strength and "substance" that are needed to actually affect the criminal justice process in their intended manner. In illustrating these themes, the book discusses both the definition of rights and the impact (or lack thereof) of those rights in the lives of individual human beings.

There is no simple division between rights that are symbolic and those that have substance. For all rights, the extent to which they are symbolic or substantive depends on two primary determining factors: first, whether the justices of the Supreme Court and judges on other courts interpret the words of the Constitution in ways that provide meaningful legal protections for individuals; and second, whether criminal justice officials fulfill their proper duties and respect individuals' legal protections in specific situations. The right to counsel, for example, is largely symbolic for a defendant who is represented by a disinterested or incompetent lawyer. By contrast, the right has substance for defendants whose appointed attorneys are conscientious and skilled. The analysis in this book illuminates the implementation of specific rights in the criminal justice process. Depending on how rights are defined, there may be varying opportunities for criminal justice officials to stretch their authority beyond the public's expectations as well as corresponding vulnerabilities for the legal protections described in judicial decisions. The first two chapters of this book discuss the nature of rights and how they are defined in the American legal system. Subsequent chapters examine the rights contained in specific provisions of the Constitution to illustrate the issues of symbolism and substance in the fulfillment of rights—or lack thereof—in the various stages of the criminal justice process. The discussions throughout the book make clear that rights by themselves do not automatically provide protection against improper actions by government officials. Instead, the knowledge, professionalism, and ethics of decision makers in criminal justice are especially important for turning the promise of legal rights into a reality for the human beings who are drawn into contact with the criminal justice system.

The book's themes are illuminated by examining popular beliefs about rights. These beliefs are characterized as propositions labeled "Conventional Wisdom" and then analyzed to determine whether they accurately reflect the reality of the nature and effect of rights. These propositions do not purport to represent the beliefs of all people in American society. However, you will recognize these statements as embodying widely shared beliefs and conclusions about what rights ought to exist under the American legal system and how these rights affect the criminal law process. As you encounter each proposition of "conventional wisdom," stop and think about whether you agree with the statement before reading the discussion of the topic.

THE LANGUAGE OF "RIGHTS"

Conventional Wisdom 1

Police officers have a right to conduct searches as a valid method of investigating crimes.

Imagine that you are a professor of criminal justice and a student approaches you after class with a question. "Hey, Professor, I need to know something. I was driving to campus when a police officer pulled me over for no reason. He claimed that I did not use my turn signal when changing lanes, but it wasn't true. He looked at my driver's license and then asked me if he could search my car. I was in a hurry to get to class so I said 'no.' I didn't have anything to hide; I was just in a hurry and I didn't have time to waste when I didn't do anything wrong. Even though I said 'no,' he searched the car anyway. Can he do that? Does he have a *right* to search my car without my permission, or did he violate *my rights* by conducting the search?"

Obviously, the student believes that the police officer acted improperly and thereby violated a right against searching a car without the driver's permission. Is the student correct? How would you answer the question?

More importantly, how would you go about finding an answer to the question? Where do you look to discover the nature and meaning of rights?

As indicated by the student's question, Americans tend to have firm beliefs about the existence and function of rights. They may not claim to know all of the details of legal rights, but they often react to perceived injustices by translating those perceptions into the language of "rights violations." In fact, however, the nature and function of rights often differ from many people's assumptions. Many Americans are surprised to learn that they do not possess the precise rights to which they believe they are entitled. Moreover, they are doubly surprised when they discover that even the legal rights to which they are entitled under the constitutional governing system do not necessarily provide the protections that people expect. One factor that complicates people's understanding of legal rights is the fact that people use the term *rights* in imprecise and inaccurate ways.

The student's choice of words reflects the fact that Americans are accustomed to talking about rights. However, the student's use of the word *right* confuses the concept with other concepts. In order to understand the nature and meaning of rights, it is useful to think precisely about when the term *right* is appropriate to use. For example, after describing the police officer's search despite the objections of the driver, the student asked: "Can he do that?" An honest, realistic answer to that question would be: "Sure. He did it, didn't he? So I guess that shows that he can." This response, albeit mildly obnoxious, reflects the reality that whether or not legal rights are supposed to exist, criminal justice officials have the ability to take actions based on their own discretionary decisions. When the student asked whether the officer had "a right" to conduct the search, the student was really inquiring about the officer's **authority.** In other words, was the officer authorized to conduct the search under the rules of law? Did the rules of law make it proper for the officer to conduct the search? The concept of **rights** in criminal justice, by contrast, actually concerns the legal protections possessed by individuals against improper actions by government officials. The police officer, who is the government official interacting with the individual in this example, does not possess rights when conducting a search. The officer possesses authority, and that authority is limited by the extent of the individual's rights. However, the officer's range of possible actions is not defined by his authority or limited by the individual's rights. The officer also has **power,** especially because the gun and the badge he carries have a coercive, threatening impact on people that usually makes them cooperate and acquiesce when given orders by the officer. Many people comply because they fear being handcuffed, arrested, or otherwise harmed or deprived of liberty if they disobey the officer, even when they believe that the officer's actions are improper. The officer's authority represents the extent of the officer's range of possible proper actions. The officer's power represents what, in reality, the officer can do, whether or not it is proper under the law. We need to recognize and distinguish the concepts of governmental authority and governmental power in order to understand the extent to which legal rights do or do not protect individuals from actions taken by government officials. An individual may be entitled to the protections of a legal right, yet because of improper assertions of power by government officials, that right is violated and unfulfilled. In effect, sometimes the honest answer to a question about the existence of a right is "Yes, you were supposed to have a legal right, but what good did it do since the officer took the actions he wanted to take anyway?"

In this book, we examine rights possessed by people in the context of criminal justice. Moreover, we see how those rights define the limits of government officials' authority. However, it is not sufficient to describe and catalog the legal rights discussed in court cases. One must also understand the processes through which rights are defined and the way in which those definitions change. Additional analysis is required to understand how those rights affect (or fail to affect) people's lives and guide their encounters with decision makers in the criminal justice system. Mere descriptions of rights that are supposed to exist can lead to misunderstandings about how the criminal justice system operates. In reality, assertions of power by criminal justice officials, especially through discretionary decisions, can significantly detract from an idealistic vision of the nature and importance of rights. Other factors can also affect whether the rights described in judges' decisions actually provide their expected protection against improper actions by criminal justice officials.

Summary

Americans often use the term right *to represent concepts other than the legal protections enjoyed by individuals against governmental intrusion. When the word* right *is used to represent the authority and power of governmental officials, the concept of rights can become confused with other concepts and thereby detract from people's ability to understand how rights actually operate within the criminal justice system.*

UNDERSTANDING THE CONCEPT OF LEGAL RIGHTS

Conventional Wisdom 2

When I have suffered a harm from someone else's wrongful behavior, my rights have been violated.

Americans frequently use the word *rights*. In conversations every day, people assert that they possess *rights* that, in some way, provide them with protections or entitlements under the law. Think about how frequently you hear the word *rights* asserted as a weapon or a shield when there are disagreements or conflicts between people.

> "I don't care if you are the owner of this movie theater. You can't tell me to shut up. I paid for my ticket and *I have the right* to whisper during the movie if I want to."
>
> "My child is a student at this private school. I pay a lot of money for tuition so *I have a right* to visit her classroom if I want to."
>
> "I don't care what the neighborhood association says. *I have a right* to paint my own house any color that I want it to be."
>
> "The advertisement did not say that you can only buy three jars of peanut butter at the sale price so *I have a right* to buy as many jars as I want."
>
> "The security guard at that rock concert violated *my rights* by digging through my backpack. I'm going to file a lawsuit against the people who run that stadium."
>
> "That blue car was supposed to yield at the highway entrance ramp. I'm the one who has *a right* to be in this lane."

Statements about rights are so common that virtually every American adult (and many children) has made them when confronted by a conflict or potential conflict with another person. In making these statements, what are the speakers asserting? The language of rights in common usage is a language of entitlement, as if the person is saying "I possess something powerful and important." It may also be a language of prerogative as if to say "I can assert my freedom to make choices without interference." Whether or not the statement makes the point explicitly, the language of rights is intimately linked to law. The person asserting the possession of a right is making a claim that this entitlement or prerogative is backed by a legitimate, powerful force. In some circumstances, people may refer to a "God-given right," as if this important possession is provided from a religious source. It is difficult, however, to know whether a right that purports to rest on an underlying religious source will be enforced in a timely manner or whether other people will recognize and respect such a right. On the other hand, the more typical reference to rights implies that the courts or another governmental entity will use the authority of law to remedy violations and to ensure that rights are respected. Lurking beneath many statements about rights is the following statement, which may be either articulated or implied: "You are violating my rights. If you do not stop, I will sue you (or otherwise call upon governmental authorities to intervene on my behalf)."

Observers of American politics and government have long noted the importance of rights in Americans' beliefs about their country. In some countries, politics and government are guided almost entirely by power, either financial or military. In other societies, governments and daily life may be guided by people's beliefs in and respect for traditional leaders or a common religion. By contrast, Americans see law, including rights, as the guiding force for government and society. According to Professor Stuart Scheingold, Americans' conceptions of rights are central to "a social perspective which perceives and explains human interaction largely in terms of rules and of the rights and obligations inherent in rules."[7] The focus on rights and law is intimately connected to central features of the political ideology underlying the American system of government. The **American ideology** emphasizes individualism. People are free to pursue their own interests, economic and otherwise, but they are sometimes obligated to surrender their goals and preferences in favor of the policy choices of central authorities. Individual freedom is limited. The maintenance of society requires that people pay taxes, serve in the armed forces when necessary, and obey laws. However, Americans can choose their own careers, start their own businesses, accumulate their own wealth, practice their own religions, and aspire to enjoy a degree of personal freedom that is not available in most of the world. Rights are regarded as legal protections possessed by individuals that protect them against improper actions by other individuals, the government, and larger society. Viewed in this way, rights play an important role in protecting individuals' opportunities to make their own decisions without undue interference. If inappropriate interference occurs, individuals can use legal processes to assert their rights and regain their freedom of action, property, and liberty.

Another key element of the American ideology is limited government. Individuals can only maintain their freedom of action to the extent that the government cannot tell them what to do. Thus, the founders of the United States began with the premise that the government should possess only those powers granted to it by the people. Moreover, those powers were to be limited in scope rather than expansively employed at the discretion of governmental leaders. Rights serve as a limitation on governmental power. As legally protected interests of individuals, rights serve to tell government officials what they cannot do in their interactions with citizens. If the government attempts to assert excessive powers by conducting improper searches, depriving people of their liberty unnecessarily, or otherwise violating individuals' legally protected interests, then legal actions filed in court can ask judges to order officials to limit their actions to those permitted under law. Obviously, Americans' beliefs about rights presume that judges are responsive to individuals when disputes about rights violations are brought to court. In addition, these pervasive conceptions of rights in the American ideology presume that judges are sufficiently neutral and powerful to act on behalf of individuals in enforcing the law against the government and other powerful entities. As is shown in subsequent chapters, these presumptions about judges may not always be correct.

Looking back at the sample statements that invoke the concept of "rights," how many of them actually concern entitlements or prerogatives protected by law? For example, what law would allow you to whisper in a movie theater after you have been asked to keep quiet? Is this an issue of freedom of speech? Do you really have a right to paint your property any color that you wish? What if the deed to your house contained restrictions that limited your choices, such as a requirement that you seek approval from the neighborhood association before painting? Would such a deed be enforceable against you in court or could you get a court order declaring the deed's limitations invalid? Is there ever a legally protected entitlement to buy unlimited quantities of a product if the store decides to limit how many may be purchased by each customer? Similar questions could be raised about the other examples. These examples all involve conflicts that relate to some aspect of law, but do these situations involve rights?

When used accurately, the word *right* usually refers to legally protected interests. By *legally protected,* we mean that these protected interests are created and protected by law and therefore are presumably enforceable in court. If someone violates your legally protected interests, then you can file a lawsuit asking a judge to order the violation to cease or requesting that a jury award you money to compensate you for the harm you suffered when your protected interest was violated. Some of these legally protected interests or rights are based on legally enforceable contracts. **Contracts** are voluntary agreements written in a manner to assure that they are enforceable in court because their terms are consistent with statutory law governing legally enforceable agreements. Thus we hear about professional sports teams that "bought the rights to" a certain player. The player signed a contract agreeing to play for a specific team and, typically, to accept that team's decision to trade the player or sell the player's contract to another team. In effect, the team has a *right* to the player's services and a court could enforce the contract by prohibiting the player from choosing to play for another team or by requiring the player to pay back money to the team if he or she refuses to obey the contract. The player also gains *rights* under the contract, such as a legally protected interest to be paid an agreed-upon salary for a specified period of time.

Legally protected interests may also stem from **statutes,** the laws enacted by the people's elected representatives in state legislatures and Congress, the national legislature. When Internet programs permitted people to download music without paying any fees, musicians and songwriters filed legal actions to protect their *right* to receive compensation for the songs that they wrote and performed. The ability of someone to "own" a song and therefore have a *right* to payment whenever it is purchased or performed is based on statutory law concerning *intellectual property rights.* These laws (and rights) also cover books, inventions, films, and other creative products.

Other legally protected interests can be created by agencies within the executive branch of government. Legislatures often delegate authority to executive agencies to determine the precise rules for government programs.

Thus the state department of corrections often creates the rules for visitors who come to prisons to visit convicted offenders as well as other rules for the daily operation of correctional institutions. Social service agencies often create many of the rules for programs that provide financial assistance, food, and housing for poor people. These rules created by government agencies are called **regulations.** Depending on how they are written, regulations may create legally protected interests for individuals that are enforceable in court if the government does not follow the rules that it created for itself. For example, a social service agency may not be able to automatically cease providing food or housing assistance to a poor person if the relevant regulation requires that certain procedures be followed before ending assistance or if the individual clearly meets eligibility requirements established by the regulations.

Despite the varied sources of legally protected interests that people refer to as *rights,* for the purposes of this book about the criminal justice system, we use the word *right* in a narrower sense. The term *right* is reserved for legally protected interests that are based on constitutional law rather than contracts, statutes, or other forms of law. **Constitutions** are the legal documents that describe the fundamental laws and governing systems of states and the federal government. Each state has its own constitution, and the entire nation is governed by the U.S. Constitution. The U.S. Constitution describes the structure of the national governing system, including the powers of Congress, the president, and the Supreme Court. State constitutions provide similar fundamental laws concerning governmental structure and authority within each state. The U.S. Constitution also contains the **Bill of Rights,** ten amendments added to the Constitution in 1791 that describe the rights possessed by individuals. State constitutions, which are often modeled on the language of the U.S. Constitution, also describe the rights possessed by people within their states. By defining *rights* as interests that find their legal basis and protection in constitutions, and especially the U.S. Constitution, this book uses the term in the manner most frequently applied by judges, lawyers, and officials in the criminal justice system. Moreover, most of the legally protected interests that are relevant to criminal justice are found in the U.S. Constitution or state constitutions. Legally protected interests that have their basis in other forms of law, including contracts, statutes, and regulations, often concern *rights* that define relationships between private citizens or businesses in society. By contrast, rights in criminal justice that are drawn from constitutions concern a different relationship.

In addition, because processes for adding formal amendments to constitutions tend to be long and difficult, constitutional rights are regarded as more reliable and enduring than legally protected interests under statutes, contracts, and regulations. These legally protected interests often can be changed relatively quickly by the actors—legislators, parties to the contract, and agency officials, respectively—who created them. Legislators can simply enact a new statute to change statutory rights. Parties to a contract can simply agree to amend their current contract or create a new contract in order to change contractual rights. Agencies can issue new regulations that change regulatory rights. By contrast, the requirements for amending the U.S. Constitution are set out in the document's Article V. Proposed amendments must originate with the support of two-thirds of the members of Congress or two-thirds of the state legislatures. If proposals can gain such super-majority support for initiation, then ratification of the amendments requires even greater support through approval by the legislatures of three-fourths of the states or by constitutional conventions in three-fourths of the states. Very few proposals can garner such consensus among the country's diverse states and divided political parties.[8] Thus, since the first ten amendments were added as a group in 1791, only seventeen additional amendments have been ratified and one of those amendments, concerning the prohibition on alcoholic beverages in the early twentieth century, was repealed in the 1930s. In light of the difficulty and rarity of ratifying formal constitutional amendments, rights contained in constitutions are considered stronger and more enduring than legally protected interests created by other forms of law. As a result, many scholars reserve the term *rights* for those special, presumptively enduring legal protections created and maintained by constitutions. Protections found in other legal sources, such as statutes and contracts, are often distinguished from "real" rights by referring to them specifically as "statutory rights" or "contractual rights." The word *right* expressed without any modifying term to identify its legal source most commonly refers exclusively to constitutional rights.

Consider the following example: Two students sit next to each other in a criminal justice class at a small, private college. The class is discussing whether the death penalty is an appropriate punishment for murder and whether capital punishment is a desirable sentencing policy for the United States. As one student begins to present criticisms of the death penalty, the neighboring student puts her hand over her classmate's mouth, wrestles him to the ground, and prevents him from speaking. In light of our definition of rights, were any rights violated in this episode? Criminal justice instructors know from experience that if this scenario is described to college students, more than 90 percent of them will quickly respond by stating that the woman violated the man's right to freedom of speech. The man was attempting to assert his prerogative to express his views verbally, and the woman's actions kept him from speaking. Although it is obvious that the man's ability to speak and express himself was stifled by the woman's actions, how do we know if this situation really constitutes a rights violation? Because we have defined rights as legally protected interests that have their basis in constitutions, we must look in one or more constitutions to see if the student's interest in expressing his opinion is, in fact, legally protected.

When asked where in the U.S. Constitution one can find the right to free speech, most students know to look in the First Amendment. Those same students are, however, typically surprised to discover that the words of the First Amendment are different than they had always presumed. The First Amendment does not say, "Everyone has a right to free speech." Instead, its words about the right to free speech say the following: "Congress shall make no law . . . abridging the freedom of speech." The student's ability to speak was impeded by the person sitting next to him, not by any action of the national legislature. Thus the words of the Constitution that define the legally protected interest do not cover the scenario in the classroom.

There are several lessons to be learned from this example. First, Americans' perceptions of constitutional rights may not match what the Constitution actually says. In order to learn whether a right actually exists, one must begin by looking at the words of the U.S. Constitution, or a state constitution if that provides the governing law. The words of the Constitution do not provide the final conclusion about the definition of rights because judges are permitted to interpret those words. But the words of the Constitution provide a necessary starting point for analyzing and understanding legally protected interests that we call constitutional rights.

Second, the example demonstrates that constitutional rights typically concern the relationship between individuals and government. This point is especially important in the criminal justice system where the government—through the police, prosecutors, judges, and corrections officials—investigates, prosecutes, and punishes people for violating criminal statutes. By contrast, as noted earlier, contracts, statutes, and regulations often concern legally protected interests relevant to relationships and conflicts between people, businesses, and other nongovernmental entities.

A third lesson arises when we ask the following question: If the student's right to free speech was not violated by his classmate, then is the student unprotected against such actions that keep him from speaking? The answer is clearly "No." The law provides protection for the student. But that protection is not in the form of a constitutional right. Instead, the student is protected by criminal laws against assault and battery. When one person makes unwanted physical contact with another person, that action may be prosecuted as the crime of battery or a related offense, depending on the crime definitions in the state's governing laws and the prosecution policies of the local district attorney. When that uninvited and unwanted touching rises to the level of physical contact that is violent and can cause injury, that action may be prosecuted as assault. Again, an actual prosecution would depend on the precise definition of the crime under relevant statutes and the prosecutor's decision about whether or not to press charges. The student's action could also trigger a civil lawsuit for battery under tort law. In sum, an absence of constitutional rights in a specific context does not mean an absence of legal protection. That protection may have its basis in criminal statutes, statutes that permit civil lawsuits for personal injuries, and other sources of law. Americans are accustomed to speaking and thinking about *rights* as encompassing the legal protections to which they are entitled. A more precise approach to understanding the nature of rights requires that constitutional rights be examined closely and distinguished from other forms of legal protections.

In light of the foregoing discussion, we are able to develop a definition that will help to illuminate the nature of rights in criminal justice. Thus, *a right is a legal entitlement originating in the U.S. Constitution or state constitutions that protects individuals against actions by government.* The examples at the start of the chapter concerning common statements about rights do not actually concern *rights* as that term is used in this book. We can re-examine them and see that they reflect assertions about legally protected interests—which may or may not actually exist—that are based in perceptions about legal sources other than constitutions.

- *"I don't care if you are the owner of this movie theater. You can't tell me to shut up. I paid for my ticket and I have the right to whisper during the movie if I want to."* The asserted *right* to whisper in the movie theater may stem from a misperception about what the First Amendment actually says about freedom of speech. Moreover, the conflict concerns an individual and a private business, not the government.
- *"My child is a student at this private school. I pay a lot of money for tuition so I have a right to visit her classroom if I want to."* The relationship between parents and private schools is based on contracts that are governed by specific statutes. The Supreme Court has spoken of certain constitutional rights possessed by parents to make decisions about their children. However, there is no specific constitutional right, either in the words of the Constitution or in judges' interpretations of those words, that amounts to a right to visit a private school.
- *"I don't care what the neighborhood association says. I have a right to paint my own house any color that I want it to be."* People are not necessarily entitled to paint their houses any color that they choose. If a homeowner's deed includes requirements imposed by the neighborhood association, then those requirements may be enforceable in court. Thus, by purchasing property that contains restrictions, the property owner is deemed to have accepted those restrictions. The homeowners' association may go to court to enforce those restrictions. Although people may assume that the Constitution protects their *right* to make their own decisions about property that they own, they may have surrendered the opportunity to make decisions under the sale contract and deed when the property was purchased.
- *"The advertisement did not say that you can only buy three jars of peanut butter at the sale price, so I have a right to buy as many jars as*

I want." If consumers rely on an erroneous advertisement to assert an entitlement to purchase additional items at a sale price, their ability to make the purchase may be preserved by consumer protection statutes. The Constitution, however, does not speak to the issue.

- *"The security guard at that rock concert violated my rights by digging through my backpack. I'm going to file a lawsuit against the people who run that stadium."* A security guard at a concert venue is typically a private sector employee, not a representative of the government. The guard's actions do not create conflicts between the individual and government. This does not mean that people are unprotected against actions by private security guards. Such guards are susceptible to lawsuits seeking compensation for personal injuries or damage to property.
- *"That blue car was supposed to yield at the highway entrance ramp. I'm the one who has a right to be in this lane."* Traffic laws, including the definition of which cars must yield to other cars, are created by state and local legislatures. These ordinances and statutes allocate responsibility when there is a dispute or collision between drivers, but they do not grant constitutional rights to drivers. Moreover, the dispute illustrated in this example concerns a conflict between two individuals rather than a situation in which an individual asserts that the government has interfered with his or her liberty, autonomy, or prerogatives.

The rights commonly associated with criminal law processes, such as rights related to searches, entitlements to representation by a defense attorney, and protections against cruel and unusual punishments, limit the government's actions against individuals. In criminal justice, the government pursues criminal investigations and presses charges against individuals who are suspected of violating substantive criminal law, which is defined by statutes. These statutes define acceptable behavior in society by identifying which behaviors are so harmful or important as to require the government to use its full coercive powers in their enforcement. The distinguishing feature of criminal law is punishment imposed by the government, including fines, incarceration, and execution.

By contrast, civil law typically concerns disputes between individuals or between individuals and businesses or other organizations. Civil law is relevant to some aspects of criminal justice because police departments and corrections agencies must obey laws concerning equal employment opportunity, pension benefits, and safe working conditions. A police officer may file a civil lawsuit against his or her employing department, for example, if there is evidence of discrimination by race, gender, or age in hiring and promotions. In one specific context, civil law can also concern the constitutional rights of individual citizens who come into contact with the criminal justice system. Civil statutes provide opportunities for lawsuits against certain governmental officials as one possible remedy for violations of individuals' rights in the criminal justice process. These **civil rights lawsuits** are most numerous and effective when the rights violation resulted in physical injuries or improper deprivations of liberty. Thus civil rights lawsuits for violations of the right against unreasonable searches less frequently provide successful remedies because juries may be disinclined to award money damages for an improper search that was merely a temporary inconvenience for the person who was forced to endure a momentary patdown or brief search of a car or luggage. Violations of these rights remain either unremedied or addressed through the exclusion of improperly obtained evidence in the resulting prosecution aimed at the rights-violation victim. However, the violations of some rights, especially those concerning "unreasonable seizures" that constitute either excessive use of force or improper arrests and "cruel and unusual punishments" in prison conditions, can produce both financial damages awards against the officials who allegedly committed rights violations and court orders mandating a change in officials' unconstitutional policies and practices.

The imprecise use of the term *rights* by many Americans indicates that they do not necessarily have a clear understanding of the legal protections provided for them by the Constitution. Their ability to seek remedies for rights violations depends, in part, on their accurate awareness that a violation has occurred. Conversely, criminal justice officials have a strong need to know the definition and application of constitutional rights. These rights define the appropriate extent of officials' authority; and, if officials' improper actions result in physical injuries or deprivations of liberty for citizens, they can trigger the risk of financial liability for individual police officers and corrections officials. In spite of the obvious importance of accurate knowledge for both citizens and criminal justice officials, the complexity and inconsistency of definitions and explanations of rights provided in judges' case opinions hinder widespread understanding. Moreover, the imagery and mythology surrounding courts and law can distort understandings of rights for both trained officials and average citizens.

Summary

People may suffer many harms that are recognizable and remediable by the law. However, only a few of these harms are likely to be constitutional rights violations. Constitutional rights refer specifically to legal protections with their source in the U.S. Constitution or state constitutions that guard individuals against actions by government. Other legal protections are found in other sources of law, particular statutes, contracts, and regulations. Although these protections may be referred to as legal rights, the term rights *in this book refers exclusively to those legal protections found within constitutions because those are the most important protections for individuals in the criminal justice process.*

The Image of Courts and Law

Conventional Wisdom 3

Judges are effective in defining and protecting rights because the judicial branch follows principles of law and is therefore different from the legislative and executive branches, which are influenced by politics.

When politicians run for office in legislatures, city councils, and other policy-making institutions, the public expects their statements and actions to be guided by their partisan political self-interest. Political candidates typically promise to reduce taxes, fight crime, and expand prosperity for all citizens. Their specific promises often represent the policy positions of their political parties, and their actions in elective office frequently benefit the constituent groups who provided them with their greatest support. Upon assuming the presidency in 2001, George W. Bush was criticized for altering energy policies to seek additional opportunities for oil and natural gas companies to drill in untouched areas of the Alaska wilderness and the Gulf of Mexico as well as national parks. Bush's position was not surprising, however, in light of his own background in the oil business and the large sums of money contributed by energy interests to the Bush campaign and the Republican Party. On the other side of the coin, the Democrats' support for a "patients' bill of rights" that included opportunities for people to sue their health maintenance organizations (HMOs) was criticized as favoring the interests of an important Democratic constituency group, trial attorneys who sue corporations on behalf of individuals. When Americans hear politicians' promises or assess elected officials' actions, they are often skeptical. They are accustomed to hearing promises that may never be fulfilled. They expect officeholders' decisions to benefit those individuals and groups that contributed large sums of money to political campaigns. The average citizen has become accustomed to unfulfilled campaign promises, government scandals, negative campaigning, and interest group politics. If you ask Americans about the lofty, unfulfilled promises of a governor, the president, or members of Congress, they are likely to say "That's just politics."

By contrast, people often have different perceptions and expectations about the judiciary. People do not typically presume that courts are guided by overt partisanship. Unlike in the elected branches of government, politics and partisanship are not so obvious in the judicial branch. Judges are presumed to use their specialized training in order to make decisions according to the principles of law, which are designed to achieve justice. A poor citizen who cannot afford to make a campaign contribution may have little hope that an elected official will listen to his or her concerns. However, if that person is arrested or files a lawsuit, there is a universal expectation that he or she is entitled to the same "day in court" that is accorded to everyone else in the country, rich or poor. Furthermore, people expect that the decisions in court will be neutral, objective, and guided by firmly established principles of law. This expectation stands in stark contrast to the public's acceptance of inconsistent statements by political candidates and elected officials whose partisanship, personal ideology, and political self-interest are clearly connected to their decisions.

Evidence of Americans' elevated view of the judicial branch can be found in studies and public opinion polls, especially those concerning the U.S. Supreme Court. A study of college students' perceptions found that they "exhibit a high degree of mythical belief about the Supreme Court."[9] Less than one-third of the students in the study acknowledged that the Supreme Court's decisions would be affected by politics.[10] In a comparison of people's views about Congress and the Supreme Court, a national survey of American adults found that twice as many respondents rated the Supreme Court's performance as "good" or "excellent," despite the fact that 40 percent acknowledged that justices' political beliefs influence the Court's decisions.[11] A national public opinion poll in June 2000 revealed that 47 percent of respondents said that they had a "great deal" or "quite a lot" of confidence in the Supreme Court. By contrast, only 34 percent of respondents gave Congress similarly high ratings.[12] The public's opinion of the Supreme Court remained high even after the Court's controversial December 2000 decision (*Bush v. Gore*, 2000) that ended the presidential election in George Bush's favor amid vote-counting problems in the pivotal state of Florida. This was a situation that could have potentially turned public opinion against the Court, especially because national vote totals demonstrated that Vice President Al Gore had 500,000 more votes than Bush. Moreover, as Bush officially held a slim 500-vote lead in Florida, the Court's decision abruptly ended a recount of votes in a state in which many voters were denied the opportunity to vote; improper ballots were counted; and a confusing, illegal "butterfly"-design ballot may have cost Vice President Al Gore thousands of votes in one county.[13] Despite the public criticism of the Republican-dominated Court by many news commentators and legal scholars for the appearance of political motives and self-interest, the Court enjoyed the same approval rating, 62 percent, that it had before the election controversy. The Court's rating was above that of both Congress and the president.[14]

The attributes of the judicial branch reinforce its image of neutrality. Judges' opinions and lawyers' arguments in court are infused with the language of neutral justice. Such phrases as "equal protection," "due process," and "rights of the accused" convey the message that law is based on principles of fairness and not on partisanship or political self-interest. These phrases are drawn from the U.S. Constitution, state constitutions, statutes, and judicial opinions. They reflect ideals that connect contemporary Americans with the revered images of the nation's eighteenth-century founders who revolted against the British king in order to attain liberty and equality under a system of laws. Judges and their lofty statements about neutral justice are not typically associated with political parties' platforms or political candidates' opportunistic, self-interested promises.

In addition, the physical surroundings of courts distinguish them from other governing institutions and reinforce the imagery of principled decision making and equal justice under law. Judges wear black robes and sit at high benches elevated above the rest of the people in the courtroom. Everyone must stand when a judge enters or leaves a courtroom and must address the judge as "Your Honor." Respectful silence is expected and frequently enforced by the judges' bailiffs, court security officers, or deputy sheriffs. These traditional formal procedures give judicial officers at all levels of state and federal courts a unique measure of symbolic deference and respect that is unmatched in the American governing system except for the formal treatment accorded the president as the national head of state. Judges' courtrooms are often majestic settings that instill reverence and awe. With wood paneling, stained glass windows, marble columns, high ceilings, Greco-Roman statues, and velvet curtains, courtrooms often look more like religious temples than like work environments of a democratic government. Courtrooms and courthouses also have inspiring slogans and quotations about justice etched in walls and walkways. High above the majestic marble columns and massive bronze door at the U.S. Supreme Court in Washington, D.C., the eye cannot miss the large letters spelling out "Equal Justice Under Law" chiseled in stone and visible from blocks away. In their image, language, and physical environment, courts and judges appear to be removed from the ugly combat of partisan politics. Instead, judges can sit above the swirling turmoil of imperfect human society in order to provide a reliable, unshakable anchor for democratic governmental processes. Judges appear to serve as the one set of authoritative decision makers who are guided by principle, in the form of law, rather than by self-interest and politics.

The image of courts as neutral, dependable institutional guardians of constitutional rights and principles of law is also reinforced by the concerted efforts of lawyers and judges. Lawyers and judges speak of the development and enforcement of law as if it is based on neutral principles of justice. Their efforts are, in part, self-interested because their high status, income, and power are linked to public acceptance of and deference to law and courts as forums for dispute resolution and authoritative decision making about the rules for society. Lawyers who accuse judges of being biased may risk being sanctioned for unprofessional conduct. In one particularly revealing example, an Ohio lawyer was barred from ever practicing law in that state again because he had violated the judicial system's dignified legal image by accusing judges of lying. According to the justices of the Ohio Supreme Court, "[W]e find the flagrant disrespect that [the attorney] demonstrated toward the entire judicial system deserving of the legal profession's most severe sanction."[15] As a newspaper report on the case noted, however, "[L]awyers found to have committed seemingly more serious offenses—like stealing money from their clients—regularly receive less severe punishment" from the state supreme court, such as only having their licenses temporarily suspended.[16] Thus, it appears that tarnishing the judicial system's dignified image may be a more serious offense for attorneys than committing an actual crime.

In part, the efforts by judges to maintain the courts' image of neutrality are very practical. The image of neutrality is considered the central element of the judicial branch's **legitimacy.** A court's legitimacy is, in essence, its acceptance in the eyes of the public as a governing institution worthy of obedience because it is operating properly according to legal principles rather than politics. In the words of Justice Felix Frankfurter, who served on the U.S. Supreme Court from the 1930s through the early 1960s, "[T]he Court's authority—possessed of neither the purse nor the sword—ultimately rests on sustained public confidence in its moral sanction."[17] Justice Harry Blackmun, who served in the 1970s and 1980s, reiterated the idea that "[t]he legitimacy of the Judicial Branch ultimately depends on its reputation for impartiality and nonpartisanship."[18] The statements by these justices reflect a widespread concern that, in practice, the judicial branch is far weaker than the other branches of government. The executive branch controls the military and police. If people disobey a law, the executive branch can take action by sending armed, uniformed personnel to force people to comply. The legislative branch controls the "power of the purse." Legislators can enact laws that impose unfavorable tax policies on people who do not cooperate with the law. They can also offer financial incentives for compliance with laws. For example, Congress used highway construction and maintenance funds as the incentive to pressure states to comply with national standards for speed limits, drunken driving laws, and other matters. Courts, however, do not possess military power in order to coerce compliance and they also do not possess the power to create the kinds of financial incentives established by Congress and state legislators. Instead, courts must usually depend on voluntary compliance with their decisions. If such voluntary compliance does not occur, the judges must hope that a governor or president will use executive authority to enforce compliance with judicial decisions. Thus it was Presidents Eisenhower and Kennedy, not the Supreme Court, who sent troops to such places as Little Rock Central High School and the University of Mississippi to ensure that segregationists could not use disobedience and violence to block the enrollment of African-American students in the 1950s and early 1960s. In other examples from American history, the judiciary's lack of power was revealed when the executive branch failed to enforce court decisions. When the Cherokee Nation won a Supreme Court decision in the 1830s to prevent whites from forcing them off of their ancestral land in Georgia, President Andrew Jackson simply refused to enforce the judicial decision and the Cherokees were forced to march at gunpoint to Oklahoma on the infamous "trail of tears." Their land, houses, and other property in Georgia were simply stolen from them; and hundreds died along the way during the difficult westward trek.[19]

Judges sometimes make explicit references to the need to maintain the image of courts and law in the mind of the public. If courts were viewed as partisan political institutions, judges fear that citizens would be less inclined to voluntarily accept and obey judicial decisions. Widespread disobedience of the law, including judicial decisions, would breed chaos and thereby weaken the stability enjoyed by American society. In a 1992 case concerning the controversial issue of abortion, three justices declined to overturn *Roe v. Wade* (1973), the precedent legalizing abortion as a component of the right to privacy, because of concerns that the public would believe that the overruling occurred only because the Court's composition had changed. These justices did not want the public to think that the law concerning an important issue would change merely because conservative justices had replaced liberal justices who had retired. They wanted the public to have faith that the rules of law would only change because of the dictates of important legal principles. According to the opinion issued jointly by Justices Sandra Day O'Connor, Anthony Kennedy, and David Souter in *Planned Parenthood v. Casey* (1992),

> A decision to overrule *Roe*'s essential holding under the existing circumstances would address error, if error there was, at the cost of both profound and unnecessary damage to the Court's legitimacy, and to the Nation's commitment to the rule of law. It is therefore imperative to adhere to the essence of *Roe*'s original decision, and we do so today.[20]

Judges' and lawyers' overriding concerns about the image and legitimacy of courts and law make them reluctant to acknowledge the impact of partisan political influences on the judiciary. Yet, such influences clearly exist and shape the definitions of law and rights for people throughout the United States. Most obviously, political influences on courts stem from the methods for selecting judges.[21] Lawyers selected to serve as judges are not selected because they are the wisest, most experienced, or most sensible decision makers in the legal profession. Judges are selected through political processes for political reasons. In many states, judges are chosen through partisan elections. The selection of candidates for judgeships is often based on individual lawyers' ability to raise campaign funds and generate support among the voters rather than knowledge, wisdom, and experience. In states that hold nonpartisan elections to select judges, political parties are typically very active behind the scenes in selecting and supporting candidates.[22] In Michigan, for example, which uses "nonpartisan" judicial elections, the Democratic and Republican parties endorse the candidates for the state supreme court and each party spends hundreds of thousands of dollars attempting to get its "nonpartisan" candidates elected. In all election systems, candidates for judicial office gather campaign contributions from lawyers, interest groups, and political parties, a practice that creates risks that the judges will have difficulty adopting a neutral stance when deciding cases that affect their electoral supporters. Election systems are often bypassed because many judges time their resignations and retirements so that a governor from their preferred political party can make an "interim" appointment of a new judge who will then have the advantage of incumbency when running to retain the seat in the next election. Other states use merit selection processes that still retain political elements because the governor appoints the committee that will review candidates and then the governor makes the final selection of judges from among the committee's recommended finalists.[23] Not surprisingly, the people selected as judges are often members of the governor's political party or share the governor's political values.

In the federal court system, judges and Supreme Court justices are nominated by the president and confirmed by a vote of the U.S. Senate. Because **Article III of the U.S. Constitution** says that federal judges serve "during good Behaviour," which effectively means for life unless they are impeached and removed from office for committing a crime, presidents can influence law and policy for years after they leave the White House by appointing federal judges who share the president's political values. Thus presidents rarely appoint any judges who are not from their own political party.[24] As in the state judicial selection systems in which political parties and governors attempt to place like-minded partisans on the bench, presidential practices in appointing federal judges reflect a widespread recognition among politicians and government leaders that judicial decisions are determined by the values and policy preferences of the judges rather than by neutral principles of law. In other words, politics rules the selection of judges because those who work in the world of politics recognize that political values also rule judicial decision making and the interpretation of law. Moreover, the accuracy of this observation has been verified by scholars who systematically study the decision making of judges on courts throughout state and federal judicial systems.[25]

It is not difficult to identify examples of changes in law and constitutional rights that stem directly from political changes in the composition of appellate courts. Many judges believe that changes in law, if they are to occur at all, should usually be gradual and incremental so that the public retains confidence that the law is evolving in response to important societal developments or newly discovered insights about legal principles. Dramatic, overnight changes in the law are viewed as especially threatening to the image and legitimacy of courts because such changes are most likely to be attributed to the arrival of a new judge or to a specific judge changing his or her mind about the law. Such changes make it especially clear that law changes because of what judges say about it and not because of neutral legal principles.

For example, the U.S. Supreme Court decided by a 5-to-4 vote that Victim Impact Statements cannot be presented during the sentencing phase of death penalty cases (*Booth v. Maryland,* 1987). As the jury considers whether to sentence a convicted murderer to death or to life in prison, friends and relatives of the victim describe how their lives have been harmed and how the community has been harmed by the loss of the victim. Such testimony can obviously be very moving and emotional. The Court declared that such testimony creates grave risks that the jurors' emotions will be aroused so that their decision will not be focused on the relevant issues of the nature of the killing and the qualities of the killer. Moreover, the use of victim impact statements creates risks that the lives of certain victims will be valued more highly than the lives of other victims. Thus the killers of whites, wealthy people, or prominent citizens may generate victim impact testimony that has a greater effect on the jury than testimony concerning the poor and members of minority groups, even if the actual crimes and killers were equally horrible.

Two years later, the Court revisited the issue and again declared that the use of Victim Impact Statements violates the Constitution (*South Carolina v. Gathers*, 1989). In dissent, Justice Antonin Scalia argued that the Court should overturn the *Booth* precedent, even though it was established only two years earlier. He claimed that a quick reversal would not harm the Court's image as the institutional guardian of stable principles of law. In addition, he explicitly referred to the role of the Court's personnel changes in affecting the reversal of established precedents. In Scalia's words, "Overrulings of precedent rarely occur without a change in the Court's personnel."[26] Scalia's words represented a surprisingly frank admission about the role of a political process, namely the selection of new justices by the president, in determining the definition of constitutional rights and other aspects of judicially interpreted law. Shortly after the decision, Scalia's wish came true because liberal Justice William Brennan retired from the Court and was replaced by President George H. W. Bush's first Republican nominee, Justice David Souter. Two years later, the Supreme Court overturned the precedent established in 1987 (*Booth v. Maryland*) and reinforced by the decision in 1989 (*South Carolina v. Gathers*). In *Payne v. Tennessee* (1991), a majority of justices approved the use of victim impact statements in death penalty sentencing hearings. In dissent, Justice Thurgood Marshall stated the obvious in criticizing the majority for changing the law through the apparent exercise of political power: "Neither the law nor the facts supporting *Booth* and *Gathers* underwent any change in the last four years. Only the personnel of this Court did."[27] Another dissenter, Justice John Paul Stevens, lamented that the majority's decision was a "sad day for a great institution" because he perceived that the victims' rights movement and popular fears about crime, both of which were central justifications within Justice Scalia's majority opinion, had replaced legal reasoning as primary influences on the Court's decisions concerning this capital punishment issue.[28] In applying his own analysis of legal reasoning, Stevens concluded that "Our cases provide no support whatsoever for the majority's conclusion that the prosecutor may introduce evidence that sheds no light on the defendant's guilt or moral culpability, and thus serves no purpose other than to encourage jurors to decide in favor of death rather than life on the basis of their emotions rather than their reason."[29] In courts, as in legislatures, the nature of evidence and arguments concerning the most appropriate definition of law may be much less important than the simple reality of which political values and policy preferences attract the most votes.

Similar examples are available from state courts. In July 2001, the Michigan Supreme Court decided that detainees in jails cannot sue the government when they are injured on jail premises. In the case at issue, *Brown v. Genesee County Board of Commissioners* (2001), a prisoner in a jail was injured when he slipped on water near a shower stall. He filed a lawsuit claiming that the county was liable for his injuries because improper drainage and the absence of a shower curtain had caused water to accumulate on the floor. Although governmental entities are immune from many kinds of lawsuits, Michigan statutes permit lawsuits for injuries sustained in governmental buildings that are "open for use by members of the public." In *Brown*, a four-member majority on the seven-member court, including three justices originally appointed to judicial office by the state's conservative Republican governor, altered thirty years of precedents by declaring that jail detainees are no longer considered members of the "public" eligible to file lawsuits for injuries sustained due to dangerous or defective conditions in jails. The dissenting opinion complained that "[o]ther than to effectuate a policy change, I see no reason for this Court to depart from the logic *Green* [*v. Department of Corrections* (1971)] used thirty years ago and that this Court has implicitly followed since. . . . [The opinion for the Court] offers nothing substantial in support of its observation that '[j]ail inmates are not members of the public for the purposes [of the statute].'" If the Michigan Supreme Court's composition had not changed in the way that it did through the influence of the governor's appointment decisions, it seems unlikely that the justices would have completely changed the law in such an abrupt fashion. Interestingly, Michigan is a state where voters choose judges through nonpartisan elections. However, key retirements permitted the governor to use the power to make interim appointments in order to give several conservative members of the state supreme court their initial foothold in judicial office.

As indicated by these examples, judicial decisions that define constitutional rights and other law relevant to criminal justice are influenced by political developments that determine which lawyers serve as judges and by the political values and policy preferences of those judges. Judges may honestly believe that they aspire to use neutral principles of justice in making decisions. However, judges' interpretive powers are so broad and, as is shown in Chapter 2, the law is so malleable that there are continuous opportunities for judges to use their own values in defining the law. Even the U.S. Supreme Court's conservative chief justice, William Rehnquist, has admitted that "[t]he law is at best an inexact science . . .

[so] [t]here is simply no demonstrably 'right' answer to the question involved in many of [the Supreme Court's] difficult cases."[30] Thus judges inevitably make decisions by determining what they think will be the "best" interpretation of law according to their own values and policy preferences. The processes of producing judicial decisions through the litigation process are different than the processes of decision making in the legislative and executive branches, but the underlying factors that shape decisions are no less political and personal than those affecting the other branches. The ideal of objective decision making according to neutral principles of law is a myth, especially when it comes to controversial issues such as the definition of constitutional rights for suspects, defendants, and convicted offenders in the criminal justice system.

Justices Clarence Thomas and Antonin Scalia claim that neutral principles of justice can guide courts' decisions but only if other judges follow their example by applying a coherent, complete, and objective philosophy of interpretation. They assert that the Constitution should be interpreted according to the original intentions of the document's authors. They claim that such an approach prevents judges from applying their own values in deciding cases. However, close analysis of their claims reveals that they do not actually apply their originalist approach in all cases. Instead, like the justices whom they criticize, Scalia and Thomas are inconsistent in their decision making and demonstrate a tendency to ensure that their conservative values and policy preferences prevail in most cases.[31] Even if it were hypothetically possible to decide legal cases consistently in accordance with neutral principles of justice, American history has yet to see any black-robed human beings on the bench who have managed to avoid imposing their own values into judicial decisions.

Summary

Many Americans have greater faith in the judicial branch of government than in the legislative and executive branches because of the judiciary's reputation as the "nonpolitical" branch of government. In reality, political influences are evident throughout the judicial branch, from the selection of judges to the processes of judicial decision making. Thus the interpretation, definition, and protection of constitutional rights are inevitably shaped by political processes.

CONCLUSION

The concept of *rights* holds an important place in the minds of Americans. As they think about the nature and operation of law in society, people tend to assert that their rights have been violated when they feel wronged by the actions of others. Unfortunately, the term *rights* is used too loosely in casual conversation to permit people to gain an accurate grasp of its meaning. Rights are legal protections originating in the U.S. Constitution and state constitutions that are possessed by individuals and protect those individuals against actions by government. In criminal justice, rights are supposed to provide protection against actions by police, prosecutors, and corrections officials. Thus police officers do not have a *right* to conduct searches when they investigate criminal cases. Instead, they have the *authority* to conduct searches when permitted by law and they have the *power* (albeit not always legitimately applied) to conduct searches whenever the coercive power of their guns and badges enables them to take action. The concept of *rights* must be carefully distinguished from *authority* and *power* in analyzing the nature of legal protections enjoyed by Americans under the law, even though the terms are often used interchangeably in casual conversation.

As indicated by the constitutional basis for rights defining the relationship between individuals and government, all legal grievances are not connected to the concept of *rights* as used in this book. Conflicts between individuals and other individuals or businesses are often handled by various aspects of civil law. When people feel aggrieved by the actions of others, the legal remedy for such grievances often comes from contract law, personal injury law, or other areas of law that are not drawn from the Constitution. Constitutional rights actually address only a limited range of protections for individuals in their contacts with government.

The concept of rights is intimately connected to the image of law and courts. Rights are presumed to be strong and enduring protections that are guarded by the principled decision making of the judicial branch. Judges and lawyers reinforce the neutral image of law and courts and simultaneously protect the public's assumptions about the importance and effectiveness of rights. Although judges and lawyers seek to enhance the perceived neutrality and majesty of courts in order to distinguish judicial institutions from the "political" branches of government, judicial decisions are actually shaped by political influences. Political developments determine which individuals will serve as judges, and those judges rely on their political values and policy preferences in shaping the law, including the definition of constitutional rights. Thus the definitions of constitutional rights do not reflect enduring principles of justice. Instead they reflect the values and preferences of the majority of decision makers who happen to be serving on a court at a particular moment in history.

THE DEFINITION OF CONSTITUTIONAL RIGHTS

For the purposes of this book, *rights* are defined as legal protections for individuals originating in the U.S. Constitution and state constitutions that apply against the actions of governmental actors. In order to identify and understand the rights that purport to protect individuals in the criminal justice process, we examine the words of the U.S. Constitution and consider what those words say about the legal protections to which individuals are entitled. We could also look at state constitutions, but our examination focuses almost exclusively on the U.S. Constitution for several reasons. The U.S. Constitution provides fundamental law for the entire nation. Americans' shared perceptions of their rights from the U.S. Constitution help to link together an ethnically and geographically diverse country. Those rights provide specific expectations and a national identity that permit people within the country to share a common definition of what it means to be an American. Rights also serve as the basis for rules that limit the authority of justice system officials throughout the nation. Thus they purport to affect all criminal justice cases. In addition, the rights in many state constitutions are modeled on the language in the U.S. Constitution. In those instances in which the language of state constitutions differs from the federal constitution, the language has limited application because it governs only the interactions between individuals and governmental officials within a particular state's borders. Thus the U.S. Constitution is exceptionally important as a source of rights that affect the criminal justice system.

RIGHTS IN THE U.S. CONSTITUTION

Most of the constitutional rights concerning criminal justice are found in the Constitution's first ten amendments, known as the *Bill of Rights*, and the Fourteenth Amendment. During the drafting of the Constitution and its subsequent ratification process, many people raised concerns that the document did not provide enough specific legal protections for individuals to adequately guard against abusive actions by the national government. A proposed list of individual legal protections that eventually became the Bill of Rights was drafted during the first Congress that met in 1789 after ratification of the Constitution.[1] Ten amendments were added to the Constitution in 1791, the first eight of which specified rights for individuals.

The **Fourteenth Amendment,** which also affects criminal justice, was added to the Constitution in 1868 after the Civil War. This amendment was drafted and ratified at a historical moment in which there was great concern about how former Confederate states of the South would treat African-Americans who had been newly freed from slavery. Within that amendment, the rights to "due process" and "equal protection of the laws" have developed special importance for criminal justice processes.

Box 2.1 presents the complete Bill of Rights and the relevant portions of the Fourteenth Amendment. Notice that the Fourteenth Amendment is different from the first ten amendments because it empowers Congress to enact legislation to ensure that "due process," "equal protection," and other aspects of the Fourteenth Amendment are enforced against the states. By contrast, the first ten amendments contain no such legislative power and, in fact, the First Amendment is clearly intended to limit the power of Congress.

When scanning the list of rights contained in the Bill of Rights and the Fourteenth Amendment, it is easy to notice specific rights that are obviously intended to protect individuals in their contacts with the criminal justice system. The Eighth Amendment's prohibition on excessive bail is a good example. Other rights are also relevant to criminal justice, but we often do not think of these rights as concerning individuals' interactions with police officers and other government officials. For example, the First Amendment right to freedom of speech has had important implications for criminal justice, although most Americans do not think of it in those terms. By giving Americans a legal right to express themselves in certain ways and specific situations, the First Amendment simultaneously limits the government's ability to define such forms of expression as crimes. Thus many First Amendment cases have arisen when people were arrested for expressing themselves and they used legal processes to challenge the government's authority to punish them for speaking. For example, a Ku Klux Klan leader in Ohio was convicted of advocating violence for verbally attacking African-Americans and Jews at a Klan rally. The U.S. Supreme Court overturned his conviction because it found that the Ohio criminal statute impermissibly violated freedom of speech (*Brandenburg v. Ohio,* 1969). This example illustrates the point that some constitutional rights affect **substantive criminal law,** which is the law that defines which acts are punishable as crimes. Other constitutional rights, such as the Eighth Amendment protection against excessive bail, concern **procedural criminal law.** Procedural criminal law concerns the proper processes

2.1 *The Bill of Rights and the Fourteenth Amendment of the U.S. Constitution*

FIRST AMENDMENT (ratified in 1791): Congress shall make no law respecting an establishment of religion, or prohibiting the free exercise thereof; or abridging the freedom of speech, or of the press; or the right of the people peaceably to assemble, and to petition the Government for redress of grievances.

SECOND AMENDMENT (ratified in 1791): A well regulated Militia, being necessary for the security of a free State, the right of the people to keep and bear Arms, shall not be infringed.

THIRD AMENDMENT (ratified in 1791): No Soldier shall, in time of peace be quartered in any house, without the consent of the Owner, nor in time of war, but in a manner to be prescribed by law.

FOURTH AMENDMENT (ratified in 1791): The right of the people to be secure in their persons, houses, papers, and effects, against unreasonable searches and seizures, shall not be violated, and no Warrants shall issue, but upon probable cause, supported by Oath or affirmation, and particularly describing the place to be searched, and the persons or things to be seized.

FIFTH AMENDMENT (ratified in 1791): No person shall be held to answer for a capital or otherwise infamous crime, unless on a presentment or indictment of a Grand Jury, except in cases arising in the land or naval forces, or in the Militia, when in actual service in time of War or public danger; nor shall any person be subject for the same offence to be twice put in jeopardy of life or limb; nor shall be compelled in any criminal case to be a witness against himself, nor be deprived of life, liberty, or property, without due process of law; nor shall private property be taken for public use, without just compensation.

SIXTH AMENDMENT (ratified in 1791): In all criminal prosecutions, the accused shall enjoy the right to a speedy and public trial, by an impartial jury of the State and district wherein the crime shall have been committed, which district shall have been previously ascertained by law, and to be informed of the nature and cause of the accusation; to be confronted with the witnesses against him; to have compulsory process for obtaining witnesses in his favor, and to have the Assistance of Counsel for his defence.

SEVENTH AMENDMENT (ratified in 1791): In Suits at common law, where the value in controversy shall exceed twenty dollars, the right of trial by jury shall be preserved, and no fact tried by a jury, shall be otherwise re-examined in any Court of the United States, than according to the rules of the common law.

EIGHTH AMENDMENT (ratified in 1791): Excessive bail shall not be required, nor excessive fines imposed, nor cruel and unusual punishments inflicted.

NINTH AMENDMENT (ratified in 1791): The enumeration in the Constitution, of certain rights, shall not be construed to deny or disparage others retained by the people.

TENTH AMENDMENT (ratified in 1791): The powers not delegated to the United States by the Constitution, nor prohibited by it to the States, are reserved to the States respectively, or to the people.

FOURTEENTH AMENDMENT (ratified in 1868): Section 1. All persons born or naturalized in the United States, and subject to the jurisdiction thereof, are citizens of the United States and of the State wherein they reside. No State shall make or enforce any law which shall abridge the privileges or immunities of citizens of the United States; nor shall any State deprive any person of life, liberty, or property, without due process of law; nor deny to any person within its jurisdiction the equal protection of the laws.° ° °

Section 5. The Congress shall have the power to enforce, by appropriate legislation, the provisions of this article.

that must be followed by criminal justice officials when investigating, prosecuting, trying, and punishing people for violating the substantive criminal law.

In addition, some rights affect both substantive and procedural criminal law. For example, the Supreme Court interpreted the Eighth Amendment's prohibition on "cruel and unusual punishments" as barring states from making it a crime to "be a drug addict" (*Robinson v. California,* 1962). States can enact criminal laws that punish *actions* people take with respect to drugs: selling drugs, carrying drugs, possessing drugs, distributing drugs, smuggling drugs, conspiring to smuggle drugs, and so on. However, the Court declared that it is unconstitutionally cruel and unusual to punish people for their *status* as addicts, particularly because some people can become addicts through no fault of their own, such as babies born to drug-addicted mothers and medical patients who are mistakenly given too much pain medication by their doctors. This example shows the prohibition on cruel and unusual punishments applied to limit substantive criminal law. The same provision also affects procedural criminal law by limiting decisions and actions by judges in sentencing criminal offenders and by corrections officials in their treatment of incarcerated offenders. In July 2001, for example, the U.S. Court of Appeals for the Eighth Circuit ruled that it was unconstitutionally cruel and unusual for Arkansas to sentence a first offender to life in prison for possession of $20 worth of cocaine (*Henderson v. Norris,* 2001). The judges decided that the punishment was too harsh and did not fit the crime.

Box 2.2 lists the constitutional rights relevant to criminal justice from the Bill of Rights and the Fourteenth Amendment, and it provides examples of questions that arise concerning these legal protections. There are a few other rights affecting criminal justice found in the main body of the original Constitution. For example, the **Ex Post Facto Clause** bars the government from applying substantive criminal laws retroactively. The legislature cannot enact a new criminal statute and then apply that statute to someone for something that he or she did before the law came into being. In another example, the Constitution prohibits the government from suspending people's right to file **habeas corpus** petitions, except when necessary during a rebellion or invasion. *Habeas corpus* provides the traditional process for people being held in prison or jail to ask judges to determine whether their confinement is legally proper. Most of the discussion in this book focuses on procedural rights from the Bill of Rights and the Fourteenth Amendment, but it is important to remember that constitutional rights can also limit the nature of substantive criminal statutes enacted by legislatures.

In addition to the rights and corresponding issues illustrated in Box 2-2, there is another context in which many of these rights as well as additional rights apply to criminal justice. Judges must interpret the Bill of Rights to identify the rights retained by people who are under correctional supervision. To what extent do people in prison enjoy freedom of speech or even a different First Amendment right, the free exercise of religion? Many people presume that convicted offenders forfeit all of their rights. Although it is true that convicted offenders possess only limited rights while in prison or on probation and parole, they do not lose all of their legal protections against excessive actions by government. According to its words, the U.S. Constitution is not based on a **social contract philosophy** in which individuals lose the protections of law when they violate their "contract" with society to obey the rules announced and enforced by the government. It would be possible to have such a legal system, but that is not the system created by the U.S. Constitution. Instead, the U.S. Constitution and the Bill of Rights are based on a **natural law philosophy.** Remember Thomas Jefferson's famous words in the Declaration of Independence: "We hold these truths to be self-evident . . . all men . . . are endowed by their Creator with certain inalienable rights." This underlying philosophy assumes that all people, by virtue of being human, have certain rights that cannot be taken away. Thus the Bill of Rights does not

Constitutional Rights in Criminal Justice

Substantive

Amendment	Right
1	Freedom of speech/press/assembly

Can the government criminalize certain statements and writings?

| 2 | Bear arms |

Can the government criminalize the ownership or possession of firearms?

| 8 | No cruel and unusual punishments |

Can the government criminalize a status by punishing someone for being a drug addict?

| 14 | Equal protection of the laws |

Can the government make an activity a crime when committed by women but not a crime when committed by men?

Procedural

Amendment	Right
1	Freedom of the press

Does the right of the press to cover criminal trials clash with the right to a fair trial?

| 4 | No unreasonable search & seizure |

Can police conduct a search or arrest someone without a warrant?

| 4 | Warrants supported by probable cause |

What information must police officers show to a judge to obtain a search or arrest warrant?

| 5 | Indictment by a grand jury |

Must a person always be indicted by a grand jury in order to be charged with a serious crime?

| 5 | No double jeopardy |

Can a person ever be tried a second time for the same criminal act?

| 5 | No compelled self-incrimination |

When can a person be pressured by police officers to provide a confession?

| 5 & 14 | Due process |

What steps must be followed in the processing of a criminal case in order to fulfill the right to due process?

| 6 | Speedy and public trial |

How soon after arrest must a trial occur and must the judge let everyone into the courtroom?

(continued)

Constitutional Rights in Criminal Justice (continued)

Procedural

Amendment	Right
6	Impartial jury

How must a jury be selected in order to make sure that it is impartial?

6	Confrontation of opposing witnesses

Can anyone ever testify against a defendant without being face-to-face with the defendant in the courtroom?

6	Compulsory process

What authority does the defendant possess to bring witnesses to court?

6	Assistance of counsel

Must a defense attorney be provided for defendants in all cases?

8	No excessive bail

How high must a bail amount be in order to be judged as "excessive"?

8	No excessive fines

How large must a fine be in order to be judged as "excessive"?

8	No cruel and unusual punishments

Which punishments are considered cruel and unusual?

14	Equal protection of the laws

If more African-Americans than whites are stopped and searched, does that violate the right to equal protection?

---

explicitly make exceptions for people who are convicted of crimes. Only one right is expressed in terms conveying the notion that "People have this right EXCEPT if they have committed a crime," and that right is the Thirteenth Amendment's prohibition on slavery that specifies an exception for requiring convicted criminal offenders to work ("Neither slavery nor involuntary servitude, except as a punishment for crime whereof the party shall have been duly convicted, shall exist within the United States . . . "). Indeed, the authors of the Constitution recognized that they themselves were "criminals" in the eyes of the British for revolting against King George. Therefore they wanted to provide protections for people who disagreed with the government and were thereby viewed as deserving of punishment by the leaders who happened to be in power at the moment. The detailed rights for criminal defendants in the Sixth Amendment demonstrate the founders' evident concern about protecting individuals from excessive prosecution by the government. More importantly, the Eighth Amendment prohibition on cruel and unusual punishments makes it abundantly clear that there are limits on what the government can do to people, even those whose criminal actions have been proven. As a result, judges face cases in which they must decide the extent to which the Bill of Rights protects convicted offenders while they are in prison or under other forms of correctional supervision.

Now that we have identified the constitutional rights relevant to criminal justice and illuminated the ways in which such rights can affect criminal law and its processes, it is time to examine how these rights are defined and applied.

THE APPLICABILITY OF THE BILL OF RIGHTS

Conventional Wisdom 4

When ratified in 1791, the Bill of Rights provided fundamental legal protections against the actions of police officers and other criminal justice officials throughout the country.

As indicated by the preceding discussion, the Bill of Rights was added to the Constitution because of concerns that the foundational document did not provide enough specific legal protections for individuals. During the first decades of its existence, the Bill of Rights attracted little attention from the Supreme Court. The early high court met for only a few months each year, and the justices spent other months traveling separately to different sections of the country to preside individually over legal proceedings. The Court's limited caseload did not require the justices to devote much attention to defining the meaning and applicability of the Bill of Rights during the first few decades in which the early amendments existed. In 1833, however, the Court addressed the meaning of the Bill of Rights in an important case concerning the Fifth Amendment.

In *Barron v. Baltimore* (1833), Mr. Barron filed a legal action against the City of Baltimore because the city's road construction efforts had directed dirt and silt into the harbor at the spot where ships loaded and unloaded their cargoes at Mr. Barron's dock. The construction dirt lowered the water level and made it impossible for ships to reach Mr. Barron's wharf. Thus Mr. Barron's business was ruined. He sought to recover money from the city by claiming that the road construction amounted to the taking of private property for public use without just compensation and thereby violated the specific words of the Fifth Amendment. In other words, Mr. Barron's private business was no longer usable because of the city's actions so he believed that the city had, in effect, taken his business away without giving him compensation.

The Supreme Court rejected Mr. Barron's claim by pointing out that the Bill of Rights applied only against actions by the federal government and not against actions by state and local governments. The first words of the First Amendment say that "Congress shall make no. . . ." The words of the amendment do not provide protections against all governments. Congress is not a generic word for government or even legislature; it refers to a very specific institutional entity, the national legislature that enacts laws on behalf of the federal government. Thus the Bill of Rights did not provide any protection against actions by state and local governments. It only applied to limit the laws that could be enacted by Congress and the actions undertaken by officials in federal government agencies. This interpretation meant that the Bill of Rights offered hardly any actual protections for people because the federal government was so small during the early nineteenth century that it touched people's lives in relatively few ways. People's daily lives were affected much more significantly by the state and local governments, which were immune from the requirements of the Bill of Rights.

With respect to criminal justice, the Bill of Rights had an especially limited impact because the federal government had so little involvement in issues of crime and justice. With the exception of smuggling, counterfeiting, and a limited list of other crimes defined by Congress, nearly all crimes were defined and enforced by state and local authorities. In the aftermath of the Supreme Court's decision in *Barron v. Baltimore,* it was quite clear that the Fourth Amendment prohibition on unreasonable searches and seizures and other rights in the Bill of Rights did not apply to the vast majority of criminal cases. The only rights possessed by most criminal defendants were those contained in individual state constitutions.[2] Thus the precise rights that applied to criminal cases varied widely from state to state.

The ratification of the Fourteenth Amendment in 1868 re-opened the issue of whether any provisions of the Bill of Rights applied against state and local officials. The Fourteenth Amendment explicitly provides legal protections against actions by state officials, but the rights contained in the amendment, such as "due process" and "equal protection," are more vague than many of the rights expressed in the first ten amendments. Lawyers began to argue that the right to "due process" in the Fourteenth Amendment should be understood to include specific rights contained in the Bill of Rights. Indeed, some scholars believe that the Fourteenth Amendment was intended by its authors to apply the entire Bill of Rights against state and local officials in the same way that it applied against federal officials.[3] However, the Supreme Court did not interpret the amendment in that fashion. In a series of decisions over the course of fifty years, the justices rejected arguments for including within the Due Process Clause of the Fourteenth Amendment such legal protections as the Fifth Amendment right to a grand jury indictment (*Hurtado v. California,* 1884) and the Fifth Amendment privilege against compelled self-incrimination (*Twining v. New Jersey,* 1908). Attorneys had argued that these rights should be considered very important to the criminal justice process because the country's founders had viewed them as important enough to be expressed in the Bill of Rights. Therefore, according to their arguments, these rights should be regarded as elements of the process due to defendants in state courts as part of the Fourteenth Amendment's right to due process. Initially, the justices did not agree with this argument and the Bill of Rights generally continued to apply only against actions by the federal government.

In the twentieth century, the Supreme Court used the process of **incorporation** to expand the applicability of the Bill of Rights. Beginning with its decision to incorporate the First Amendment right to freedom of speech into the Fourteenth Amendment in 1925 (*Gitlow v. New York*), the Court gradually began to interpret the Due Process Clause to include specific provisions of the Bill of Rights. Most criminal justice rights, however, were not incorporated into the Fourteenth Amendment's Due Process Clause and applied against state and local officials until the 1960s. The justices applied the Fourth Amendment's prohibition on unreasonable searches and seizures against the states in 1949 (*Wolf v. Colorado*), but it was not until 1961 that the Court required state and local police to follow the same rules as federal law enforcement officers with respect to the exclusion of evidence as the penalty for failing to conduct reasonable searches (*Mapp v. Ohio*). The Eighth Amendment prohibition on cruel and unusual punishments was applied to the states in 1962 (*Robinson v. California*). The Sixth Amendment right to counsel was enforced against the states in 1963 (*Gideon v. Wainwright*). The Fifth Amendment privilege against compelled self-incrimination was incorporated in 1964 (*Malloy v. Hogan*); and it was followed by the Sixth Amendment rights to confront adverse witnesses in 1965 (*Pointer v. Texas*), to a speedy trial in 1967 (*Klopfer v. North Carolina*), and to a trial by jury in 1968 (*Duncan v. Louisiana*). By the end of the 1960s, nearly every right relevant to criminal justice in the first eight amendments had been incorporated into the Due Process Clause of the Fourteenth Amendment and applied against the states except for the Fifth Amendment right to a grand jury and the Second Amendment provision concerning firearms. This means that states are not required to use grand juries and they can freely regulate ownership and possession of firearms unless they have their own state constitutional provisions or statutes that provide people within their states with legal protections concerning these two issues.

This history of the Bill of Rights illustrates the point that many of the rights that Americans take for granted and assume have been available since 1791 actually provided little protection for people until the last half of the twentieth century. For most of American history, nothing in the U.S. Constitution prevented state and local police officers from conducting warrantless searches at their own discretion and questioning witnesses as they wished without worrying about any rights concerning self-incrimination or defense counsel. Abusive police practices were widespread during much of American history. The Supreme Court occasionally intervened into cases concerning state and local law enforcement officers, such as when the justices found a violation of the Fourteenth Amendment right to due process when officers in Mississippi tortured African-American suspects into confessing in the 1930s (*Brown v. Mississippi,* 1936). Because in many states the right to a defense attorney did not develop until the mid-twentieth century, most criminal suspects who were victimized by police had little hope of using the legal process to assert that their rights were violated or that they were otherwise mistreated.

Summary

Americans are justifiably proud of the emphasis on the protection of individuals' legal rights that has been evident in the nation's governing documents since the eighteenth century. However, the existence of words defining and protecting constitutional rights cannot be equated with the actual existence of legal protections for individuals. For most of American history, the rights contained in the Bill of Rights applied only against the federal government. Individuals' legal protections against actions by state and local officials depended on the definition and implementation of rights from state constitutions. As a result, the existence and protection of rights varied from state to state. Most of the criminal justice–related rights that Americans take for granted in the twenty-first century did not apply universally throughout the country until the 1960s.

INTERPRETING THE CONSTITUTION'S WORDS

Conventional Wisdom 5

The literal meaning of the Constitution's words control the definition of rights unless the words are ambiguous and therefore require interpretation by judges.

Some words in the Bill of Rights are clearly ambiguous. There is no way to avoid interpreting the word *unreasonable* when defining the meaning of the Fourth Amendment right against "unreasonable searches and seizures." Similarly, the entire Eighth Amendment requires interpretation in order to determine when bail and fines are "excessive" and which punishments are "cruel and unusual." Other words and phrases, however, seem relatively clear. The Fifth Amendment says, in part, "No person shall be held to answer for a capital, or otherwise infamous crime, unless on a presentment or indictment of a Grand Jury." Although the word *infamous* would require interpretation, the rest of the clause clearly appears to require that evidence be presented to a grand jury before someone can be charged with a capital offense. In this case, the words are relatively unambiguous but the protection provided by the right is limited because, as already mentioned, this portion of the Fifth Amendment is one of the few rights that has never been incorporated into the Fourteenth Amendment. The grand jury requirement applies only to federal cases, which comprise only a small fraction of the total number of serious criminal cases, capital and otherwise, each year in state and federal courts. Individual states use grand juries if required to do so under their own state laws.

Another portion of the Bill of Rights that people regard as relatively unambiguous is the First Amendment's statement that "Congress shall make no law . . . abridging the freedom of speech." As previously noted, the word *Congress* no longer limits the applicability of the amendment to the federal government because the Supreme Court has interpreted the Fourteenth Amendment as expanding the reach of the First Amendment. In *Gitlow v. New York* (1925), the Court effectively used the word *Congress* to stand for all government, including state and local governments, when the First Amendment was incorporated into the Due Process Clause of the Fourteenth Amendment in order to give it nationwide applicability. The phrase "freedom of speech" provides an additional illustration of the interpretive power of judges. In *Texas v. Johnson* (1989), for example, a political protester at the 1984 Republican national convention was arrested and convicted for burning an American flag in violation of a Texas statute that made it a crime to dese-crate the national flag. The U.S. Supreme Court issued a controversial deci-sion that invalidated the criminal conviction because a majority of justices defined Johnson's actions in burning the flag as expressive conduct that they considered to be protected "speech" under the First Amendment. Clearly, burning a flag is an action that would not be considered "speech" in the ordi-nary use of that term, which implies communicating orally with words. However, the justices possess the authority to examine the underlying purpose of an amendment in order to define its meaning. Here, the justices recognized that the First Amendment emphasizes serious concerns about the government preventing people from communicating their ideas to each other. Because communication can involve forms of expression that extend behind the use of words expressed orally, the justices interpreted the word *speech* as encom-passing a broader array of expressions, including expressive conduct. This is a defensible approach to interpretation, but it also illustrates the authority of judges to say that words mean what the judges believe that they should mean.

In *Adderley v. Florida* (1966), the Court upheld the convictions of civil rights protesters who demonstrated on the grounds of a local jail that held people who had been arrested for protesting against racial segregation and discrimination against African-Americans. The Court's decision rested on the conclusion that the government can impose reasonable time, place, and man-ner restrictions on speech. This principle has been followed in subsequent cases, but how is it derived from the words of the First Amendment? The amendment does not say that "you can have freedom of speech except when you are standing outside of a jail." The First Amendment's words express an absolute: Congress shall make no law. The Fourteenth Amendment and the Supreme Court's incorporation decisions expanded this limitation to state and local governments. Yet it turns out that the apparently absolute prohibition on government regulation abridging speech is not actually as strong or expansive as one might presume from the words. Supreme Court justices have asserted the authority to create additional unexpressed terms and conditions in conjunction with the interpretation and definition of constitutional rights. These additional conditions and limitations are typically supported by a rationale intended to permit the government to carry out necessary functions, such as transporting prisoners to and from jails without any risk of interference from the public. However, it is the judicial officers themselves who determine what conditions and limitations are appropriate and necessary. The identification of these factors vary and change depending on the composition of the Court because they are based on each individual justice's values and "best judgment" about what is good for society. This authority to add (or subtract) elements to constitutional rights further diminishes the public's ability to rely on the literal words of the Constitution as a source for understanding the definition and nature of constitutional rights.

Another example of the introduction of interpretive limitations on constitutional rights comes from the context of corrections. Since the Supreme Court began examining the constitutional rights of incarcerated offenders in the 1960s, it has consistently defined the scope of those rights by balancing the safety and security interests of the institution against the legal protections provided by the Bill of Rights. For example, the First Amendment says that "Congress shall make no law . . . prohibiting the free exercise [of religion]." The amendment does not include the phrase "except in jails and prisons." The authors of the Constitution were unlikely to add any such phrase because they were not familiar with the use of prisons as a means of long-term punishment. In the late eighteenth century, colonial America applied physical punishments to convicted offenders. Such punishments included hanging, whipping, branding, and locking for short periods in public stocks. Jails were used to hold debtors and offenders awaiting punishment for relatively short periods of time. The first dedicated use of incarceration as a criminal punishment began in Pennsylvania at the end of the eighteenth century. The concept of the American prison began at this time but did not fully develop until the mid-nineteenth century. Thus modern judges find themselves attempting to reconcile the language from a Constitution written before there were any prisons with the contexts of modern correctional institutions. As a result, the Supreme Court has recognized *limited* religious rights for prisoners. When prison regulations collide with prisoners' desire to practice their religion, such as when a Muslim prayer service conflicts with prisoners' work schedules, the Court is very deferential to the policies and preferences of corrections officials. The First Amendment is written in absolute terms, but the Supreme Court says that prison regulations that impinge on religious freedom are acceptable when they advance important institutional interests in security and order and they provide prisoners with other opportunities to engage in religious practices (*O'Lone v. Estate of Shabazz*, 1987). Judicial decision makers can use their interpretive authority to advance societal interests even when those interests collide with the plain language of the Constitution.

Justices can also use their interpretive authority to expand constitutional rights, including the provision of legal protections that are not evident in the document's specific words. In 1965, the Supreme Court invalidated a Connecticut statute that made it a crime for a doctor to counsel married couples about contraception (*Griswold v. Connecticut*). Justice William O. Douglas's majority opinion concluded that the statute violated the constitutional right to privacy. However, the word *privacy* does not appear anywhere in the Constitution or the Bill of Rights. Although Justice Hugo Black argued that a right to privacy cannot exist unless such a right is explicitly stated in the Constitution, other justices agreed with Douglas's conclusion that rights exist in the Constitution by implication. According to Douglas, various provisions of the Bill of Rights explicitly protect specific aspects of privacy. For example, the First Amendment protects freedom of association; the Third Amendment prevents the government from quartering troops in people's homes; and the Fourth Amendment prohibits unreasonable searches in order to protect people, their homes, and their personal papers. Because Douglas saw various elements of privacy explicitly protected by the Constitution's words, he declared that the cumulative effect of the existence of these specific rights was the creation of a generalized right to privacy. Justice Arthur Goldberg had a different but related rationale for the same result. He concluded that the right to privacy was one of the unnamed "other rights" mentioned in the Ninth Amendment as being reserved for the people. Again, he identified and defined the right through interpretive implication rather than through the Constitution's specific words.

In another example of judges' ability to announce the definition of rights by inferring their existence by implication rather than specific constitutional language, the Supreme Court's requirement that police officers provide *Miranda* warnings is not based on specific language in the Fifth Amendment. Instead, a majority of justices see the right to receive warnings as an essential element for the protection of the constitutionally specified privilege against compelled self-incrimination and the right to counsel.

Summary

The literal words of the Constitution do not define the constitutional rights enjoyed by Americans. The words must be interpreted by judges, especially the justices on the U.S. Supreme Court. The U.S. Supreme Court possesses significant authority to interpret and define rights, even if the definitions appear to clash with the apparent meanings of the Constitution's words. The Supreme Court can also use its interpretive power to identify and define rights that are not evident from the Constitution's words.

THE PROCESS OF CONSTITUTIONAL INTERPRETATION

Conventional Wisdom 6

When the words of the Constitution are ambiguous, justices interpret and define rights by following the precedents established in prior court decisions over the course of history.

The concept of **stare decisis,** or adherence to case precedent, is important in American law. The United States inherited the common law system of England through which judges created legal rules as they decided cases concerning disputes over contracts, property, and personal injuries. Subsequent judges then followed these rules in similar cases. Constitutional law is not the traditional common law, because it is based on the interpretation of a document rather than simply judge-created law. However, American constitutional law, like other areas of American law, draws from the common law process by treating previously decided cases as establishing authoritative rules of law that should be followed. This does not imply that the rules in prior decisions must be followed in all cases. Sometimes a majority of justices on the Supreme Court decide that a new rule would embody a better interpretation of the Constitution and provide a more beneficial result for society. Thus the common law process of reliance on case precedent also allows for changes in legal rules through decisions in new cases.

Case precedent can be a very useful guide for judicial decision makers. By relying on case precedent, justices provide stability in the rules for society and protect the interests of people who have taken actions in reliance on existing rules. One of the underlying purposes of law is to provide social stability by guiding people in their interactions and transactions with other individuals, businesses, and government. If the law frequently changed quickly and drastically, disputes within society would be exacerbated rather than preempted and resolved. As a result, people might rely on means other than law in order to protect their property, personal safety, and other interests. When a society lacks a common set of reliable rules and people choose their own means to advance their self-interest, chaotic results are likely to follow, much to the detriment of peaceful coexistence and civility. Such results would also harm the legitimacy and image of courts as governing institutions and increase the likelihood that people would not voluntarily obey court orders. Thus Supreme Court justices sometimes rely on case precedent in making decisions with which they personally disagree. When the Supreme Court faced its first reconsideration of the decision in *Booth v. Maryland* (1987) that barred the use of victim impact statements in capital sentencing hearings, Justice Byron White voted to maintain the ban in *South Carolina v. Gathers* (1989) because he felt it was required by the *Booth* precedent even though he disagreed with the Court's decision in *Booth*.

Although adherence to case precedent arguably serves a valuable function for judges and society, it is not treated as an inviolable obligation for judges. When judges—especially those on a state supreme court or the U.S. Supreme Court—disagree with a decision, they frequently attempt to persuade a majority of their colleagues to produce a new rule by either overruling the prior precedent or by making an incremental adjustment in the legal rule while leaving the prior case precedent in place. For example, the Court's decision in *Payne v. Tennessee* (1991) flatly overruled the prior precedents established in *Booth v. Maryland* and *South Carolina v. Gathers* when it endorsed the use of victim impact statements in capital sentencing.

By contrast, when the Supreme Court reconsidered the precedent established by *Enmund v. Florida* (1982) that barred the application of the death penalty to a felony-murder accomplice (i.e., the driver of the getaway car) who did not actively participate in the killing, they changed the underlying rule while claiming to keep the *Enmund* precedent intact. In *Tison v. Arizona* (1987), the Court claimed to merely alter the *Enmund* precedent by permitting the death penalty for felony-murder accomplices who were found by the jury to show "reckless disregard for human life." Justice Sandra O'Connor's opinion declined to overrule and eliminate *Enmund* because she needed to persuade the author of the *Enmund* opinion, Justice White, to provide the decisive fifth vote for opening the possibility of executing felony-murder accomplices. Rather than risking the loss of White's crucial vote by stating forthrightly that *Enmund* was decided incorrectly, O'Connor claimed to preserve White's *Enmund* precedent even as she created a rule that made it irrelevant. The *Enmund* precedent had made the imposition of the death penalty rest on whether or not the accomplice took an active role in the killing. After the rule was "adjusted" by the *Tison* decision, the only question was whether the jurors disliked the defendants' actions enough to label those actions as showing "reckless disregard for human life," regardless of the extent of the defendants' involvement in the actual homicide.[4]

The *Tison* example illustrates the point that the process of adherence to case precedent also serves another, less recognized function. Because of the malleability of the language of law, precedents help to provide legitimacy for new decisions by judges, even if those decisions are disconnected from legal rules established in prior cases. Justices can claim to adhere to precedents such as *Enmund* even as they define rights in new ways and take the law in new directions. By citing precedents, justices give the appearance that their decisions are guided by and perhaps even dictated by existing law when, in fact, the decisions simply reflect the justices' preferred rules and outcomes based on their values and policy preferences.

Case precedents may dictate the outcomes of many cases for lower court judges. Even when these judges disagree with a rule of law, they may feel constrained from making a decision to change the rule because they know that an appellate court above them will simply reverse their decision. If they believe that a majority of judges on the court above them may be sympathetic to a new rule, then they may use a case decision to establish the rule with the hope that the rule will be solidified on appeal through endorsement by a higher court. By contrast, judicial decision makers on **courts of last resort,** such as the U.S. Supreme Court and state supreme courts, possess the authority to overrule precedents and alter legal rules established in prior cases because there are no higher courts to overturn their decisions. They may be reluctant to change precedents if, as in the case of abortion discussed in Chapter 1 (*Planned Parenthood v. Casey,* 1992), they fear that the public will not accept their new ruling as a legitimate legal decision or if they fear adverse public reactions, such as disobedience to the rules of law. Precedents do not dictate outcomes to courts of last resort, but justices may accept and respect precedents for various reasons, such as protecting the judiciary's legitimacy or maintaining stability in the law concerning a specific issue, even if some of them do not agree with the established rule. If, however, they feel strongly that a new legal rule would be most beneficial to society, then they will adjust or overturn precedents despite the risks of adverse public or political reactions. The Supreme Court's famous decision in *Brown v. Board of Education* that declared racial segregation in public schools to be a violation of the Equal Protection Clause was made by the justices in 1954 despite their knowledge that the decision would generate widespread opposition and possibly violent resistance, especially in southern states. In making the decision, the Court effectively overturned a fifty-eight-year-old precedent that had permitted governmental institutions to discriminate by race (*Plessy v. Ferguson,* 1896).

Summary

In making decisions, American judges rely on the rules established by prior cases. The reliance on precedent is a legacy of the English origins of American law and serves the purpose of promoting consistency and stability in law. Precedents are, however, not sacred. In fact, judicial reasoning is very malleable. Judges have opportunities to alter, ignore, or overturn precedents as they seek to produce the case outcomes that they believe are most appropriate. Courts of last resort, such as the U.S. Supreme Court and state supreme courts, are best positioned to overturn and alter precedents because there are no higher courts to overturn their decisions that move the law in new directions.

Conventional Wisdom 7

When there are no precedents to guide the Supreme Court about an issue presented in a legal case, the justices follow a well-established philosophy of constitutional interpretation that leads them to the proper result.

As indicated by the foregoing discussion, the justices do not feel obligated to follow precedent, even when it exists. They *use* precedents to develop the justifications for their decisions, but they do not necessarily *follow* the logic and rules of prior case decisions. When they consider the cases presented to them, whether or not a relevant precedent exists, judges draw from their beliefs about the proper approach to constitutional interpretation, their views about the best law and policy for society, their concerns about the need to maintain the Court's image of neutrality and legitimacy, and their interactions with each other. There is no simple, agreed-upon approach that leads to the "proper" result. The justices often disagree with each other about the proper approach for constitutional interpretation as well as about the most appropriate result.

Two justices, Clarence Thomas and Antonin Scalia, strongly advocate the use of a single approach for interpreting the Constitution. They assert that all judges should interpret the Constitution, including the Bill of Rights, according to the intentions of the people who wrote each provision. By following the intentions of the framers, they claim that they are able to avoid the risk of injecting their own values and policy preferences into constitutional interpretation. Although their arguments sound coherent and plausible when described as a philosophy of constitutional interpretation, the "original intent" approach, sometimes referred to as **originalism,** is problematic.

A basic problem for an originalist interpretation is the question of whether we actually know what the framers intended each provision of the Constitution to mean and, more importantly, whether the framers agreed about precise meanings. There is no authoritative source to tell us what the framers intended. Among the available historical sources, the notes of James Madison, for example, are useful in some ways but cannot be presumed to represent the views of everyone involved in the constitutional convention. Similarly, other notes about the debates concerning the Constitution and the Bill of Rights demonstrate that various people expressed divergent opinions and concerns. The Constitution and the Bill of Rights were written and approved by legislative bodies. Thus it is difficult to believe that every participant shared precisely the same views about the meaning of ambiguous words and phrases. Moreover, some critics argue that a "true" originalist approach should be more concerned with the intentions and understandings of the ratifiers within each individual state since their act of approving the Constitution and its amendments gave the document its legal authority.

Neither Thomas nor Scalia actually follows the Constitution's original intent in all of their decisions. In specific cases, each of them deviates from their purported adherence to originalism in order to support outcomes that advance their conservative policy preferences.[5] Thomas, for example, interprets the Equal Protection Clause according to an idealistic view of a color-blind Constitution that is at odds with the more complex attitudes and behavior of the Fourteenth Amendment's authors who supported both racial segregation and forms of race-based special assistance for former slaves. In addition, both justices concede that the framers' original intentions for specific constitutional provisions are not known. In such cases, even Thomas and Scalia must rely on alternative approaches to interpretation.

Originalism is also controversial because of debates among judges and legal scholars about whether the twenty-first-century Constitution should be interpreted through eighteenth-century eyes. Many of the legal issues and problems of contemporary American society would have been unimaginable to the authors of the Constitution. How could anyone possibly know what the authors of the Fourth Amendment would have said about the use by modern law enforcement officers of sophisticated electronic surveillance and thermal-imaging devices? Harvard law professor Archibald Cox argues that the genius of the framers was their recognition that their own values and understandings of the world could not dictate the meaning of law as society changed over the decades. According to Cox, the framers created a short document with general words and phrases in order to permit future generations to interpret and utilize constitutional principles in a manner most appropriate to the social conditions and problems of their own era.[6] According to Laurence Tribe, another Harvard professor who is considered a leading critic of originalism,

> I think a judge's role is to identify the basic values that are expressed in the document and to give those values life in the context of contemporary society. He or she should not pretend to be merely a pipeline for some distant voices of giants who walked the land in the 18th century, but instead take personal responsibility for explaining what it is about a particular exercise of governmental power that does or does not clash with basic constitutional principles.[7]

Rather than follow a specific theory of constitutional interpretation, justices typically make *ad hoc* decisions that reflect their understandings about history, the role of the Court, and the needs of society. Within some justices' decisions about the definition and scope of rights in criminal justice, one can see the aspiration to provide broad, strong protections for individuals, even if it sometimes means that guilty offenders will go free because the police cannot obtain evidence against them through legal means. These justices, such as the late Justices William Brennan and Thurgood Marshall, arguably demonstrate suspicion and skepticism about the motives and actions of government officials, including officials within the criminal justice system. By contrast, other justices, such as Chief Justice William Rehnquist and Justice Sandra Day O'Connor, regard the Constitution as providing less expansive rights because they are more concerned about ensuring that law enforcement officials have sufficient power to combat crime effectively.

At the outset of each case, the characterization of the issue by the opposing attorneys affects the outcome of the case. Attorneys' characterizations and arguments place the legal issue in context for the justices and provide the justices with persuasive justifications that they could use in writing an opinion in support of a specific outcome. A study of the Supreme Court's death penalty cases, for example, shows how the attorneys' choice of arguments ultimately shapes the Court's decisions by framing the way the justices see and analyze a legal issue.[8] In a case concerning the constitutionality of Georgia's statute that made sodomy a felony punishable by a sentence of twenty years in prison, even for consenting adults and married couples, the majority and dissenting justices had divergent views about the real issue in the case (*Bowers v. Hardwick*, 1986). The case arose when a gay man was caught in bed with another man by a police officer who had entered the man's home and bedroom in order to carry out an arrest warrant. The warrant was based on inaccurate court records that erroneously reported that the man had failed to appear in court for the minor offense of drinking alcohol in public out of an open container. Justice White's majority opinion characterized the issue as whether homosexuals had the constitutional right to commit acts of sodomy. Based on this characterization of the issue, he and four other justices concluded that no such right existed. By contrast, Justice Harry Blackmun's opinion on behalf of three other justices characterized the issue as whether the statute violated the right of privacy of consenting adults to make their own decisions about their sexual behavior in the privacy of their own bedrooms. When characterizing the issue in this manner, these justices concluded that the statute violated the constitutional right to privacy. Nearly two decades later, after changes in the Court's composition, a different majority of justices made the *Bowers* dissent into the law of the land by invalidating a Texas sodomy statute (*Lawrence v. Texas*, 2003).

The importance of attorneys' arguments in the *Bowers* case was made especially clear by Justice Lewis Powell's concurring opinion. Powell said that he might have found the law to be unconstitutional if the attorneys had argued that the possibility of a twenty-year prison sentence violated the Eighth Amendment's prohibition on cruel and unusual punishments rather than focusing their arguments on the right to privacy issue. If other justices had been preoccupied with the Eighth Amendment issue, they might have based their decision on the Cruel and Unusual Punishments Clause no matter what arguments were made—or not made—by the attorneys. However, Powell's view of the appropriate role of judges apparently constrained the range of possible arguments and rationales that he felt he could legitimately use in making his decision. He felt obligated to decide the case based on the arguments provided by the attorneys, although he later admitted during an interview that he had made a mistake when he supported the constitutionality of the Georgia law. Because he changed his mind about the case after he retired, his new views had no impact on the development of constitutional law.

Justices' decisions may also be influenced by their interactions with each other. During oral arguments, justices may pose specific questions to an attorney for reasons other than their own desire to hear the attorney's answer. They may, in fact, believe that specific kinds of arguments will appeal to a particular colleague whom they wish to persuade to support their preferred outcome. If they can induce the attorney to provide an argument that they believe to be attractive to a colleague, they may increase the likelihood that they can gather the five needed votes to prevail in determining the outcome. Justices also discuss the cases together in conference and, occasionally, in one-to-one encounters within the Supreme Court building. The justices claim, however, that most of the persuasion occurs in the process of writing draft opinions that are circulated among the justices. A justice may change or solidify his or her vote in a case after reading a particularly persuasive draft opinion written by a colleague.

Judicial decision making and the definitions of rights are further complicated by the fact that individual justices are not always consistent in the way in which they interpret the Constitution. Justice O'Connor wrote an opinion concurring in part and dissenting in part to express concern about constitutional rules created by the Court that do not give police clear guidance about permissible behavior (*New York v. Quarles,* 1984). In *Quarles,* she said that the Court created vague rules about when suspects must be informed about their *Miranda* rights and these rules were causing confusion. She indicated that the Court should favor clear-cut rules that all officers can readily understand and easily follow. Although the particular case at hand had raised this concern in her mind, in fact, she had previously endorsed many of the Court's decisions that created the confusing patchwork of rules concerning searches and interrogations.

Rather than present consistent conclusions about the interpretation of a particular constitutional amendment, the Court's decisions sometimes create apparent contradictions because one or two justices perceive a small difference in the facts from one case to another. For example, a majority of justices ruled that there was no violation of the Eighth Amendment's prohibition on cruel and unusual punishments when Texas sentenced a man to life in prison as a habitual offender for the commission of three theft offenses over a nine-year period in which the total amount stolen was less than $250 (*Rummel v. Estelle,* 1980). A few years later, a majority of justices found that South Dakota violated the Eighth Amendment for giving a life sentence to an offender with a half-dozen drunk driving and theft convictions (*Solem v. Helm,* 1983). The second decision did not overturn the Court's earlier decision on the constitutionality of life sentences for habitual offenders. One wing of the Court consistently concluded that states possess the authority to choose when to impose life sentences. Another wing of the Court consistently concluded that life sentences for a series of nonviolent lesser offenses always violate the Eighth Amendment. The conflicting outcomes of the two cases and the confusing rule produced by the decisions were determined by the two justices in the middle of the Court who concluded that the Texas approach was permissible because it included the possibility of parole but the South Dakota scheme was unconstitutional because the life sentence included no possibility of parole. Sometimes it only takes one justice in the middle of an evenly divided Court who perceives subtle differences in an issue to produce decisions embodying rules that the rest of the Court regards as contradictory.

Individual justices can also change their minds about issues. They may arrive at the Court with one approach to interpreting specific constitutional amendments, but over time they develop a new view about the impact of their interpretation upon society. Justice Harry Blackmun, for example, spent nearly twenty years on the Court endorsing the constitutionality of capital punishment. Although his colleagues William Brennan and Thurgood Marshall consistently wrote dissenting opinions arguing that capital punishment always violates the Eighth Amendment prohibition on cruel and unusual punishments, Blackmun did not support their conclusion. Just prior to his retirement in the early 1990s, shortly after both Brennan and Marshall had departed from the Court, Blackmun announced that he had changed his mind. After two decades of deciding cases concerning capital punishment, Blackmun concluded that it was impossible for the American criminal justice system to impose the death penalty fairly, consistently, and in a nondiscriminatory manner. In the case of capital punishment, Blackmun's announced switch did not affect the Court's decisions because too few justices on the Court shared that view to impact the outcomes of cases. However, such individual changes can affect other issues concerning constitutional rights when the switch concerns an issue about which the Court is evenly divided.

Summary

The justices on the U.S. Supreme Court do not agree on a single judicial philosophy or approach to constitutional interpretation. When faced with cases, they inevitably apply their values and policy preferences to reach the result that they believe fits most closely with the Constitution's purposes and the needs of American society. Even those justices who claim to follow a consistent, coherent judicial philosophy in order to minimize the intrusion of their own values and beliefs are not completely consistent in following that purported philosophy. The definition of rights, like other judicial outcomes, is determined by the rule or result that can attract the support of a majority of justices.

CONCLUSION

The definition of constitutional rights is not determined by the literal words of the Constitution or a specific approach to constitutional interpretation. Supreme Court justices do not agree on a common approach for interpreting the Constitution. Moreover, even justices who claim to follow a coherent interpretive approach do not always actually remain faithful to that approach when specific issues trigger the expression of values to which they strongly adhere. Justices use their interpretive authority to produce case outcomes and rules for society that they believe embody the principles of the Constitution *as they see them.* Because each justice sees the Constitution in a slightly different light, according to their individual understandings of history, the Court's role, and the values underlying the Bill of Rights, the Court produces opinions on an *ad hoc* basis as the majority coalitions for each decision shift and change. Justices' decisions are shaped by their values and policy preferences as well as by the arguments of attorneys and the persuasiveness of other justices. Thus the justices alter the meaning of apparently clear words in the Constitution, add exceptions to rights expressed in absolute terms, create rights by the perceived implications of the Constitution's purposes, and change previously established interpretations whenever five of the nine justices deem such changes to be appropriate. Obviously, we cannot think of rights as fixed and enduring legal protections. The existence of the Bill of Rights does not guarantee that Americans will enjoy any specific rights because Supreme Court justices possess the authority to give meaning to, and even ignore, the specific words of the amendments. The definition of constitutional rights flows from malleable processes determined by fallible human beings. As is shown in subsequent chapters, the malleability of constitutional interpretation contributes to confusion and inconsistency in the definition of rights as well as deficiencies in the recognition, understanding, and implementation of rights by criminal justice officials.

THE IMPLEMENTATION OF CONSTITUTIONAL RIGHTS

The traditional study of law often meant gaining an understanding of the wording and interpretations of constitutions, statutes, and judicial opinions. These documents are the most important sources of law. Historically, many legal scholars limited their analysis to wording and interpretation without taking the next important step of considering whether and how those words and interpretations affect the lives of human beings. Since the 1960s, many social scientists have studied the impact of law on society. Their research provides significant insights about both human behavior and the limited effectiveness of legal rules. Although contemporary scholars have greater awareness of the human consequences of law, discussions of law—by both scholars and judges—often emphasize words and interpretations without adequately presenting important issues about human consequences. The emphasis on law as words and interpretations rather than as a practical force in society contributes to the public's misperceptions and unmet expectations about the nature of constitutional rights. This chapter provides an overview of a crucial link between law as words and law as a force affecting human beings: **implementation.** Subsequent chapters discuss implementation issues with respect to specific rights affecting criminal justice. The implementation, or lack thereof, of constitutional rights is one of the most important factors that determines the extent to which rights are symbolic or substantive.

With respect to constitutional rights, the word *implementation* means the processes and factors affecting the translation and application of law on paper into a force that affects people's lives. If a constitutional right, as stated by the words of a constitution or judicial opinion, is translated and applied so that people's actions and fates are affected in a manner that matches the words of the legislature or judge, then the law has been implemented effectively and the constitutional right has substance. In many cases, however, the words that describe and interpret a constitutional right do not match what actually happens to people in the real world. Rights are symbolic to the extent that there is a gap between the definition of the right and the application of the right to human beings' behavior and fates in the criminal justice system. The extent to which a right is symbolic is defined by the extent of the gap between its formal definition and its effective implementation. If a constitutional right defined in a judicial opinion does not provide any protection for individuals in the criminal justice system, either because it is ignored, unenforced, or distorted through implementation processes, that legal protection can be labeled as a **symbolic right.** It would be difficult to argue that any specific right is completely symbolic for all individuals. However, for specific suspects, defendants, and convicted offenders in the criminal justice system, individual rights may be entirely symbolic if these rights are effectively absent from the processes of their cases. Moreover, there are certain rights that are largely symbolic because of common impediments to implementation that affect large numbers of cases.

OVERVIEW OF THE IMPLEMENTATION PROCESS

Conventional Wisdom 8

The Supreme Court's decisions that define constitutional rights determine when and how those rights will be applied.

Judges' decisions interpreting constitutional provisions provide the formal definitions of rights. The process of implementing judges' decisions inevitably reshapes and limits the effectuation of court decisions. Because judicial decisions are not self-implementing, they must pass through the hands of various influential actors in the implementation process before they affect people's lives. The involvement of actors with varying political attitudes, values, and partisan interests can lead to inconsistent and unpredictable outcomes that diminish judges' ability to ensure that their decisions accomplish intended goals. In a useful model for illustrating the implementation and impact of judicial policies, Professors Charles Johnson and Bradley Canon identified interpreters, implementers, and consumers who, along with external political actors, determine precisely if and how judges' decisions will affect society.[1]

Interpreters

After judges issue a decision, the judicial opinion and its implications must be communicated and explained to the people who will carry it out. Police officers, for example, cannot follow closely the developing case law affecting search and seizure, *Miranda* warnings, and the other aspects of their jobs that are shaped by judicial decisions. Police officers, corrections officers, parole officers, and other lower level criminal justice officials do not have easy access to judges' opinions on such issues; nor do they have the time or training to study and interpret the judges' intended meanings. Thus, other actors assume the task of interpreting and explaining judicial decisions.

The most far-reaching pronouncements about the definition of rights come from the Supreme Court and other appellate courts. Frequently, if a trial judge makes a decision defining constitutional rights, the decision is often not implemented until the issue has been examined by higher courts on appeal. When appellate courts issue decisions about rights, their decisions are often limited to broad announcements that describe a rule imposed on governmental officials or provide a declaration concerning rights within a particular case. Thus there is uncertainty about how the appellate decision is to apply to other cases with factual circumstances that are similar but not necessarily identical to the case decided by the appellate court. The interpretation and explanation of the constitutional right are developed gradually by the trial judges who must apply the appellate decision to the individual circumstances within new cases that arise concerning that policy issue. In *Brown v. Board of Education,* the Supreme Court explicitly acknowledged this interpretation and implementation process by instructing the federal district courts to examine alleged racial segregation within school systems and to develop remedies on a case-by-case basis. In other issue areas, such as criminal justice, the interpreting role of trial judges is equally inevitable but based on less explicit instructions. When the Supreme Court declared that criminal suspects must be informed of their rights prior to questioning in the *Miranda* decision, trial judges subsequently had to decide precisely when the warnings had to be given, whether the warnings had to be phrased in a precise fashion, whether any questions could be asked of suspects prior to the warnings, and other issues that were not specifically spelled out by the Supreme Court. Some of these issues received clarification from the Supreme Court in subsequent cases concerning police interrogation of criminal suspects. However, trial judges inevitably determine the application of *Miranda* warnings and other rights in some cases because not all defendants fully pursue the appeal process or initiate other actions to challenge their convictions in higher courts.

Other officials may also serve as interpreters. These officials include state attorneys general, city attorneys, police chiefs, and other officials to whom police officers, prosecutors, and other officials look for advice and guidance. Unlike trial judges, these other interpreters—except for state attorneys general who issue official advisory opinions—do not make authoritative interpretations that purport to pronounce rules of law. Instead, their interpretations merely guide the behavior of officials charged with carrying out judicial decisions. Although their interpretations may turn out to be incorrect if a trial court reaches a different conclusion about the same issue, these interpreters still affect how constitutional rights impact citizens' lives. For example, city attorneys advise police departments about the meaning and implications of judicial decisions. State attorneys general interpret decisions and provide instructions to state and local officials about how they must follow judicial pronouncements. Thus police officers, parole officers, probation officers, and other officials who have daily contact with citizens use the interpretations they are given—whether accurate and authoritative or not—to establish policies and practices that affect people in society.

What are the consequences of this interpretation process? The various interpreters may interpret and explain the constitutional rights decisions in different ways. Moreover, some interpreters may not hear immediately about specific judicial decisions, especially if they are busy with various responsibilities rather than serving as an attorney-advisor for a police department who is specifically focused on monitoring new case law. The spread of computerized legal research services make U.S. Supreme Court decisions readily available. However, decisions by state supreme courts, state courts of appeals, and federal courts of appeals are often not highly publicized and therefore a delay may occur before some officials realize that a new decision has been issued that affects their work. While some city attorneys may not be immediately aware of all relevant decisions, others quickly learn about new decisions and produce interpretations for their own police departments. These interpretations may be different from those produced by other city attorneys. As a result, the actual meaning and implementation of specific constitutional rights may vary from city to city.

The varying interpretations of the judges' intentions may stem from ambiguity in the wording of the judicial decision, mistaken perceptions on the part of interpreters, or even willful efforts by interpreters to shape the meaning of the judicial decision to fit the interpreter's own policy preferences. If city officials object to a judicial decision, they may intentionally interpret it as applying only to a limited range of circumstances. This may force a citizen to go back through the lengthy litigation process again in order to force the officials to follow a precise directive from the courts in various specific circumstances in which the right may be relevant. In the meantime, the city officials have succeeded in weakening and delaying implementation of a policy that they oppose. For example, in 2003 a California Supreme Court case revealed that police officers were taught to violate *Miranda* rights by ignoring suspects' requests for access to defense attorneys during interrogations (*People v. Neal*).

Implementers

Even if judicial opinions are explained, they do not affect society according to the judges' intentions unless the officials responsible for carrying out the policies implement the directives properly. The *Miranda* decision, for example, is primarily a symbolic declaration unless police officers follow through with their instructions to inform suspects about the right to counsel and the right against self-incrimination. The substance or symbolism of constitutional rights can depend on whether implementers have heard about the judicial definitions of rights, whether they understood the explanations concerning the meaning of the rights, and whether they comply with their instructions to respect these rights.

A failure to comply with judicial decisions may stem from a lack of understanding or from an intentional effort to resist the court's decision. When federal courts issued orders to desegregate public schools, many school systems in the South initially refused to comply. They knew what they were supposed to do, but the judicial policy did not take effect because the implementers opposed equal rights for African-Americans and intentionally failed to follow the judges' directives. This willful noncompliance was premised upon a hope that other political actors, such as Congress, would combat the courts' decisions and prevent desegregation through a constitutional amendment or other means. Eventually, it took additional judicial decisions to levy fines on school systems, legislative and executive actions to withhold funds, and even the actions of law enforcement officers or military forces to initiate compliance in several cities.

Failure to implement judicial policies can occur in more subtle ways as well. For example, an unethical police officer who makes an arrest in an alley with no witnesses present may have the opportunity to mistreat the suspect in violation of judicial decisions concerning suspects' rights. If the suspect asserts that the police officer never informed him of his rights and the police officer says the suspect is lying, the judge will simply decide which witness is more credible. Such decisions are likely to go against a criminal suspect whether or not the suspect is telling the truth. Because of the varying contexts in which suspects are arrested and questioned, the Supreme Court cannot protect the rights of criminal suspects. The Court can issue rules that, if followed, would protect suspects' rights. However, the actual protection of such rights rests primarily in the hands of individual police officers who control implementation of those rights according to whether or not they understand and obey the Supreme Court's directives.

Sometimes an individual police officer's failure to follow judicial policies in areas such as search and seizure may stem from a lack of knowledge about the most recent court decisions explaining the technical details of appropriate police behavior. Police cannot be expected to read and understand the most recent judicial decisions, especially because certain areas of law are refined every year by new decisions. There are likely to be weaknesses in the processes for communicating the details of judges' decisions to implementers, and these weaknesses reduce the effectiveness of constitutional rights. The spate of decisions by conservative judicial officers in the late 1980s and early 1990s exacerbated the difficulties experienced by police officers. These decisions reduced the scope of several constitutional rights. By creating exceptions to previously clear-cut rules, the Court eliminated some of the restrictions on police behavior with respect to questioning suspects, search and seizure, and other areas. For example, the Court changed from a clear-cut **exclusionary rule** mandating the exclusion from court of improperly obtained evidence to a series of exceptions that permit the use of illegally obtained evidence in certain circumstances. Thus the boundaries of proper law enforcement practices are less clear.

It is also possible that unethical police officers will intentionally disregard rules about constitutional rights. Although all evidence indicates that most officers attempt to fulfill their responsibilities properly, there are risks that some officers will mischaracterize events in order to protect themselves against being disciplined by their superiors for making mistakes.

"Did you read that suspect his *Miranda* rights before you questioned him?"

Rather than reply with "Uh, oh. We were so busy trying to keep bystanders out of the way and prevent the crime scene from being disturbed that we forgot to do the *Miranda* warnings at first," even an officer who generally tries to do his or her job properly might be tempted to say, "Yeah, of course."

As periodic police scandals reveal, some officers lack a commitment to ethics and professionalism. These officers may violate policies, give dishonest responses to their superiors and on the witness stand, and otherwise violate constitutional rights intentionally. Even if such officers constitute only a tiny percentage of the police force nationally, they place rights at risk for anyone who encounters them. As an average citizen, how do you know what kind of officer has stopped you when you are pulled over for a traffic violation? The underlying point is that implementation of constitutional rights rests in the hands of criminal justice officials and there are risks that some of those officials will fail to fulfill the requirements established by courts in defining rights and dictating rules for the permissible range of authority for criminal justice officials.

Consumers

The people directly affected by court decisions can also influence implementation. Although government officials are affected by judicial decisions, their roles as authoritative decision makers place them in the implementer category. Consumers are the private citizens and corporations affected by judicial decisions. For example, in regard to decisions affecting the rights of criminal suspects, consumers would be the individuals investigated, questioned, or arrested by the police. In school desegregation cases, consumers would be the parents and schoolchildren directly affected by a court order within a specific school system. Consumers may hear about important judicial decisions that are reported by the news media, but frequently they have no ability to learn about the most recent court cases. Thus, if the implementers fail to respect the consumers' rights in accordance with judicial directives but the consumers do not realize that their rights have been violated, the constitutional right will not be effectuated because there is no one to complain about the lack of implementation. For example, if a police officer conducts a search of an automobile without proper justification, the driver's Fourth Amendment right against unreasonable search and seizure has been violated. However, if the driver does not know the constitutional rules governing police searches, the driver has no basis to make a complaint to the police department. If the search uncovers evidence of illegal activity, the defense attorney, who is trained in law, is positioned to identify rights violations and challenge the validity of the search in court. But if no illegal evidence is found and no prosecution is pursued, the driver's right has been violated with virtually no possibility of a remedy.

In addition, if a consumer recognizes a rights violation but is frustrated by resistance from a school system or other government agency or, alternatively, cannot afford to hire a lawyer to seek enforcement in court, the consumer may not follow through with additional efforts to ensure that the policy is fully implemented. For example, a driver may believe that her car was illegally searched by police officers without any justification. If the driver complains to the police department and no action is taken against the officer, the driver may feel frustrated by the agency's lack of responsiveness. Yet, the driver may have no alternative course of action to protect her rights.

For certain kinds of rights violations, criminal justice officials' fears about consumers' reactions may help to ensure implementation.[2] These fears are aroused primarily when rights violations may lead to lawsuits that produce substantial financial awards. Such lawsuits are likely to be undertaken and successful only when the consumer can prove physical injury, property damage, or improper deprivation of liberty as a result of a constitutional rights violation. Thus, consumers may play an important role in the implementation, or lack thereof, of specific constitutional rights.

Secondary Groups

Many external political actors influence the development and implementation of constitutional rights. The president and state governors are important enforcers of judicial decisions. Their commitment, or lack thereof, to the enforcement of judicial decisions can significantly affect whether the judges' intentions are implemented. Interest groups frequently bear the burden of pressing for implementation of judicial decisions. Because the consumers who are supposed to be directly affected by these decisions frequently are not aware of court decisions or they lack the resources to seek enforcement of such decisions, interest groups utilize their organizational expertise and resources to initiate additional legal actions, publicize government officials' failure to obey judges' orders, lobby elected officials for enforcement, and otherwise seek to effectuate the judicial decisions that favor their policy preferences. With respect to the rights of individuals in the criminal justice system, organizations such as the American Civil Liberties Union and the NAACP Legal Defense and Education Fund undertake litigation designed to persuade judges to issue decisions that provide greater protection for constitutional rights.

The public relations activities of interest groups may educate consumers as well as influence interpreters and implementers. A state prosecutors' association, for example, may publish a newsletter describing recent court decisions and these descriptions may influence the way county prosecutors and city attorneys interpret decisions concerning constitutional rights. The news media play an important role in disseminating information about judicial decisions so that interpreters, implementers, and consumers learn about recent policy directives. The slant that reporters take in their stories may also shape the knowledge and perceptions of police officers and others about the latest judicial developments concerning constitutional rights. Moreover, the news reports help to keep the judges themselves informed about the consequences of their decisions and may thereby influence future judicial decisions, including actions to accelerate implementation.

Legislators, scholars, and others are also part of this rights implementation process through their actions, which influence and inform the actors most directly responsible for the interpretation and implementation of judges' decisions. Law professors may, for example, write articles analyzing and explaining judicial decisions that influence how state attorneys general and city attorneys understand judges' written opinions that define rights.

Summary

The Supreme Court's definition of a constitutional right is just one element in the process of determining how people's lives will be affected by that right. As illustrated by the roles of the interpreters, implementers, consumers, and secondary groups, the implementation of judicial decisions concerning constitutional rights is neither easy nor automatic. Numerous factors can influence whether there is a gap between the words of the judges' decisions and the actual legal protections enjoyed by citizens in their encounters with criminal justice officials.

FACTORS AFFECTING IMPLEMENTATION

Conventional Wisdom 9

If Supreme Court justices wrote their decisions with greater clarity, interpreters and implementers would understand their responsibilities. Thus constitutional rights would be implemented effectively.

The human activities comprising the process of interpreting and implementing constitutional rights cannot be undertaken with scientific precision. These processes involve people making decisions in difficult situations. These decisions are many and varied. Judges interpret the Constitution and apply it to complicated factual circumstances. Police consider the commands of constitutional rights while making quick, stressful decisions about whether to search, arrest, or even shoot a criminal suspect. Citizens serving on juries decide the fate of criminal defendants even when the evidence is not crystal clear. These decisions cannot be made with consistency and precision. They require the decision makers to make situational judgments, and these judgments are shaped by values, attitudes, and emotions.

Myriad human decisions and reactions determine whether and how constitutional rights are implemented. These decisions and reactions are shaped by a variety of factors that both preclude clarity in Supreme Court decisions and hinder consistent compliance by interpreters and implementers. The primary factors that affect implementation begin with the process of producing the Supreme Court's decisions and influence every aspect of the implementation process through the point of police officers, corrections officers, and other officials either respecting or violating individuals' constitutional rights.

The Context and Processes of Constitutional Interpretation

The characteristics of the judicial process affect the clarity of Supreme Court decisions. First, when interpreting constitutional rights, the Court focuses on a specific case with unique factual circumstances. The specific facts in a case may influence how particular justices view the existence (or lack thereof) of a right. Some justices may write opinions focused on specific facts in a case, while others may attempt to use the same case to establish broad principles of law that they intend to cover many other similar cases. In addition, the focus on a specific case may make it impossible for lower court judges to understand how to apply a case precedent in the context of a different fact situation. Because there are infinite variations in potential factual situations that may arise, the Supreme Court's justices cannot write opinions that accurately anticipate all of the situations in which an alleged rights violation may occur. For example, the Fourth Amendment's words indicate that the amendment intends to protect people in their homes. But does the amendment protect guests? What if the guests stay overnight? What if they are visitors only during a single day? What if they are at the house for only five minutes? The Court's decisions have distinguished between overnight guests who share the homeowner's privacy protections and brief visitors who do not enjoy the same Fourth Amendment protections (*Minnesota v. Carter,* 1998), yet there may be other kinds of factual situations concerning invited guests and other visitors that will require courts to continue to clarify the applicability of the Fourth Amendment.

The American legal system says that judges are not supposed to attempt to create rules that govern situations that have not been presented in court. Otherwise, the decision makers are interpreting the Constitution without giving attorneys the opportunity to present evidence and arguments favorable to each side in the adversarial process. Thus the Supreme Court does not issue **advisory opinions** so there is no easy opportunity to ask the justices to clarify aspects of their decisions. There must be an actual **"case or controversy"** in order for the Supreme Court to make a decision. Clarifications of constitutional rights definitions come from subsequent cases that raise new issues. It often takes years for these clarifying questions to make it to the Supreme Court, as each case must work its way through every stage of the state or federal court system before it can be accepted for hearing by the U.S. Supreme Court.

Second, the lawyers for each side carefully craft arguments about the words and reasoning that the justices should use in producing a decision. By focusing on the arguments of the opposing attorneys, the justices may overlook alternative interpretations that might have produced more clarity. The attorneys are not advisors to the justices who purport to present the most clear and comprehensive articulation of constitutional rights. Instead, they are hired advocates whose responsibility is focused on persuading the justices that their side should win. They may even argue persuasively against clear and comprehensive opinions if such opinions would be adverse to their client's interests. The **adversarial legal process** induces advocates to hide information, overstate favorable evidence and reasoning, and criticize reasonable alternatives that do not advance their clients' interests. If the advocates are skilled and effective, they may contribute to doctrinal confusion in the course of pursuing a narrow victory for their clients.

The Supreme Court is a **collegial court** with nine members. Unlike trial courts with a single judge as the sole decision maker, the justices must work together to reach a decision and write a majority opinion interpreting the Constitution. Thus the justices may need to compromise and accommodate in order to produce a result that attracts the support of at least five members. Such compromises may involve consciously using ambiguous language that is acceptable to justices who do not see eye to eye rather than strongly and clearly stating a definition or rule that exacerbates disagreements within the Court. The participation of multiple decision makers also creates the opportunity for multiple opinions. Sometimes justices write concurring opinions in which they attempt to present an alternative interpretation of the Court's rule or an explanation of how the decision does or does not apply to other factual situations.

The rule of law established by a case is called its **holding.** The holding provides the answer to the question or "issue" that was the basis for the court's acceptance of the case for hearing. Everything else in a judicial opinion is technically considered to be **dicta,** merely discussion that explains the decision but does not establish a precedent that must be followed. Concurring and dissenting justices may emphasize the narrowness of a holding in a case in order to send a message to officials and the public that they need not obey all of the discussion contained in the majority opinion. This may cause confusion for people who read the case because they are not sure whether to follow the entire majority opinion or to follow the explanation in the concurring or dissenting opinion that gives them more options for action that may, in subsequent cases, clash with what the majority intended to express. For example, the Supreme Court decided a case concerning the legality of distributing marijuana to people who claim to need it as treatment for medical conditions such as glaucoma and nausea from cancer chemotherapy (*United States v. Oakland Cannabis Buyers' Cooperative,* 2001). The Court unanimously decided that a marijuana buyers' cooperative could not claim that "necessity," a traditional defense under Anglo-American criminal law, provided a justification that would permit the cooperative to distribute marijuana despite the prohibition on such activity in the federal Controlled Substances Act. In a concurring opinion joined by Justices David Souter and Ruth Bader Ginsburg, Justice John Paul Stevens emphasized the narrowness of the Court's holding and argued that there might be other situations in which the necessity defense would apply, despite the fact that majority opinion said otherwise. According to Stevens,

> Lest the Court's narrow holding be lost in its broad dicta, let me restate it here: "[W]e hold that medical necessity is not a defense to *manufacturing* and *distributing* marijuana." . . . (emphasis added). . . . [A]t least with respect to distribution, this holding is consistent with how the issue was raised and litigated [in the lower courts]. . . . Because necessity was raised in this case as a defense to distribution, the Court need not venture an opinion on whether the defense is available to anyone other than distributors.
>
> Most notably, whether the defense might be available to a seriously ill patient for whom there is no alternative means of avoiding starvation or extraordinary suffering is a difficult issue that is not presented here.

Does such an opinion contribute to the clarity of a ruling and its consistent implementation? In all likelihood, such opinions serve as invitations for those who agree with the concurring or dissenting perspective to treat the majority opinion as if it has limited applicability. Although the concurring opinion in this case provided encouragement for individuals in conflict with the government, other such opinions encourage police officers to view constitutional rights narrowly. In those cases, concurring and dissenting opinions may provide a justification for limited implementation of constitutional rights by those who disagree with the purposes of the majority opinion.

In addition to all of the other factors that contribute to ambiguous and incomplete definitions of constitutional rights and rules for criminal justice officials' behavior, the vague phrases in the Constitution defy precise definition, especially when considered in light of the varying factual circumstances that can arise. The Court cannot easily define a phrase such as "probable cause" in the Fourth Amendment because there is no easy way to predetermine the nature and amount of evidence that may exist in each criminal case that will lead police to seek search or arrest warrants. Thus the flexible definitions for many vague constitutional phrases require continuing interpretation and application by lower court judges whose decisions may subsequently be appealed to higher courts for clarification.

Communication Problems

In theory, Supreme Court declarations concerning the definitions of constitutional rights take effect the moment that the decision is announced in Washington, D.C. In reality, it may take days or weeks for prosecutors and police chiefs to realize, amid all of their other busy responsibilities, that the high court has issued a new decision relevant to their work. After relevant decisions are identified, state attorneys general, city attorneys, prosecutors, police chiefs, and other supervisory officials must figure out what the decision means for the personnel under their supervision. Sometimes they may make errors in attempting to interpret and understand the court decisions, especially because the decisions are written in "legalese" for an audience of lawyers and cannot always be easily translated into terms that criminal justice personnel can readily understand. There is a significant risk that interpreters will not accurately characterize the constitutional rule and corresponding requirements produced by a Supreme Court decision.

The time lag between the Supreme Court's decision and the dissemination of information about new constitutional rules necessarily means that police officers and corrections officers may operate under "old" rules until they are educated about new definitions of rights. As an example of this process in another context, it was not until three weeks after Michigan's new statute concerning citizens' entitlement to carry concealed weapons took effect that the Michigan Sheriffs Association was able to organize a training session to explain the new law to police officers.[3] There would be a further time lag as the 330 sheriffs, prosecutors, police officers, and county clerks who attended the session returned to their home counties and organized events to explain the law to officials in their home jurisdictions. Even if the Michigan Sheriffs Association representatives understood the new law completely, did their presentation explain the law in a way so that all 330 participants understood the law completely? Were all 330 participants skilled communicators who subsequently did a complete job of explaining the law to their personnel at home? Communication processes that rely on information being passed from person to person result in changes, distortions, and omissions in the messages that are delivered to some of the recipients of the information. The same process operates with respect to decisions about constitutional rights. The information must pass through various people who not only interpret the decision but also must communicate the meaning of the decision effectively in order for it to be implemented properly. An early study of local police departments' compliance with the Supreme Court's decision in *Miranda v. Arizona* (1966) found differences in the way departments communicated information about and implemented the requirements of informing suspects of their rights. Highly professionalized departments with systematic training programs were most effective in communicating information about the latest Supreme Court decisions.[4]

The interpretation and communication of judicial decisions about constitutional rights can also be distorted by the self-interest of those responsible for interpreting and conveying the underlying principles and rules. In a police academy training program or a seminar to update officers about new court decisions, will the instructor present the new constitutional right and corresponding rules for police procedure in a manner to give the broadest application of the right? Such a presentation would make sense if the objective was to avoid the risk of even inadvertently violating a citizen's rights. In reality, many officers who have gone through training programs comment that their instructors tell them how to engage in conduct that avoids the court's rule or obeys the rule in a technical manner while undercutting the purpose of the rule. The Supreme Court's purpose in deciding *Miranda v. Arizona* (1966) was to prevent uneducated and naive criminal suspects from being coerced into incriminating themselves.[5] By contrast, police training programs may treat the rule as a technical matter of reading suspects their rights. Officers may be taught to give the warnings in a casual or confusing manner while they receive training on how to induce suspects to waive their rights and confess. The training may teach techniques of pressure and persuasion—such as falsely telling a suspect that several witnesses observed him commit a crime—that clash with the original purpose of *Miranda*. Alternatively, formal coursework may teach about *Miranda* in a straightforward fashion but the socialization and practical on-the-job training provided by a senior supervisor may informally communicate strategies for avoiding the underlying purpose of *Miranda*. In this context, criminal justice officials are not necessarily taught to value and protect rights but to regard constitutional rights as obstacles to investigation that can be avoided through specific "tricks" and techniques that are likely to be accepted by many judges. Do such communications encourage officials to respect rights or to experiment with their own methods of "getting around" the protections provided by the Constitution?

An early study of police compliance with *Miranda* found the following results:

> There were important personal advantages to police officers for maintaining a relatively low degree of compliance with the *Miranda* decision. Police efficiency was still primarily measured by clearance rates, and officers were rewarded no less for solving a case by means of interrogation. . . . By encouraging the

suspect to make a hasty decision on whether to request counsel or the right to remain silent, the interrogation facilitated a relatively quick solution to many cases. Perhaps greater police agreement with the policy would also mean a greater degree of compliance, but there were few positive attitudes toward the [*Miranda*] decision [among the officers studied]. . . .[6]

One could adopt the position of saying, "As long as the technical rules imposed by courts are obeyed, there's nothing wrong with officers aggressively seeking confessions in order to solve crimes." This position, however, creates risks of abusive police behavior. In Prince Georges County, Maryland, for example, a newspaper investigation in 2001 revealed that at least four innocent men had been pressured into confessing to murders that they did not commit. Among those who wilted under hours of intense police interrogation were two teenagers, including one with learning disabilities, and an illiterate janitor who signed a confession that was written out for him by a police detective.[7] Such interrogations may be legal as long as the police have informed the suspect about *Miranda* rights and obtained the suspect's agreement to waive those rights by saying such things as "But why would you request a lawyer or refuse to talk to us if you have nothing to hide?" The way in which the definitions of constitutional rights are communicated to police officers, corrections officers, and others can have a profound impact on their attitudes about the desirability and necessity of respecting those rights.

Discretion

One of the most important and pervasive characteristics of the criminal justice system is the discretionary decision-making authority possessed by criminal justice officials. Police officers use their own judgment to decide whom to stop, search, and arrest. Defense attorneys use their discretion to determine strategies in plea bargaining and trial tactics. Prosecutors use discretion in determining which suspects to charge with crimes, which charges to apply, and whether to offer a plea agreement. Judges use discretion in ruling on motions, and they often have discretion in imposing sentences. Corrections officers employ discretion in determining which prisoners to search, cite for rules violations, or commend for exemplary behavior. Discretion is a necessary and inevitable aspect of the system. There is no way for police supervisors to watch officers all day to ensure that discretion is used properly, especially when officers are out on patrol. Similarly, corrections supervisors cannot observe the actions of corrections officers. The officers are scattered throughout institutions and bear responsibility for their own interactions with the prisoners.

The existence of discretion opens the possibility that criminal justice officials will not implement constitutional rights properly. Police officers may decide to search someone without adequate justification. This assertion of their power cannot be stopped. Police officers with guns and badges can do

whatever they want to do as long as they are prepared to deal with the consequences of their actions. After the fact, it is possible that they may be sanctioned
by their supervisors for disregarding rules or, if their actions cause physical
injuries or an improper loss of liberty, they may face civil rights lawsuits from
citizens. These remedies are imperfect, especially because officers often deny
that they have done anything wrong even when their actions violated proper
procedures. If an unethical officer strikes a citizen without a proper justification, such as self-defense, he or she may simply claim that the blow was never
delivered or that the citizen struck the officer first. If it is the officer's word
against the citizen's, the officer may be believed, especially if the citizen is
young, poor, a member of a minority group, or someone with a criminal
record. Similarly, an officer may stop a car merely because he or she has a
hunch that there is something suspicious about the driver. Because that justification is not legally sufficient for a reasonable stop, the officer may claim that
the driver failed to use his turn signal when changing lanes. Thus the stop
would be justified on the assertion that a traffic violation occurred. Even if that
claim is false, how can the driver prove otherwise?

Discretionary decision-making authority is a powerful tool for officers to
use in investigating crimes, but its existence also creates risks that it will be mis-
used in ways that violate citizens' constitutional rights. Unfortunately, criminal
justice officials who disagree with the Supreme Court's definitions of specific
constitutional rights often have opportunities to defeat the enjoyment of those
rights by suspects, defendants, and offenders. There is no foolproof way to control discretion and protect rights from being violated by criminal justice officials
who value crime control more than they value constitutional rights.

Resources

The scarcity of resources can hinder the implementation of constitutional
rights. Time is one resource for criminal justice officials. Police officers,
prosecutors, judges, and other officials are busy fulfilling their responsibilities
for investigating, prosecuting, and punishing lawbreakers. They do not necessarily have extra time to dedicate to the study of new constitutional rules just
because the Supreme Court has issued a new decision refining the definition
of a constitutional right. It can take time to organize training sessions for police
officers and corrections officers. Such sessions may disrupt normal work
schedules and require state and local governments to pay overtime wages to
personnel who must take classes to learn about new constitutional rules.

Other resources may also be scarce, especially because state and local governments usually have limited budgets. Just because the Supreme Court
announces that suspects are entitled to have a defense attorney appointed to
represent them at certain identification lineups (e.g., *United States v. Wade*,
1968) does not mean that state and local governments instantly have attorneys

available or the money with which to pay them. In 2003, one county in Mississippi filed a lawsuit against its state government claiming that the state should pay for defense attorneys because the county had no money with which to fund representation for indigent defendants.[8] Other rights decisions that impose affirmative obligations on criminal justice officials, such as court decisions mandating conditions and services in prisons and jails, provide similar financial challenges for state and local governments.

Summary

Because of the nature of judicial reasoning and the ambiguous terms in the Bill of Rights, it is not possible for Supreme Court decisions to be completely precise, clear, and effective. Moreover, various problems with communication, interpretation, resources, and other issues can affect whether and how constitutional rights are implemented.

AN ILLUSTRATIVE EXAMPLE: VICTIMS' RIGHTS

One way to understand the impediments to implementation of constitutional rights is to analyze closely a specific constitutional provision. Subsequent chapters of this book examine in detail the constitutional amendments most relevant to criminal justice. However, the consideration of actual effects of constitutional rights is also important when examining proposed amendments to the Constitution that seek to create new rights. One such amendment is the proposed Victims' Rights Amendment that was presented to Congress and endorsed by President Bill Clinton but, as yet, has not been approved by the necessary super-majority of Congress to initiate the amendment process. This proposed amendment provides a useful example for many of the interpretation and implementation issues that affect existing constitutional rights.

PROPOSED VICTIMS' RIGHTS AMENDMENT—U.S. CONSTITUTION

To ensure that the victim is treated with fairness, dignity, and respect, from the occurrence of a crime of violence and other crimes as may be defined by law pursuant to section 2 of this article, and throughout the criminal, military, and juvenile justice processes, as a matter of fundamental rights to liberty, justice, and due process, the victim shall have the following rights: to be informed of and given the opportunity to be present at every proceeding in which those rights are extended to the accused or convicted offender; to be heard at any proceeding involving sentencing, including the right to object to a previously negotiated plea, or a release from custody; to be informed of any release or escape; and to a speedy trial, a final conclusion free from unreasonable delay, full restitution from the convicted offender, reasonable measures to protect the victim from violence or intimidation by the accused or convicted offender, and notice of the victim's rights.

Interpretation

The words of the proposed amendment are relatively clear when compared to those of other constitutional provisions, but there are many words and phrases that will require interpretation and definition.

- *"Fundamental rights to liberty, justice, and due process."* How are these "fundamental rights" defined and applied for crime victims?
- *"Opportunity to be present."* Does the "opportunity to be present" mean that a hearing or trial cannot take place if the victim is unable to attend? Alternatively, if the victim is informed of the time and date for the hearing or trial, does that provide sufficient "opportunity" even if the victim happens to be in the hospital recovering from injuries suffered during the course of the crime?
- *"Right to be heard."* Does the right to be heard at any proceeding involving sentencing mean that the victim can say whatever he or she wants to say, even if it is inflammatory, emotional, racist, sexist, or factually inaccurate? What if the victim says in front of the judge and jury that "this guy has always hated me and he has planned for weeks to rob my house," but it simply is not true? Could a judge require the victim to speak only on the witness stand, under oath, and in response to questions so that the statements are limited to those that are admissible as evidence?
- *"Right to object to a previously negotiated plea."* Is this simply a right to say, "I object!" or does it give the victim any actual power over whether the court will accept the plea? If it is just a right to say the words, "I object," does that mean that the right is merely symbolic because it will have no impact on the processing and outcome of the case?
- *"Right to a speedy trial."* How will a court determine when this right is violated? How much time must pass before there has been too much delay in the trial? What if the defense attorney requests continuances (court-approved delays) in order to interview witnesses and investigate the case? Can the victim insist that the trial be held on a specified date even if the defense has not had time to prepare?
- *"A final conclusion free from unreasonable delay."* What is an "unreasonable delay"? What if such a delay occurs? What is the remedy? If the delay is caused by the prosecutor, can the crime victim sue the prosecutor even though prosecutors traditionally have had immunity from most lawsuits concerning their official actions?
- *"Reasonable measures to protect the victim from violence."* What are "reasonable measures"? Could this ever require the police to provide around-the-clock personal guards if a person was threatened by drug dealers or organized crime figures? What will such a right do to the

ability of the police to determine for themselves how to deploy their personnel? Who will the victim sue for violations?

- *"Notice of the victim's rights."* What information must be conveyed to the victim? Who is responsible for conveying that information? When must the information be given?

Imagine that the first case that comes to the Supreme Court concerning this amendment is a case in which a victim of an assault has filed a civil rights lawsuit against police officers for violating his rights under the Victims' Rights Amendment by failing to inform him of his rights. He claims that the failure to inform him of his rights as a crime victim caused him to miss his opportunity to be present at his assailant's bail hearing. The police department defended against the action by claiming that it was the responsibility of the prosecutor's office to inform victims of their rights and that the police are, therefore, not at fault. At trial, a district court judge found that the police are responsible for informing victims of their rights but she delayed a determination of remedy until the police had an opportunity to appeal because the amendment had not previously been interpreted. The court of appeals affirmed the finding of police liability. Thus, in this hypothetical case, the lower court judges concluded that the civil rights lawsuit could move forward to determine what damages (money), if any, would be owed to the crime victim by the police department.

The Supreme Court issued an 8-to-1 decision with a majority opinion, a concurring opinion, and a dissenting opinion. The majority of justices affirmed the lower court decisions and thereby approved the order by the court of appeals that the case should continue in the district court to make a determination of damages. Imagine that the following excerpts are from the Supreme Court opinions.

MAJORITY OPINION (on behalf of five justices): . . . The intention of the Victims' Rights Amendment is to place responsibility on *both* the police department and the prosecutor's office for informing crime victims of their rights. Police officers have the initial contact with crime victims on behalf of the criminal justice system. Therefore they are best positioned to provide immediate information to victims. However, many of the rights in the amendment concern *court processes* for which the prosecutor's office is responsible. Police officers cannot reasonably be expected to inform crime victims about the times and dates of hearings and trials, especially when those times and dates are set after the police no longer have contact with the victim. Moreover, those times and dates often change as attorneys request continuances. Thus the prosecutor's office is the sole entity that can reasonably be expected to inform victims about the proceedings at which they have the opportunity to appear, the sentencing proceedings at which they have the opportunity to be heard, and the opportunities to object to negotiated pleas. Police officers' constitutional duty is limited to informing crime victims about the existence of the Victims' Rights Amendments and the nature of the rights contained in the amendment. After that initial notice provided to victims, the prosecutor's office then assumes the constitutional responsibility for informing victims about the nature and timing of the specific rights within the amendment. Thus, in this case, the police officers are liable for failing to inform the crime victim of his rights, but the damages must be limited to the harm caused by the police officers' failure. If the primary harm in this case stemmed from a failure to give adequate notice about a bail hearing, the police officers cannot be held solely responsible for that fact. The damages held against the police must be limited to the extent of the harm caused by their failure to fulfill their duty. The respective duties of the police and prosecutor must be taken into consideration in the subsequent proceedings to determine damages.

CONCURRING OPINION (on behalf of three justices): . . . We agree with the majority opinion's conclusion that the nature of the rights in the Victims' Rights Amendment logically implies that the prosecutor shares with the police a duty to inform crime victims about their rights under the amendment. However, as a practical matter, the entire responsibility for informing victims of their rights should rest with a single entity and that entity is the police. Under American law, prosecutors are generally immune from civil rights lawsuits. If this Court says that prosecutors bear a primary responsibility for informing victims of their rights, we are creating a right without a remedy. When prosecutors fail to fulfill that duty by forgetting to communicate with a victim, as will inevitably happen in the busy bureaucracies that characterize prosecutors' offices, that victim will have no recourse other than to complain after the fact to the prosecutor's office about the lack of information. If a victim misses a sentencing hearing or other proceeding for lack of notice, there is no way to go back to conduct the proceeding over again. Such actions would cause administrative difficulties for prosecution, judicial, and corrections officials. Moreover, such proceedings could violate due process and other rights of criminal defendants. Thus, crime victims have no effective recourse against prosecutors for any rights violations. These practical concerns lead us to conclude that the police must assume the entire responsibility for informing victims about their rights. Police are susceptible to lawsuits, and their legal vulnerability provides a legal recourse that will make the Victims' Rights Act meaningful in the lives of crime victims. In our view, the lower courts appropriately concluded that the determination of damages should focus solely on the police without any consideration of the prosecutor's role in the rights violation.

DISSENTING OPINION (one justice): . . . The majority opinion is quite correct in observing that the specific rights in the Victims' Rights Amendment relate to stages of the criminal justice process that are under the supervision and control of prosecutors. By concluding that the police and prosecutor share responsibility for informing victims of their rights, the majority has needlessly created confusion in its initial interpretation of the new amendment. In the aftermath of this opinion, it is not clear exactly what police officers must tell crime victims and when they must tell it to them in order to avoid the risk of liability. Because the rights at issue concern prosecutorial processes, the prosecutor should have the sole duty to inform victims about their rights under this amendment. The unworkable administrative complexity of dividing the constitutional duty between police and prosecutors can be avoided by placing the entire duty upon the single entity most closely connected to the rights at issue, and that entity is the prosecutor's office. The concurring justices' argument that we are creating a right without a remedy should have no role in our interpretation of this amendment. We often interpret and define constitutional rights for which there is no concrete remedy in the real world. For example, when was the last time anyone won a lawsuit against the police for an improper stop-and-frisk on the street? An unreasonable search that delays a pedestrian for thirty seconds violates a constitutional right but does not cause sufficient harm to produce damages in a lawsuit. Our role is to educate and remind officials about their duties, not ensure that money damages will be available for every kind of constitutional violation. If prosecutorial immunity is an impediment to the effectiveness of the Victims' Rights Amendment, then it is up to Congress to enact legislation that would create and define the appropriate bases for prosecutors' liability under civil rights statutes. The lawsuit in this case should be dismissed because the police do not bear responsibility for informing crime victims of their rights.

In considering the processes of constitutional interpretation, can you say that any of these hypothetical judicial opinions is "wrong"? The justices reached three distinctly different conclusions about the duties of criminal justice officials under the proposed Victims' Rights Amendment. Yet all three opinions are supported by reasoning that many people could agree is sensible and logical. Obviously, the application of logic and sensibility to any issue does not necessarily drive a decision maker to a single, inescapable result. The vagueness of constitutional language and the malleability of legal reasoning frequently produce divergent analyses and conclusions that are all supported by plausible justifications.

If you were a city attorney or a police chief, what would you tell police officers about their responsibilities under the Victims' Rights Amendment? One key sentence in the majority opinion is as follows: "Police officers' constitutional duty is limited to informing crime victims about the existence of the Victims' Rights Amendment and the nature of the rights contained in the amendment." This sentence and other phrases in the majority opinion seem to indicate that police officers' duty is limited to telling crime victims as soon as possible about the fact that they have rights under the Victims' Rights Amendment. Some police departments might, for example, instruct their officers to make it part of their systematic crime response procedures to read out loud and hand a card to crime victims that says: "You need to be aware that you have specific rights under the Victims' Rights Amendment. These rights include the right to be present at court proceedings against anyone accused of the crime against you. The prosecutor's office will inform you about the full range of victims' rights. They will also inform you about the dates and times of any relevant proceedings. If you have any questions about your rights as a crime victim, you can contact the prosecutor's office at 555-1234."

Would such notice be adequate according to the Court's opinion? Perhaps. But perhaps not. Frequently, the victim of a violent crime is injured, in a state of emotional upset or shock, or otherwise unable to focus clearly on everything going on around him or her. If an injured crime victim filed a lawsuit against the police claiming that the card provided inadequate notice because the victim was incapable of understanding the information in the midst of the chaos at the crime scene or while lying injured in a hospital bed, might the Court decide that the police could be liable for rights violations because they did not account for the circumstances in which the information could be presented effectively? How could a police chief possibly predict what the Court would say in a different factual situation?

Another potential problem may lurk in the majority's use of the following phrases highlighted in italics: *"Police officers' constitutional duty is limited to informing crime victims* about the existence of the Victims' Rights Amendment and *the nature of the rights contained in the amendment."* Does this language mean that the police officer must actually give the victim a copy of the entire Victims' Rights Amendment to make sure that he or she has been informed about "the nature of the rights contained in the amendment"? On the other hand, reading the entire amendment aloud may simply add to confusion. It could produce ineffective efforts to provide too much information at a moment when communication and comprehension are inherently difficult.

As a police chief, would you have any concerns about the concurring opinion? Three justices expressed the view that the entire duty should fall on the police. If these justices manage to persuade two other justices or if two other justices retire and are replaced by new justices who agree with the concurrence, the interpretation could quickly change to one that creates tremendous liability risks for the police. Would you try to protect your agency by teaching your officers to give detailed information about all of the rights contained in the amendment? On the other hand, will a long conversation with the victim about the Victims' Rights Amendment detract from the officer's ability to gather necessary information for the investigation of the crime? You would not want your officers to become so preoccupied with talking about the amendment that they lose their focus on solving the crime or apprehending the perpetrator.

Discretion and accountability issues would also play a role in the implementation of any procedures mandated by the police chief. If an officer was busy questioning witnesses and preparing a report about the investigation of the crime, it is possible that the officer could forget to inform the victim about the Victims' Rights Amendment. If a victim later filed a lawsuit against the officer, the officer might attempt to cover himself or herself by falsely claiming that he or she informed the victim about his or her rights. If the issue arose in litigation, it might be the officer's word against the victim's. However, the officer could claim that the victim was so upset or distracted in the aftermath of the crime that the victim does not remember the few moments when the officer talked about the Victims' Rights Amendment. If you were a judge or a juror, how would you know whether the officer informed the victim or not? If you were uncertain, would you decide the case against the officer? Probably not.

Imagine a 911 call about an assault at a home. When the officers arrive, a woman meets them at the door and tells them that it was just a misunderstanding. She was having an argument with her husband and she got so angry that she called the police in order to frighten him. She is apologetic but asks the police leave them alone. The officers notice discoloration on her cheek that they believe indicates that the man struck the woman in the face. Both the man and the woman deny that an actual assault occurred. The officers follow their department's procedure by arresting the man and taking him to the patrol car. The woman slams the door to the house and yells at the officers that she is going to call her attorney and get them into "big trouble" for making a false arrest. If you were one of the officers, would you go back to the front door, ring the doorbell, and attempt to inform the woman about her rights under the Victims' Rights Amendment? Some officers might simply say to themselves, "Why bother? She says that she's not a victim."

In another situation, the officers are sent to an alley. A caller reported hearing yelling and gunshots from the alley. Upon arriving, the officers find a young man sitting against the wall bleeding from a superficial gunshot wound to his arm. They are familiar with the man because he has been arrested numerous times for minor theft and drug offenses. Would they inform him of his rights under the Victims' Rights Amendment? What if there was a warrant out for the young man's arrest because of evidence that he committed a murder? Officers might use their discretion to make determinations about whether a specific victim is worthy of hearing the full explanation of victims' rights. When discretion is applied in this manner, there are risks that officers' actions will be discriminatory. Will officers give a careful, complete, and helpful explanation to "respectable" middle-aged, middle-class people while neglecting to explain victims' rights or delivering the words in an incomprehensible, rapid-fire manner when dealing with people who are young, poor, or otherwise unconnected to a particular officer's sympathies?

Resource issues may also hinder implementation of the right. Must prosecutors incur extra expenses by hiring a "Victim Assistance Coordinator" or some other official to assume responsibility for monitoring case schedules and communicating with victims? Some courthouses are so large that a single official could never handle the task. Instead, an entire new agency would need to be developed within the prosecutor's office with multiple personnel, office staff, office space, computers, and other expenses. In addition, the victim assistance staff must undergo continuing training and produce information booklets to distribute to victims and their families. If prosecutors do not have extra funds to create such offices, they might attempt to fulfill their obligations in an ineffective fashion, such as through the use of less-than-dependable volunteers under the supervision of one paid employee.

The obligation to include crime victims in court in specific ways may impose new costs on the criminal justice process. If victims regularly object to plea agreements and elected prosecutors fear the possibility of gaining a reputation for being insensitive to victims, more cases might be forced to trial or plea negotiation processes may become drawn out. Permitting victims to speak at any proceeding involving sentencing may prolong such events. If the amendment is interpreted to require officials to accommodate victims in scheduling hearings and trials, then some cases may face further complications and delays from scheduling coordination issues. The right to "reasonable measures to protect the victim from violence or intimidation" may create new pressure to expend more money and personnel on reassuring victims about their personal safety and, potentially, taking action to protect them.

CONCLUSION

As indicated by the example of the proposed Victims' Rights Amendment, the effective implementation of constitutional rights depends on many factors. The ultimate implementation of rights is influenced by the interpretive processes that define rights in appellate courts, the motives and knowledge of the interpreters who must explain judicial decisions to street-level personnel, the discretionary decisions of those personnel, and agency resources. There is nothing easy or automatic about the translation of judicial decisions defining rights into actual legal protections for people in American society. Any right can lose its essential substance and become merely symbolic if these factors and processes create significant gaps between the stated definition of the constitutional right and the actual implementation of that right. In the chapters that follow, these factors and processes are examined to determine how they impact constitutional rights from the First, Fourth, Fifth, Sixth, Eighth, and Fourteenth Amendments.

THE FIRST AMENDMENT

Congress shall make no law respecting an establishment of religion, or prohibiting the free exercise thereof; or abridging the freedom of speech, or of the press; or the right of the people peaceably to assemble, and to petition the Government for redress of grievances.

The First Amendment is presumed to have special importance among the provisions specifying protections for individuals in the U.S. Constitution. The amendment's placement as the initial description of rights added to the Constitution appears to say something about the importance of these rights to the framers of the Bill of Rights. In adding individual protections to the Constitution, which rights did they choose to highlight by listing first? Freedom of religion and freedom of speech. Over the decades, Supreme Court justices have debated the extent to which other rights, such as the right to counsel or the right to trial by jury, must apply in all circumstances in order to achieve the Constitution's purposes. With respect to First Amendment rights, however, special care is often taken in considering their interpretation because of a widely shared belief that these are the rights that are essential to a democratic free society. This sensitivity is reflected in the fact that freedom of speech was the first personal right in the Bill of Rights incorporated for application against state governments in the same manner as it already applied against the federal government (*Gitlow v. New York*, 1925). In theory, you could have a free society that has trials by judges rather than juries for some or all cases. Indeed, as is shown in a later chapter, the right to trial by jury does not apply to all criminal cases. By contrast, democracy rests on free expression. How can you have free and fair elections without freedom of speech and press to permit campaigning, discussions, and dissemination of information about candidates?

In addition, many early European settlers came to North American colonies to avoid religious persecution in their home countries. The Puritans of Massachusetts, the Quakers of Pennsylvania, and the Catholics of Maryland, among others, envisioned their new land as a place where they could enjoy religious freedom. Thus religious freedom, much like free expression, has long been considered an essential element in the American conception of a free society. This does not mean that there was never religious persecution in the United States. Over various periods of American history, Mormons, Jehovah's Witnesses, Muslims, and others endured discrimination and hostility, including acts of violence. Despite these regrettable examples of when American society fell short of its expressed values, the idea of religious freedom has been central to conceptions of freedom in the United States since the founding of the nation.

The First Amendment's relevance to criminal justice primarily concerns substantive criminal law rather than criminal procedure. When legislatures criminalize conduct associated with religion or expression, does it violate the Constitution? Judges have had many opportunities to examine the constitutionality of laws and governmental practices that arguably intrude on First Amendment protections. There are other contacts between the First Amendment and criminal justice. For example, freedom of the press can collide with the fair trial rights of the Sixth Amendment if excessive publicity about a criminal case in the news media threatens the possibility of obtaining an unbiased jury. Related problems arise when the government seeks to exclude the press from hearings when criminal cases concern purported national security issues or when prosecutors want to protect the privacy of child victims or adult sex crime victims. Additional criminal justice issues concerning the First Amendment arise in the context of corrections. To what extent, if any, do prisoners retain rights to religious freedom and freedom of expression? Such cases often pose difficult challenges for judges and corrections officials.

As discussed in Chapter 2, a key feature of the First Amendment is its absolutist language: "Congress shall *make no law.*" A literal interpretation of the amendment might prevent the government from criminalizing any conduct concerning religious exercise, verbal and written expression, and peaceful assemblies. However, provisions of the Constitution are seldom interpreted in a literal fashion. Thus issues inevitably arise when government regulations and practices are alleged to conflict with individuals' asserted First Amendment rights.

FREEDOM OF RELIGION

Conventional Wisdom 10

The government cannot restrict people's opportunities to conduct the services, rituals, and other practices of their religions unless those practices inflict harms on other people.

Despite the First Amendment's literal language, few people would be surprised that the Free Exercise of Religion Clause has not been interpreted to permit human sacrifices, cannibalism, or other practices that might be claimed to have a religious basis yet impose significant harms, such as homicide, on other people. In the Supreme Court's earliest interpretation of the right to free exercise, the high court endorsed statutes that made polygamy a crime. Presumably, legislatures enacted such statutes because they viewed plural marriages as harmful to individuals and society. There is a risk, of course, that the statutes also reflected intolerance of the religious beliefs and practices of Mormons. Mormons were persecuted in many places, including being subjected to murderous attacks by violent mobs. Their persecution led them to move westward to Utah to establish their own communities. The anti-polygamy statutes were aimed at Mormons whose early leaders interpreted religious texts to require men to have multiple wives. The Court's opinion in *Reynolds v. United States* (1879) concluded that it would not interpret the First Amendment in a manner that permitted people in one religion to engage in an activity that would be enforced as criminal conduct against people in other religions: "If [Mormon polygamists] are [excepted from the operation of the statute], then those who do not make polygamy a part of their religious belief may be found guilty and punished, while those who do, must be acquitted and go free. This would be introducing a new element into criminal laws." The Court justified its conclusion by stating that the First Amendment protects religious *beliefs,* but it does not necessarily protect religious *practices.*

Regarding the *Reynolds* case as a useful guiding precedent is difficult because it was decided decades before the Supreme Court began to give careful attention to the interpretation of the Bill of Rights in the mid-twentieth century. When the Court actually began to give significant attention to civil liberties issues in the twentieth century, it became more protective of the religious beliefs and practices of minority religions. In 1943, the Court protected Jehovah's Witness schoolchildren from punishment for declining to salute the flag and say the Pledge of Allegiance, activities that the Jehovah's Witnesses saw as violating their religious obligation to reserve their praises for God (*West Virginia Board of Education v. Barnette*). In effect, the Court concluded that the government's desire to foster patriotism and citizenship values could not take priority over people's religious beliefs. Later, in the early 1960s, the Supreme Court articulated a test for restrictions on free exercise of religion that provided potentially significant protections for people's religious beliefs and practices.

In *Sherbert v. Verner* (1963), the Supreme Court forbade South Carolina to deny unemployment compensation benefits to a Seventh-Day Adventist who lost her job in a textile mill because her religious beliefs would not permit her to work on Saturdays. In denying her benefits, the state treated her as if she had merely refused to work according to her employer's required work schedule. In deciding the case in favor of the individual, Justice William Brennan's opinion applied a **strict scrutiny test** to determine whether the government's rule could stand despite its collision with an individual's religious freedom. Under the strict scrutiny test, the government must demonstrate a "compelling state interest" to justify any infringement of the right to free exercise of religion. According to Brennan,

> We must next consider whether some compelling state interest enforced in the eligibility provisions of the South Carolina statute justifies the substantial infringement of appellant's First Amendment right. It is basic that no showing merely of a rational relationship to some colorable state interest would suffice; in this highly sensitive constitutional area, "[o]nly the gravest abuses, endangering paramount interest, give occasion for permissible limitation" [citation omitted]. No such abuse or danger has been advanced in the present case.

This test is also applied by the Court in other First Amendment cases concerning freedom of speech and Fourteenth Amendment equal protection cases concerning unequal treatment of people because of their race. In all of these circumstances, the limitation on rights, if it is to be upheld, must be based on the government's demonstration that the attainment of some supremely important government objective can only occur by limiting First Amendment or Fourteenth Amendment rights. The strict scrutiny test is generally difficult for the government to overcome. Although laws against homicide that prevent human sacrifice in the name of religion could be justified under the strict scrutiny test, many other potential government restrictions on religion would not survive such close examination. From the 1960s through the mid-1980s, in the words of constitutional scholars, "The strict scrutiny test of *Sherbert [v. Verner]* was seemingly a settled part of the Court's free exercise jurisprudence."[1] After the Supreme Court's composition changed from President Ronald Reagan's appointments to the Supreme Court during the 1980s, however, the Court's approach to free exercise cases changed in a way that created more opportunities for government to regulate religious practices.

In *Bowen v. Roy* (1986), the Supreme Court endorsed the government's requirement that Native American parents provide Social Security numbers for their children, despite the parents' religious belief that the assignment of such numbers served to rob individuals of their spirit. The Court rejected the strict scrutiny test by saying, "In the enforcement of a facially neutral and uniformly applicable requirement for the administration of welfare programs reaching many millions of people, the Government is entitled to wide latitude." Because the sanction applied to the individual in this case was loss of welfare benefits rather than criminal punishment, the Court implied that strict scrutiny could still apply in cases concerning criminal statutes: "We conclude then that government regulation that indirectly and incidentally calls for a choice between securing a governmental benefit and adherence to religious beliefs is wholly different from governmental action or legislation that criminalizes religiously inspired activity or inescapably compels conduct that some find objectionable for religious reasons." Chief Justice Warren Burger's opinion in *Bowen v. Roy* was merely a **plurality opinion** because it was supported by the largest number of justices in the majority but did not gain a full five-member (or larger) majority. Other justices favored the government without endorsing Burger's clear rejection of the strict scrutiny test. Plurality opinions do not establish binding precedents. However, soon thereafter, other cases gained majority support for governmental infringements on free exercise without the strict scrutiny test's required justification of a compelling state interest.

In *Lyng v. Northwest Indian Cemetery Protective Association* (1988), the Court endorsed the U.S. Forest Service's decision to construct a road that would "cause serious and irreparable damage to sacred areas which are an integral and necessary part of the belief systems and lifeway of Northwest California Indian peoples." Although the road could have been built elsewhere and it clearly would destroy a forested area traditionally used by Native Americans for religious practices, Justice Sandra O'Connor's majority opinion said that there is no free exercise violation unless a governmental policy coerces people to undertake activities that violate their religious beliefs. In effect, there is no rights violation in government actions that prevent religious practices by destroying a sacred sanctuary.

Later, in *Employment Division of Oregon v. Smith* (1990), Justice Antonin Scalia's majority opinion clearly set aside the previously applied strict scrutiny test by declaring that "the right of free exercise does not relieve an individual of the obligation to comply with a 'valid neutral law of general applicability on the ground that the law proscribes (or prescribes) conduct that his religion prescribes (or proscribes).'" In other words, the government does possess the authority to impose laws and regulations on the entire citizenry, even if those laws prevent some individuals from engaging in practices essential to their religious beliefs and those practices impose no harm on other people. In the case, a Native American substance abuse counselor had lost his job and been denied unemployment compensation for using peyote, a natural hallucinogenic substance that has been an important element in some Native Americans' religious ceremonies for centuries. Oregon made it a crime to possess and use peyote. However, if pressed to provide a compelling justification for refusing to permit Native Americans to use their traditional substance in religious ceremonies, Oregon would have had difficulty because twenty-three other states and the federal government permit Native Americans to use peyote in religious ceremonies and there is no evidence that these religious practices cause any medical problems for the individuals involved or social problems such as drug trafficking.[2]

According to the Supreme Court's interpretation of the Free Exercise Clause, the government could regulate or even criminalize many religious practices. If, for example, in the interest of fire safety, the government made it a crime to burn candles inside a building, it is difficult to see how the Supreme Court's interpretation of the Free Exercise Clause would enable various Christian denominations to continue their practice of lighting Advent candles and other candles used as essential, traditional components of their ceremonies and observances. It is highly unlikely that this issue would arise, however. The low probability of such laws is not because the government lacks a legitimate interest in fire safety but because legislative actions are unlikely to limit religious practices of mainstream Christians. There are laws that prohibit the handling of poisonous snakes in ceremonies of small, obscure Christian sects, such as Kentucky's law that makes it a misdemeanor to handle reptiles as part of a religious service.[3] However, legislators would avoid clashing with the interests of the mainstream Christian majority to which most of them belong. Because majoritarian interests dominate legislatures, it is minority religions' practices that are placed most at risk by free exercise legal doctrines that accept across-the-board statutes that interfere with religious practices. Thus it is no surprise that, as indicated in the foregoing discussions, minority religious groups such as Mormons, Jehovah's Witnesses, and Native Americans have seen their opportunities to practice their religions freely most adversely affected by legislative actions.

In criminal justice, claims about religious freedom frequently arise in correctional institutions. Corrections officials control the daily schedules of convicted offenders, including their access to religious literature and worship services. Not surprisingly, the Supreme Court does not require prison officials to prove the necessity of imposing restrictions on prisoners' religious practices. Judges, including the justices on the Supreme Court, generally show deference to corrections officials' claims that rules and procedures are necessary to preserve order and security. The Supreme Court's most important decision concerning religion behind prison walls instructs judges to defer to officials' claims that prison procedures must take precedence over opportunities to attend worship services or other aspects of free exercise of religion.

Beginning in the 1960s, federal judges recognized that convicted criminal offenders possess First Amendment rights to free exercise of religion even when they are confined to prisons. The early cases, usually filed on behalf of Black Muslims, demonstrated that prison officials would provide access to worship services and religious materials for Christian prisoners but would not give equal treatment to adherents of other faiths. The Muslims' lawsuits helped to establish the principle that corrections officials could not discriminate against minority religions (*Fulwood v. Clemmer,* 1962). Other lawsuits emphasized the same point on behalf of Buddhists and adherents of other minority religions (*Cruz v. Beto,* 1972). However, these decisions did not ensure actual equality because some prison rules affect specific minority religions but do not directly impact Christian beliefs and practices. For example, prison regulations concerning hair length or head coverings affect the religious practices of Native Americans, Rastafarians, Orthodox Jews, and others but not adherents of mainstream Christian denominations (*Iron Eyes v. Henry,* 1990).

In *O'Lone v. Estate of Shabazz* (1987), a New Jersey prison would not permit minimum security Muslim prisoners assigned to work details outside of the prison to return to the prison for Jumu'ah services on Fridays. Although the Court acknowledged that attendance at these religious services was a central component of the prisoners' religion, the majority of justices deferred to corrections officials' claims that it would be too disruptive to permit the prisoners to return early from their outside work assignments. The Court did not question the officials' claim that the prisoners' return to prison would threaten order and security or require proof of that assertion. They merely noted that officials had presented a legitimate reason, that Muslim prisoners could still practice other aspects of their religion, and that accommodation of the Muslims' request would be viewed as favoritism by other prisoners. The dissenters then complained that no problems have occurred anywhere in the federal prison system from permitting prisoners to attend Friday services and, indeed, this very New Jersey prison had experienced no problems when it previously permitted participation in the services for a five-year period. The dissenters also complained that Muslim prisoners were being denied participation in an essential component of their religion in a manner that would never be applied to Catholic prisoners and other Christians. Overall, the case clearly communicated that prisoners' religious freedom rights must be subordinate to any claims about safety and security that are asserted by corrections officials, even if those claims are unsubstantiated or contradicted by other available evidence.

After the Supreme Court's clear rejection of the strict scrutiny test in *Employment Division of Oregon v. Smith* (1990), liberal and conservative members of Congress joined forces to enact legislation that sought to require federal judges to apply strict scrutiny in religious freedom cases. The **Religious Freedom Restoration Act,** which applied to prisoners' cases as well as to cases for people outside of prison, was eventually struck down as unconstitutional by the Supreme Court (*City of Boerne v. Flores,* 1997). Because so many members of Congress feared that the Supreme Court provided inadequate protection for the right to free exercise of religion, they enacted a new statute called the **Religious Land Use and Institutionalized Persons Act.** This law applied explicitly to prisoners' free exercise rights and again sought to require federal judges to apply a strict scrutiny test in their cases. By 2003, litigation under the statute had produced mixed results with some judges in the lower federal courts declaring the statute to be unconstitutional and others endorsing its legality.[4] It remains to be seen whether the Supreme Court will rule on the issue.

Summary

The U.S. Supreme Court's rejection of the strict scrutiny test for evaluating claims concerning the free exercise of religion appears to enable the government to criminalize religious practices, including those that cause no demonstrable harm to other people or society. Because of the power of majoritarian Christian influences over the legislative process, statutes impeding the free exercise of religion are most likely to affect adherents of minority faiths. In the prison context, the Supreme Court's automatic deference to corrections officials' claims about safety and security makes it extremely difficult for prisoners to successfully challenge limits on their religious practices, even if those practices cause no problems when used in other correctional institutions.

FREEDOM OF SPEECH

Conventional Wisdom 11

> *Because the United States is a free country, people can say what they want to say even if it is something that the government does not like.*

The protection for freedom of speech in the First Amendment clearly sought to prevent the government of the United States from punishing people for expressing their opinions, even if those opinions were critical of the government. Indeed, the right's placement in the First Amendment and its absolutist language ("Congress shall make *no* law . . . abridging the freedom of speech" [emphasis supplied]) underscore the importance of this legal protection in the eyes of the American revolutionaries who fought for their freedom against the British royal governing system that they viewed as unduly oppressive. Despite Americans' general belief in their right to free speech, it easy to see that opportunities for expression are not unlimited. Think about the permissibility of the following statements, which are merely words spoken by individual Americans:

> "Hey, military officer from a foreign country. I'm going to tell you the secret computer codes that will permit you to gain access to the Pentagon's computers. They are . . ."
> "I'll give you five thousand dollars if you murder my business partner."
> "I saw Joey Johnson commit the crime" [a false statement made in court by an individual on the witness stand who had just taken an oath to tell the truth].
> "A house is on fire on East Main Street" [a false statement made by a caller to a 911 operator].

Should people be punished for making the foregoing statements? You are probably aware that people can be punished for such statements, but how does the criminalization of such statements fit with the absolutist language of the First Amendment? In essence, the U.S. Supreme Court interprets the Free Speech Clause in a non-absolutist fashion. Instead, the Court examines governmental restrictions on speech and asks whether the government's justification is legitimate and outweighs the individual's constitutional interest in free speech. In the foregoing examples, judges would find that national security interests outweigh freedom of speech when individuals seek to reveal secret information to foreign governments. Similarly, society's interests in preventing crimes of violence and punishing those responsible for such crimes would permit the criminalization of statements concerning an offer to hire a "hitman" to commit a murder. The government also has compelling interests in ensuring truthful testimony in legal proceedings and in protecting public safety officials and the general public from harms that may flow from false emergency reports (e.g., firefighters and others can be killed in traffic collisions while rushing to the scene of a false alarm). In 1919, Justice Oliver Wendell Holmes wrote that "The most stringent protection of free speech would not protect a man in falsely shouting fire in a theater, and causing a panic" (*Schenck v. United States*). As implied by Holmes's statement, governmental interests can outweigh individuals' interests in expressing themselves and this principle serves as the basis for limiting and criminalizing specific kinds of speech.

Since the mid-twentieth century, the Supreme Court has shown sensitivity to the importance of political speech. The underlying purposes of the First Amendment are not presumed to focus on all possible forms of speech, despite the amendment's absolutist language. Instead, there is a recognition that speech presenting information and opinions about politics and policy represents the aspect of free speech that is essential to democracy and embodies the core purpose of the Free Speech Clause in the First Amendment. In the early twentieth century, people were prosecuted and imprisoned for expressing opposition to the government's policies. The Supreme Court regarded such criticism, when made by socialists, communists, and others who wanted a new government in the United States, as unduly threatening to national security (*Abrams v. United States*, 1919). Similar prosecutions continued through the 1950s as many people feared that communists were seeking to take over the country and the rest of the world (*Dennis v. United States*, 1951). After overt expressions of governmental criticism became more widespread and accepted during the civil rights movement and the Vietnam War protests of the 1960s, the Supreme Court eventually revised its analysis of political speech. In a case concerning a Ku Klux Klan leader, the Supreme Court declared that "the constitutional guarantees of free speech and free press do not permit a State to forbid or proscribe advocacy of the use of force or of law violation except where such advocacy is directed to inciting or producing imminent lawless action and is likely to incite or produce such action" (*Brandenburg v. Ohio*, 1969). Thus the interpretation of the First Amendment gradually moved from permitting the government to imprison its critics to protecting political speech as long as it was not likely to cause immediate lawless action, such as a riot.

The Supreme Court has faced more difficult problems with respect to symbolic speech that did not involve merely spoken words. During the Vietnam War, the Court overturned criminal convictions of war protesters who had expressed their views through such means as performing a street play depicting American soldiers killing Vietnamese civilians (*Schacht v. United States*, 1970) and placing a peace symbol on an upside down American flag (*Spence v. Washington*, 1974). The Court's most controversial protection of symbolic speech came in decisions that forbade governments from prosecuting people who expressed their criticism of the United States by burning American flags (*Texas v. Johnson*, 1989; *United States v. Eichman*, 1990). Justice Brennan's majority opinion in *Texas v. Johnson* declared that "If there is one bedrock principle underlying the First Amendment, it is that the Government may not prohibit the expression of an idea simply because society finds the idea itself offensive or disagreeable." He rejected governmental claims that state interests in preserving the flag as a national symbol or in protecting national unity outweighed Johnson's constitutional right to express himself symbolically. According to Brennan, "We do not consecrate the flag by punishing its desecration, for in doing so we dilute the freedom that this cherished emblem represents."

These decisions did not mean, however, that all forms of symbolic speech are protected by the First Amendment. In 2003, the Supreme Court considered a case that challenged Virginia's statute making the burning of crosses a felony (*Virginia v. Black*, 2003). Cross burning is a traditional expressive activity used by the Ku Klux Klan as part of its ceremonies expressing a belief in white superiority and a desire to harm African-Americans, Jewish people, interracial couples, and others against whom they direct their hatred. The Supreme Court concluded that states can make it a crime to burn crosses when such burnings are intended to intimidate people. Although the burning of a cross at a Klan rally may be protected as a form of symbolic speech, the burning of crosses in the yards of African-Americans or interracial couples may be prosecuted as a crime if the prosecutor can prove that there is an intent to intimidate. The mere burning of a cross does not automatically fulfill the requirement that it show an intent to intimidate in order to be the basis for prosecution. Thus the context of the cross burning determines whether it is protected by the First Amendment. The majority opinion justified its limitation of free expression by relying on precedents that discussed the so-called "fighting words" doctrine (*Chaplinsky v. New Hampshire*, 1942). In relying on this doctrine, Justice Sandra Day O'Connor noted that "a State may punish those words 'which by their very utterance inflict injury or tend to incite an immediate breach of the peace' . . . [including] 'personally abusive epithets which, when addressed to the ordinary citizen, are, as a matter of common knowledge, inherently likely to provoke a violent reaction.'" Justice O'Connor analogized cross burning motivated by an intent to intimidate to the "fighting words" doctrine because it is a "type of true threat, . . . with the intent of placing the victim in fear of bodily harm or death." The Court's decision did not explain what other types of symbolic expression might be subject to pro-hibition and criminal prosecution, but it clearly establishes opportunities for the criminalization of certain expressions that are deemed harmful because of their threatening intentions. In effect, the Court viewed society's interests in preventing harms (i.e., threats of violence) as outweighing individuals' right to express themselves in this manner.

Prosecutions under these kinds of limitations on expression need not be based on symbolic speech that is dramatic or historically associated with vio-lence such as cross burning. For example, in 2003 a student at Michigan State University pleaded guilty to misdemeanor harassment for posting a racially offensive flier on a dormitory bulletin board. The flier advertised a fictitious meeting and used offensive racial stereotypes concerning African-Americans.[5]

Additional limitations on speech may be imposed on private property, even if that property is open to the public, such as a shopping mall. In 2003, a lawyer was arrested and charged with trespassing in a shopping mall in Albany, New York, when he refused to obey security guards' orders to remove a T-shirt that said "Give Peace A Chance."[6] The mall eventually asked to have the crim-inal charges dropped after it became the focus of national publicity and pub-lic protests. However, the case illustrates a further limitation on Americans' assumptions about their freedom to express their opinions.

Summary

Despite its absolutist language, the First Amendment does not provide com-plete freedom of speech. Government-imposed limitations on speech, including the criminalization of certain kinds of speech, are permissible when courts determine that the government's interests outweigh those of the individual. Asserted governmental interests in national security, public safety, and truth-fulness in legal processes are among those that may be the basis for imposing criminal punishments on individuals for statements that they make. Political speech and symbolic expression are generally protected unless they constitute threats to individuals or otherwise create imminent incitement to lawless action, such as riots.

FREEDOM OF THE PRESS

Conventional Wisdom 12

The American press is free to write or broadcast whatever material it chooses without restrictions by the government.

Like freedom of speech, freedom of the press is regarded as an essential element of a democracy. People need information in order to make choices about candidates for elective office and to hold government officials accountable in elections. Since the 1930s, the Supreme Court has examined critically any governmental efforts to prevent the news media from publishing or broadcasting information. In *Near v. Minnesota* (1931), concerning a newspaper editor who was prosecuted for publishing material that was allegedly "malicious and scandalous," the Court made its classic statement that "the chief purpose of the [freedom of the press] guaranty [is] to prevent previous restraints upon publication." In some circumstances, a compelling governmental interest might justify placing limitations on the freedom of the press. In particular, the government may have reason to muffle the press when national security interests are threatened or when significant harms to society may be produced, such as through the creation and publication of child pornography. However, even in these circumstances, the Supreme Court does not reflexively endorse the government's claimed justifications.

For example, in June 1971, the *New York Times* and the *Washington Post* began to publish the "Pentagon Papers," materials from a top secret study entitled "History of U.S. Decision-Making Process on Vietnam Policy." The materials had been given to the news media by a man who worked on the study for the Central Intelligence Agency (CIA) but later came to conclude that the American people needed to know the truth about the Vietnam War. The federal government sought court orders to prevent the newspapers from publishing the materials. However, a majority of justices on the Supreme Court rejected the government's effort to halt publication. These justices did not believe that the government provided sufficient proof of harm to national security from publication of the study (*New York Times v. United States*, 1971). Although these newspapers believed that the Pentagon Papers needed dissemination in order for the public to recognize and understand its government's actions related to a controversial issue, reporters and editors often restrain themselves and keep quiet if they discover information that they believe will cause actual damage to national security.

In 2002, the Supreme Court struck down provisions of the Child Pornography Prevention Act that prohibited not only pornographic images made using actual children but also other images, such as computer-generated images or images using youthful-looking adults, that appear to depict minors (*Ashcroft v. Free Speech Coalition*, 2002). The Court found that the restrictive legislation was overly broad and included prohibitions on materials that were not "obscene" under constitutional standards. Anything deemed to be **obscenity** is not protected by the First Amendment, but the Court is very cautious about applying that label—even to explicitly sexual material—because of a limited willingness to permit the government to engage in censorship.

In considering the extent to which freedom of the press receives support from judicial decisions, one must remember that the news media are often better positioned than individual citizens to protect their First Amendment rights. As private businesses that are often part of national corporations, newspapers and television stations usually have attorneys and the resources necessary to file lawsuits to challenge formal limitations on their access to information. Moreover, they can use their own facilities and resources to publicize issues of freedom of the press. For example, when a federal judge sealed and kept secret court documents in a criminal case concerning the tragic hijackings and suicide attacks on New York and Washington on September 11, 2001, the judge's decision was challenged collectively by ABC News, The Associated Press, The Hearst Corporation, The *New York Times,* The Tribune Company, and The *Washington Post* as well as the Reporters Committee for Freedom of the Press.[7] These organizations possess far more resources and political influence than the typical individual who seeks to challenge an alleged violation of constitutional rights.

The Supreme Court is cautious about limiting freedom of the press even in circumstances in which the First Amendment right may clash with a defendant's Sixth Amendment right to a fair trial. If there is too much publicity about a criminal case prior to trial, there is a risk that the court will be unable to find a sufficient number of open-minded jurors who have not already developed assumptions and conclusions about the defendant's guilt based on news reports. In the 1960s, there were several cases in which the Supreme Court overturned criminal convictions because excessive, inflammatory news coverage made the trial unfair. In one case involving a highly publicized confession to six murders, eight of the twelve jurors indicated prior to the trial that they believed the defendant to be guilty (*Irvin v. Dowd,* 1961).[8] Despite the examples in which freedom of the press interfered with the right to a fair trial, the Supreme Court is extremely reluctant to permit judges to prevent the press from gaining access to courtrooms or to issue "gag orders" concerning judicial proceedings. In general, the Court expects trial judges to employ all other alternatives before considering the possibility of restraining the press (*Nebraska Press Association v. Stuart,* 1976). Such alternatives include limiting the number of cameras and reporters in a courtroom—in order to avoid a "circus atmosphere"—and moving the trial to a different county where potential jurors have not been exposed to as much news coverage as those people who live near the scene of the crime. A change in locations for a trial is called a **change of venue.** The general presumption against limiting press coverage was evident in a 2002 decision by the U.S. Court of Appeals for the Sixth Circuit. In the aftermath of the September 11, 2001, suicide attacks on the World Trade Center and the Pentagon, the federal government used a national security justification to hold deportation hearings for Middle Eastern men who had violated immigration regulations. In a lawsuit filed by four newspapers and a member of Congress, the appellate court declared that the government had violated the First Amendment by restricting public and press access to the proceedings (*Detroit Free Press v. Ashcroft*).[9]

Despite the presumption against withholding court access from the press, courts keep some proceedings and information secret if judges conclude that there is a compelling reason to do so. In the preparations for the trial of Zacarias Moussaoui, a man who allegedly planned to participate in the September 11th hijackings, the federal district judge placed much of the court record under seal, thereby making information unavailable to the press and public. After news organizations claimed that the judge's orders violated the First Amendment, in April 2003 the government agreed that most of the documents could be revealed to the public. However, the government still sought to keep several documents secret because of national security interests.[10]

Unlike in Great Britain and Canada, where there are significant legal restrictions on the news media's ability to publish pretrial information about criminal cases,[11] judges in the United States seldom impose limits on American news coverage. This protection of freedom of the press may impose costs on some defendants. For example, when Timothy McVeigh and Terry Nichols were charged with killing more than 150 people in Oklahoma City in 1995 by bombing the federal building, the trial was moved to Denver in an effort to find open-minded jurors. However, there is little doubt that potential jurors in Denver, just like other Americans throughout the country, had been exposed to detailed news reports concerning the tragic story that captured the attention of the national media. The attorney for Nichols reportedly suggested moving the trial to the Upper Peninsula of Michigan apparently in the hope that people in a more isolated location might have less exposure to publicity. In an age of cable and satellite television and twenty-four-hour news channels, however, there is little doubt that pretrial information about the case was available everywhere. The emphasis on freedom of the press does not automatically mean that defendants in highly publicized cases cannot get fair trials. Instead, it means that the right to a fair trial may depend on lengthy and careful jury selection procedures, including asking potential jurors many questions about their knowledge and opinions, as the price for emphasizing freedom of the press.

The most significant limitations on the press do not arise from formal rules that prevent reporting by newspapers and broadcast journalism outlets. Instead, other constraints limit what information the press supplies to the public.

One legal constraint is the law of **defamation.** Defamation, commonly referred to as *slander* for spoken words and *libel* for written statements, provides a civil cause of action for people harmed by information that is communicated to other people. In other words, individuals may file civil lawsuits seeking the recovery of money damages when newspapers, magazines, broadcast reports, or even other individuals communicate information that is both false and harmful to their reputations. Defamation lawsuits do not prevent the publication of news stories. There is no prior restraint or censorship by the government. Instead, such lawsuits deter news outlets from publishing harmful, false stories by posing the threat of financial liability for being insufficiently careful in investigating stories and verifying facts. In order to give the press sufficient freedom to pursue stories about public officials without the risk of lawsuits for minor or inadvertent factual errors, the U.S. Supreme Court has said that public officials, unlike average citizens, must prove in defamation lawsuits not only that harmful stories are false but also that the stories were published with knowledge that they were false or with reckless disregard for the truth (*New York Times v. Sullivan,* 1964).

A more significant limitation on the ability of the press to report stories about politics and public policy stems from the government's success in hiding information from the press and public. Freedom of the press makes newspapers and broadcast outlets generally free to communicate the information that they can discover, but the purposes and benefits of freedom of the press within a democracy can be drastically curtailed by governmental efforts to shield information from disclosure. Thus the right to freedom of the press can have a symbolic quality when the press is free to report but they lack access to information about governmental processes and decisions.

The administration of President George W. Bush provides instructive examples of governmental efforts to prevent the disclosure of information. All presidential administrations as well as state governors, members of Congress, and other governmental officials make efforts to control the nature and timing of information about their activities and decisions. However, the Bush administration became noted for its successful efforts to limit access to information. Although the Presidential Records Act of 1978 declared that the records of a former president belong to the public, President Bush signed an executive order in November 2001 that allows former presidents and the families of deceased presidents to block public access to selected records.[12] Some critics wondered if the order was intended to prevent disclosure of documents that would reveal his father's role in the Iran-Contra scandal and other matters during the elder Bush's prior service as vice president and president. In October 2001, Bush's attorney general, John Ashcroft, instructed federal agencies to resist and delay requests from the press and public for government documents under the Freedom of Information Act, even if it meant going to court to slow the release of information. The prior presidential administration had, by contrast, instructed agencies to release requested information unless they could present a strong reason for contesting the request.[13] In addition, the Bush administration fought a lawsuit against the government's own General Accounting Office in order to keep secret the names of oil company officials and others who advised Vice President Cheney on the development of the administration's energy policy and it removed hundreds of thousands of previously available documents from government Web sites. The government also fought in court to keep the press blocked from court proceedings concerning the deportation of Middle Eastern men with expired visas and to prevent public release of the names of foreigners held in American jails.[14] As indicated by these examples, the First Amendment right to freedom of the press, even when interpreted broadly, does not ensure that the press and public will gain access to information about their government's activities.

Summary

The government may restrain the press from publishing materials related to national security and other matters that provide compelling justifications, but this rarely occurs. The Supreme Court expresses a strong presumption against prior restraint and censorship by government. Generally, the Supreme Court would require extremely persuasive evidence about a compelling government interest and significant risk of harm before even considering the approval of prior restraint. Indeed, the importance of freedom of the press in judicial decisions looms so large that the United States tends to risk harm to the fairness of trials by permitting significant publicity about pending criminal cases rather than place limitations on the press. Although the law does not impose significant restrictions on the press, other influences limit the information that is reported by newspapers and broadcast outlets. The threat of defamation lawsuits encourages reporters to take care in gathering their facts before filing reports. In addition, the government can limit the practical effectiveness of freedom of the press merely by hiding information from public view. Thus the right to freedom of the press, even if strongly protected in court decisions, does not ensure that the press and the public will have access to information about the government's activities and decisions.

FREEDOM OF ASSEMBLY

Conventional Wisdom 13

The right to freedom of assembly permits people to gather together, especially when they intend to express their views about governmental actions and other public issues.

The Supreme Court decided several cases emphasizing the right of people to gather and engage in peaceful protests during the era of the Civil Rights Movement of the 1960s in which African-Americans and their supporters sought legal equality and voting rights (*Cox v. Louisiana*, 1965; *Brown v. Louisiana*, 1966). However, many of the Supreme Court's decisions that affect people's freedom to gather together have been decided as free speech cases that concern "speech plus conduct." For example, in *Madsen v. Women's Health Center* (1994), the Court examined an order issued by a Florida court that created a "36-foot buffer zone" on a public street in front of an abortion clinic and barred anti-abortion protesters from entering that zone in their efforts to express their views about abortion policies. The Court upheld the buffer zone around clinic entrances in order to prevent protesters from blocking access to the clinic and interfering with traffic on the street. However, the Court rejected the imposition of buffer zones on the back and sides of the clinic. As is often the case in litigation concerning constitutional rights, the Court sought to strike a balance between First Amendment rights and important societal interests. Despite the case's relevance to people's right to assemble, in invalidating some of the buffer zones the Court's language referred to freedom of speech:

> We hold that on the record before us the 36-foot buffer zone as applied to the private property to the north and west of the clinic burdens more speech than necessary to protect access to the clinic.

The Court also decided cases concerning people's right to assemble as claims concerning the right to due process. For example, the Chicago City Council enacted a Gang Congregation Ordinance in 1992 that prohibited "criminal street gang members" from "loitering" with other persons in any public place (*City of Chicago v. Morales*, 1999). As described in the Supreme Court's opinion striking down the ordinance, the law clearly sought to limit people's ability to assemble in public:

> The ordinance creates a criminal offense punishable by a fine of up to $500, imprisonment for not more than six months, and a requirement to perform up to 120 hours of community service. Commission of the offense involves four predicates. First, the police officer must reasonably believe that at least one of the two or more persons present in a "public place" is a "criminal street gang membe[r]." Second, the persons must be "loitering", which the ordinance defines as "remain[ing] in any one place with no apparent purpose." Third, the officer must then order "all" of the persons to disperse and remove themselves "from the area." Fourth, a person must disobey the officer's order. If any person, whether a gang member or not, disobeys the officer's order, that person is guilty of violating the ordinance.

Despite the absolutist words of the First Amendment that appear to protect broadly Americans' right to "peaceably to assemble," the Supreme Court did not use this case to declare that the government may not regulate people's ability to gather together in public. Instead, the Court struck down the ordinance for being unconstitutionally vague by giving police officers too little guidance and too much discretion about defining "criminal street gang members" and "loitering." Indeed, the Court left open the possibility that a city could create a narrowly tailored ordinance that might advance the types of objectives that the Chicago ordinance sought to achieve. In the words of the majority opinion, "We agree with the city's submission that the law does not have a sufficiently substantial impact on conduct protected by the First Amendment to render it unconstitutional." The Court ultimately endorsed the conclusion of the Illinois Supreme Court that "the gang loitering ordinance violates the due process of law in that it is impermissibly vague on its face and an arbitrary restriction on personal liberties." Despite striking down this ordinance, the Court, in effect, endorsed governmental authority to regulate, prohibit, and punish assemblies of people in certain situations because it said that this ordinance did not violate the First Amendment.

As indicated by the foregoing example, there is no broad, clearly defined right for people to assemble. The Supreme Court permits what it calls "reasonable time, place, and manner" restrictions on assemblies and related activities, including those involving the expression of political viewpoints. Not surprisingly, the Court's interpretation of the First Amendment does not permit people to block public streets, interfere with governmental functions, and violate private property rights. Thus, for example, cities may require people to apply for permits before organizing assemblies that will affect traffic on public streets. Assemblies of people near jails, military installations, and some other governmental facilities may be prohibited because of the risk of interference with important governmental functions (*Adderley v. Florida,* 1966). These situations involve efforts to strike a balance between First Amendment rights and important societal interests. At the same time, however, they also grant power to government officials to determine when and if public assemblies will be permitted. These restrictive decisions can only be contested by individuals who have sufficient time, money, and legal expertise to make use of the costly, time-consuming litigation process to challenge the officials' decisions. In other cases, even overly restrictive decisions by government officials stand because the affected individuals lack the resources necessary to pursue a legal action. For cases examined in court, the determination about the reasonableness of the restrictive regulation is made by an individual trial judge or a panel of appellate judges, all of whom possess their own attitudes, values, and theories about the scope of First Amendment rights. A restriction that would be struck down by one court may be permitted to restrict the right to assembly by another court.

Governmental efforts to restrict assembly, especially with respect to political protest, are illustrated in the life story of Brett Bursey, an outspoken political activist in South Carolina. In 1969, he held an anti–Vietnam War sign at Columbia Metropolitan Airport when President Richard Nixon arrived for a visit. Bursey was arrested and charged with trespassing. The South Carolina Supreme Court eventually ordered the charges dropped because protesters on public property could not be charged with trespassing due to their First Amendment rights.[15] In October 2002, Bursey was arrested again for trespassing at the same location for carrying a "No War for Oil" sign amid a crowd of people waiting for the arrival of President George W. Bush. The police claimed that Bursey should have held his sign in a "protest zone" that had been designated by the local government for such assemblies on this day. However, the "protest area" was on the edge of a highway one-half mile away from the where the president was to speak so that the corralling of protesters away from the event could prevent them from expressing their views to the country's top elected official.[16] The trespassing charges were dropped again, but this time the federal government prosecuted Bursey under a statute that permits the Secret Service to restrict access to areas the president is visiting. Bursey faced the possibility of six months in jail and a $5,000 fine despite the fact that Bush supporters were assembled in the same purportedly restricted location and not arrested. Cases such as Bursey's highlight the risk that limitations on First Amendment rights to assembly and speech may be based on the ideas being expressed in those activities. Government supporters can receive favorable treatment in the awarding of parade permits and in assembling freely while government critics may not enjoy the same treatment. For example, in 2003 a group called "United for Peace and Justice" was denied a permit to hold a protest march in New York City based on the city's purported need to protect security in the post-9/11 era. However, the city had previously approved permits for the St. Patrick's Day Parade and the National Puerto Rican Day Parade, two events that each attracted up to 100,000 participants and spectators.[17] Was the permit denial based on the political views being expressed by United for Peace and Justice? It is impossible to know. But such examples raise questions about whether rights to assembly and speech are always equally protected and applied.

Summary

The Supreme Court interprets the First Amendment to permit "reasonable time, place, and manner" restrictions on the right to peaceably assemble as well as the right to free speech, including speech that is associated with specific conduct such as a protest march. The Court typically presents itself as seeking an appropriate balance between First Amendment rights and the protection of important societal interests. This balancing approach and its acceptance of prohibitions and regulations on certain assemblies conflict with the absolutist language of the First Amendment that declares that "Congress shall make no law" prohibiting the right to peaceably assemble. Statutes and ordinances that prohibit or otherwise restrict assemblies typically place discretionary authority in the hands of law enforcement officers or other government officials who decide when and against whom to apply the restrictions. Some of these restrictions may be challenged successfully in court by people with sufficient time, money, and legal expertise to make use of the litigation process. Other restrictions stand, either because the affected individuals cannot afford to challenge their validity or because the judicial officers who consider such challenges follow interpretive theories of the First Amendment that facilitate governmental regulation.

CONCLUSION

None of the rights in the First Amendment receive the level of protection indicated by the amendment's absolutist language that purports to bar the enactment of prohibitions by Congress (or other governmental entities—see the discussion of incorporation in Chapter 2). The Supreme Court's interpretations of the First Amendment's provisions permit government to restrict and prohibit religious exercises, speech, press freedom, and assemblies under various circumstances in which societal interests are determined to outweigh individuals' rights. The Constitution itself says nothing about weighing individuals' rights against society's interests, but judges possess the authority to interpret the Bill of Rights and other constitutional provisions according to their own theories, values, and policy preferences.

When assertions of First Amendment rights collide with governmental laws, policies, and practices, the Supreme Court often imposes on the government the burden of justifying restrictions on constitutional rights by demonstrating a "compelling" state interest. In other words, the government is required to show why it *must* have a particular law or policy in order to protect society against a *significant harm.* With respect to free exercise of religion, however, the Supreme Court has weakened First Amendment protections to make religious freedom generally subordinate to a variety of governmental laws of "general applicability." Although the Supreme Court previously applied the "strict scrutiny" test to require the government to demonstrate its compelling state interest, decisions in the 1990s set aside that test and, in effect, imposed a constitutional doctrine that gave government greater authority to impose laws and policies that restrict the exercise of religion. Because Christian denominations possess majoritarian influence over the legislative bodies that enact laws, minority religions are most likely to find their practices prohibited or limited by legislative enactments that cannot be invalidated through judicial processes because of the Supreme Court's interpretation of the Free Exercise Clause.

Speech can be regulated or prohibited in order to protect national security, public order, and other societal interests. Moreover, the government can impose "reasonable time, place, and manner" restrictions on speech and assembly rights. These restrictions are often implemented according to the discretionary decisions of law enforcement personnel and other governmental officials. Some people affected by these restrictions lack the resources to use the litigation process as a means to protect their rights. Moreover, judges do not interpret and apply First Amendment doctrines in identical fashion, so even those individuals or groups who manage to file court challenges to restrictions on speech and assembly do not necessarily gain protection for their rights.

Newspapers and broadcast corporations are often well positioned to mount court challenges to governmental restrictions on freedom of the press. In general, court decisions do not permit the imposition of governmental restraints or censorship on the news media. Indeed, American courts tend to favor freedom of the press even in situations in which there are arguable clashes between dissemination of information about criminal cases and a defendant's right to a fair trial with an unbiased jury. The general tendency to favor freedom of the press in formal interpretations of the First Amendment does not mean, however, that the press can gain access to and publish materials concerning governmental activities and matters of public interest. The First Amendment's underlying intent to preserve a free press in order to make sure citizens in the American democracy are fully informed about their government and society can be hindered by governmental and corporate efforts to keep information secret, including information about public policy issues. Thus, even freedom of the press, the First Amendment right that arguably receives the greatest judicial protection, cannot necessarily achieve the intentions of the Bill of Rights' authors because of officials' ability to hide information from the press and public. Broad judicial interpretations alone cannot always prevent the operation of other factors that reduce the substance and enhance the symbolism of specific constitutional rights.

THE FOURTH AMENDMENT

The right of the people to be secure in their persons, houses, papers, and effects, against unreasonable searches and seizures, shall not be violated, and no Warrants shall issue, but upon probable cause, supported by Oath or affirmation, and particularly describing the place to be searched, and the persons or things to be seized.

The underlying purpose of the Fourth Amendment is presented in its very first line. The amendment provides a constitutional right for the security of people, their homes, and their possessions against unreasonable intrusions by the government. However, all people are not equally protected by the prohibition on unreasonable searches. For example, the California Supreme Court has said that school officials do not need any reasonable suspicion to provide the basis for stopping, questioning, and searching students.[1] The amendment's words do not provide any exceptions that exclude students from its legal protections or that treat public school officials differently than other government officials whose authority is limited by the amendment. But judges possess the power to give meaning to constitutional amendments and, in supplying definitions of rights, judges may reduce the coverage of rights. Thus the fact that the U.S. Supreme Court's incorporation decisions gave the Fourth Amendment universal coverage across all states and localities does not mean that this coverage is uniform for all categories of people and all specific situations that might arise. Judges often define the Fourth Amendment by attempting to strike a balance between the protection of individuals' rights and other policy objectives. In the eyes of the California court, concerns about school violence clearly outweigh the personal legal protections enunciated in the Fourth Amendment.

In examining the Fourth Amendment, a primary interpretive problem for judges involves defining the word *unreasonable*. If a search is unreasonable, then it presumably violates the Fourth Amendment. If a search is reasonable, then it is permissible. The nature of the constitutional right frequently hinges on judges' decisions about the reasonableness of law enforcement officers' actions.

93

It would be useful if the Supreme Court could produce a clear rule about which searches and seizures will be deemed "unreasonable." However, the factual circumstances underlying searches and seizures are so varied that the Court often finds itself developing separate rules for different situations. The proliferation of rules and exceptions can make it difficult for police officers to know whether a particular search will be labeled as "reasonable" or "unreasonable."

The Fourth Amendment also governs seizures, which include seizures of property as well as seizures of people through stops and arrests. As in the situation of searches, police officers may use their discretion in ways that defeat the implementation of Supreme Court decisions concerning seizures. For example, in 2001 it was revealed that the Detroit police department engaged in the practice of arresting *witnesses* in murder cases in order to hold them in jail as a means to force them to talk.[2] Arrests must be supported by probable cause, which means sufficient reliable information to believe that it is more likely than not that a particular individual committed a crime. Yet Detroit homicide detectives testified under oath in court that they arrested witnesses and held them in jail for days without any probable cause.[3] In a related issue concerning the treatment of arrestees while in custody, the year 2001 also produced the revelation that Philadelphia police engaged in a long-standing practice of driving erratically and making sharp turns while driving arrestees to the police station so that the handcuffed suspects would fall all over inside the police van and thereby suffer pain and injuries. Arrestees had suffered injuries ranging from broken tailbones to permanent paralysis as a result of the police officers' efforts to injure them.[4] In both the Detroit and Philadelphia situations, it is clear that police officers can use their discretion to violate constitutional rights no matter what the Supreme Court has directed them to do. However, both Detroit and Philadelphia found themselves paying hundreds of thousands of dollars to settle lawsuits filed against them as a result of these rights violations. Because these rights violations involved either personal injuries or improper deprivations of liberty, victims have the possibility of recovering money damages through litigation. Thus the rights violations are remedied after the fact through compensation. By contrast, many other rights can be largely symbolic because of a lack of effective remedies. As you read about issues concerning Fourth Amendment searches, think about the extent to which remedies are applied when rights violations occur.

WARRANTS AND PROBABLE CAUSE

Conventional Wisdom 14

In order to obtain a search or arrest warrant, police officers must provide clear evidence to a judge concerning the suspect's guilt.

✳The purpose of the Fourth Amendment's warrant requirement is to interpose a neutral decision maker between law enforcement officials and the individual whom they wish to search or arrest. This neutral decision maker is responsible for ensuring that adequate justification exists to justify the search or arrest. Warrants are issued by judicial officers, but these officials are not always judges. Many states use "magistrates" or "referees," who may be attorneys serving as part-time judicial officers in a limited capacity. The Supreme Court has said that warrants may also be issued by court clerks and other nonlawyers (*Shadwick v. City of Tampa,* 1972). These judicial officers must decide whether the sworn evidence provided by law enforcement officers constitutes "probable cause" as required by the Fourth Amendment for the issuance of a warrant. Like the word *unreasonable* in the Fourth Amendment, the term *probable cause* is inherently vague and requires interpretation. The Supreme Court has attempted to provide guidance about the nature and amount of information needed to support probable cause, but judicial officers in lower courts throughout the country must still use their judgment in evaluating the information.

The information presented in support of probable cause for obtaining a warrant is not formal evidence, as in a trial, in which witnesses testify and actual documents are presented and challenged in court. Instead, police officers present a statement of the facts that they have obtained about the case when they meet with the judicial officer. Warrants may also be issued based on sworn oral testimony presented to the judicial officer by telephone. Other than supervision by a prosecutor, who may share the police officers' desire to conduct a search, there is no external control to ensure that the police officers are completely truthful and accurate in presenting their statement of facts. There is no defense attorney to challenge the reliability and propriety of the information. It is presumed that the judicial officer will consider the rights of the suspect in determining whether or not to issue the warrant. The accuracy of this presumption obviously varies, depending on the knowledge and actions of the judicial officer and his or her relationship with the police and prosecutor. Some judicial officers may develop reputations for assisting police and prosecutors by readily granting requests for warrants. Others may be viewed as more skeptical of the police and therefore prosecutors and police take greater care in preparing and justifying warrant applications to be presented to these judicial officers. The differences in these judicial officers' orientations toward the police and prosecutors are, in effect, differences in the nature of probable cause required to obtain warrants in different courts. Some police and prosecutors are even known to "shop around" by steering warrant applications to a specific, sympathetic judicial officer when they fear that they do not have enough information to constitute probable cause in the eyes of a different judge or magistrate. For example, if there is an investigation of an ongoing criminal enterprise, such as drug trafficking, the judge assigned to handle a multijudge court's warrants for a specific week may be especially strict about defining probable cause. If the investigation will not be disrupted by waiting for a few days, the police and prosecutor may wait until the following week to seek a warrant when a more sympathetic judicial officer is in charge of warrants for the week.

Probable cause is a vague and flexible concept. The nature and amount of information needed to establish probable cause can vary depending on the seriousness of the crime and the urgency of the perceived need for the warrant. According to one federal court decision (*Llaguno v. Mingey*, 1985, U.S. Court of Appeals, 7th Circuit),

> The amount of information that prudent police will collect before deciding to make a search or an arrest, and hence the amount of probable cause they will have, is a function of the gravity of the crime, and especially the danger of its imminent repetition. If a multiple murderer is at large, the police must compress their investigation and make the decision to search or arrest on less information than if they could investigate at their leisure.

If the meaning of probable cause differs from case to case, judicial officers obviously must use their own judgment in determining when a warrant is justified. Thus there cannot be any precise formula that tells them when the facts presented by the police are sufficient for Fourth Amendment purposes.

As summarized by law professors Charles Whitebread and Christopher Slobogin,

> [P]robable cause to search exists when the facts and circumstances in a given situation are sufficient to warrant a person of reasonable caution to believe that seizable objects are located at the place to be searched. . . . Literally interpreted, this term seems to require a more likely than not showing that the evidence sought will be found.[5]

In legal terms, this is an "objective" standard because it requires the decision maker to ask how a "reasonable person" would evaluate the information rather than asking the decision maker to simply apply his or her own judgment. In reality, however, it is an inescapable fact that the judicial officers must incorporate their own judgments into the assessment of the information, if only to reach a conclusion about what the average reasonable person would think. Thus the vagueness of the term and its application to varied factual circumstances mean that the implementation of and protection provided by the Fourth Amendment's probable cause requirement will vary from person to person. For some individuals, the probable cause requirement may ensure that strong and accurate information supports the search. For other individuals, search warrants may be issued relatively easily on questionable grounds. For these individuals, the Fourth Amendment right has less substance.

In theory, any errors made by police and prosecutors in preparing warrants and by judicial officers in issuing warrants will be detected and corrected as the case proceeds through the criminal justice process. Because the Fourth Amendment explicitly requires that a warrant particularly describe the place to be searched and the things to be seized, there are no general warrants that authorize "fishing expeditions" for random explorations of people's homes and possessions. Thus, if the police intend to seize items that are not listed on the search warrant, those items should be excluded from evidence when challenged by the defense attorney in court. Similarly, if a judicial officer issues a warrant based on information that is not sufficient to constitute probable cause, then evidence obtained in the search should be excluded. The U.S. Supreme Court endorsed the exclusionary rule as the remedy for improper searches by federal law enforcement officers in 1914 (*Weeks v. United States*) and applied the same rule to state and local officers in 1961 (*Mapp v. Ohio*).

In reality, however, the warrant justifies the officers in searching in places where the things listed on the warrant might be. If the objects sought are small, such as drugs, bullets, or stolen jewelry, then the officers might be justified in searching almost any location in a dwelling. While it is true that they could not search for an elephant in a bread box, most searches concern smaller articles of evidence that might be in the bread box, dresser drawer, and numerous other locations. Moreover, if the officers encounter evidence other than that listed on the warrant while looking in places authorized by the warrant, they are permitted to seize the evidence. The rule was established in a case in which officers saw weapons while executing a warrant to search for stolen coins and jewelry (*Horton v. California*, 1990). The *Horton* rule is derived from the **plain view doctrine,** which says officers can legally inspect and seize any contraband that is plainly visible to them as they stand at a location where they are entitled to be (*Coolidge v. New Hampshire*, 1971). Thus the specificity requirement for warrants provides less practical protection than one might presume from the words of the Fourth Amendment.

In addition, individuals' rights are not automatically protected when court decisions subsequently determine that judicial officers issued warrants without sufficient information to constitute probable cause. In *United States v. Leon* (1984), a judicial officer issued a search warrant based on stale, five-month-old information from an informant of unproven reliability. A federal court of appeals later decided that the information could not support probable cause, the search warrant should not have been issued, and therefore the criminal evidence found during the improper search should be excluded from evidence. The U.S. Supreme Court subsequently reversed the decision by the court of appeals. The Supreme Court created a new exception to the exclusionary rule. According to the majority of justices, evidence need not be excluded when the police officers acted in "good faith" by honestly presenting information to a judicial officer in applying for a search warrant. There are concerns that the decision diminished the incentives for officers to make sure that their information is current and reliable. When the error is made by the judicial officer in issuing the warrant and the police have done nothing wrong, then, under the **good-faith exception,** the police are allowed to conduct the search and seize incriminating evidence while executing the defective warrant. In effect, the Court acknowledged that the individual's Fourth Amendment right was violated because a search was conducted under the authority of a mistakenly issued warrant that was not supported by probable cause. However, the Court eliminated the usual remedy for that right. Thus the individual could be convicted of a crime based on evidence obtained through a search that violated the Fourth Amendment. For individuals whose homes are searched as a result of warrants improperly issued by judicial officers, the Fourth Amendment is largely symbolic and does not protect their "persons, houses, papers, and effects."

Summary

The probable cause and warrant requirements of the Fourth Amendment provide uncertain protection for individuals. Warrants are not necessarily issued by experienced judges. In many jurisdictions, warrants may be issued by attorneys acting as part-time judicial officers or even by court clerks and other nonlawyer magistrates. Probable cause is a vague, flexible concept that is interpreted and applied differently by different judicial officers who must use their judgment in determining whether sufficient and proper information has been presented to justify a search or arrest. Although the Fourth Amendment says that the warrant must describe with particularity the items to be sought, officers can actually seize other contraband and evidence during a search of authorized locations. In addition, the good-faith exception to the warrant requirement permits Fourth Amendment rights to be violated because evidence found during some improper warrant-authorized searches can be used against defendants anyway.

WARRANTS AND THE NEUTRAL DECISION MAKER

Conventional Wisdom 15

Despite its weaknesses, the warrant requirement in the Fourth Amendment ensures that a neutral decision maker will determine when searches and arrests will occur.

A primary purpose of the Fourth Amendment's warrant requirement is to ensure that a neutral decision maker will determine when a warrant will be issued. There is a fear that police officers may be too focused on investigating crimes and apprehending lawbreakers to take the time to consider whether searches or arrests might violate the Fourth Amendment. Thus a decision maker from the judicial branch is placed between the individual and the police to make sure that the police are acting properly. As described in the previous section, these judicial officers are not necessarily neutral and objective in making their decisions. They cannot avoid using their values in making judgments about the sufficiency of information presented to justify a warrant. More importantly, there are many kinds of searches in which no warrant is sought or used. The Supreme Court has never treated the Fourth Amendment's warrant requirement as a mandatory step for all searches and arrests. Instead, the requirements of probable cause and particular descriptions apply only in those situations *in which a warrant is sought.* When the police conduct searches and make arrests without seeking a warrant, then there is no "neutral" judicial decision maker. For warrantless searches and arrests, the Supreme Court merely focuses on the Fourth Amendment prohibition on "unreasonable searches and seizures." Thus warrantless searches and arrests are permissible as long as they are deemed "reasonable" upon subsequent evaluation in court.

The Supreme Court has approved an entire list of situations in which no warrant is needed in order to conduct a search:

- *Stop and frisk.* When officers have reasonable suspicion that an individual is armed and involved in criminal activity, they may stop the person and do an exploratory "patdown" search of the surface of the person's clothing to detect any weapons that might be used to harm the officers or bystanders (*Terry v. Ohio,* 1968).
- *Incident to a lawful arrest.* When officers make a lawful arrest, they may search the person arrested and the area around that person to seize any weapons and prevent the destruction of evidence (*Chimel v. California,* 1969).
- *Special needs of law enforcement.* Officers may conduct warrantless searches in specific, defined situations when it would not be practical to obtain a warrant but a strong justification exists for a search. Such situations include searches at international borders, airports, and school lockers, and drug tests for customs agents and railroad personnel (*Skinner v. Railway Labor Executives' Association,* 1989).
- *Exigent circumstances.* Various situations may arise when officers may conduct warrantless searches because of urgent circumstances, such as officers' "hot pursuit" of an armed suspect who enters a house. Upon chasing the suspect into the house, officers would be justified in undertaking an immediate search for weapons (*Warden v. Hayden,* 1967).
- *Consent.* Officers may search without a warrant whenever a person with proper authority over the place (or person) to be searched voluntarily consents to the search (*United States v. Mendenhall,* 1980).
- *Motor vehicles.* Officers have significant authority to search motor vehicles incident to arrests and to search containers as well as entire

vehicle compartments and trunks when they make their own determination that there is probable cause to conduct such searches (*California v. Acevedo,* 1991).

By identifying these situations for permissible warrantless searches, the Supreme Court has placed people's Fourth Amendment protections substantially in the hands of police officers and their discretionary decisions. Each of these warrantless search situations can create potential problems for the fulfillment of constitutional rights.

Stop and Frisk

Officers must make a determination about whether they have reasonable suspicion about a person's involvement in criminal activity and potential dangerousness in order to stop the person and conduct the patdown search. If an officer stops and frisks a person without justification, thereby violating the Fourth Amendment, no issue will arise in court unless the officer finds weapons or evidence of a crime. The person has been briefly inconvenienced and his rights have been violated, but there is no practical remedy for the violation. A civil rights lawsuit would not be fruitful because the potential damages for the brief detention are not likely to amount to enough money to justify the financial costs of litigation. The person could file a complaint with the police department about the officer's conduct. However, the officer can easily claim that he or she had reason to believe that the person was armed or involved in a crime, even if the officer had no basis for such a suspicion at the time that the search occurred. Moreover, will the police department punish an officer based on the word of one citizen, since there is not likely to be any corroborating evidence that the search was unjustified?

If incriminating evidence is found on a person, an unethical officer can readily invent "facts" about the circumstances of the search that provide the basis for the reasonable suspicion to justify the search. The Supreme Court has not said that officers can stop and search whomever they want, whenever they want. For example, officers cannot rely solely on an anonymous tip as the basis for a stop-and-frisk search, even if the tip turns out to provide good information (*Florida v. J. L.,* 2000). However, officers could rely on the tip and then make their own observations of the suspect before conducting the stop and the search. Indeed, the Supreme Court has provided police officers with great flexibility and a wide range of factual justifications to support the formation of reasonable suspicion to justify the search. For example, if officers see a person run away when they enter a "high crime" area, that person's action can be a factor considered in the decision to stop and frisk, even if the officers have no other specific observations about the person's appearance, demeanor, or behavior (*Illinois v. Wardlow,* 2000). The Supreme Court claims that seeing a person running, by itself, does not provide reasonable suspicion. The running must occur in a context in which it reasonably arouses suspicion, such as running in a neighborhood with crime problems. In reality, however, it would be easy for officers to use running as a justification for a stop and frisk as long as they claim that they were investigating criminal activity or otherwise assert that a context existed in which running was suspicious. Thus a jogger could be subjected to a stop-and-frisk search by running away from officers in a context in which the officers could claim a reason to suspect that criminal activity might be afoot. Obviously, individuals' protection against unjustified warrantless searches depends on police officers' discretion, professionalism, and honesty. The Supreme Court has given officers ample opportunity to undertake patdown searches with limited possibilities for individuals to challenge the validity of those searches after they have already occurred.

Incident to a Lawful Arrest

An arrest is a form of seizure that requires probable cause. However, unless officers seek a warrant prior to making an arrest, they make their own initial determinations of probable cause. Unless the suspect is released soon after arrest, either on bail or on a promise to appear in court, a warrantless arrest will be followed within a few days by a probable cause hearing so that a judicial officer can determine whether the arrest was justified. Probable cause for a warrantless arrest can come from an officer's own observations, such as when an officer observes someone fleeing from the scene of a crime, or from reliable information from an informant, victim, or witness. When an officer believes that he or she has probable cause to arrest and proceeds to make the arrest, the officer is authorized to search the arrestee, the immediate vicinity of the arrestee, and the area that the arrestee just left. Police officers' discretion is applied both in determining whether to make the arrest and in defining the immediate vicinity of the arrestee that is subject to search.

In 2001, the Supreme Court expanded opportunities for officers to undertake searches incident to lawful arrests because the Court approved officers' authority to arrest people for minor offenses for which the punishment is merely a small fine (*Atwater v. City of Lago Vista*, 2001). In the case, a mother was arrested because an officer observed that her children were not wearing seatbelts in her car. State law in Texas provided a punishment of only a $50 fine for such a failure to use seatbelts. However, the Supreme Court permitted the officer to deprive the individual of her liberty through arrest and transport to the police station, despite the fact that conviction for the offense would entail a lesser penalty than the arrest process itself. Moreover, because the Supreme Court authorized arrests for such minor offenses, the Court, in effect, simultaneously approved searches incident to those arrests. Depending on the crimes defined by state law, it seems possible for officers to make arrests for traffic violations, littering, and other minor offenses as a means to conduct searches. Indeed, the unethical officer intent on conducting a search could falsely claim that a driver was not wearing a seatbelt or failed to use a turn signal. There is no way for the driver to prove otherwise without credible witnesses to contradict the officer. Thus the Court has increased the opportunities for officers to use their discretion to initiate searches.

A good-faith exception was also applied to a search incident to an arrest (*Arizona v. Evans*, 1995). After a traffic stop, the police called to check whether a motorist was being sought for any past offenses. The officers were informed that there was a warrant for the motorist's arrest. They arrested the man and searched his car incident to the arrest. During the search, they found a small quantity of marijuana that was used to prosecute and convict him of a drug offense. It turned out that there was no warrant for his arrest. An unidentified clerk in the county sheriff's office had neglected to erase an invalid warrant from the county's computer records even though the office had been notified seventeen days prior to the arrest that the warrant was invalid. The Supreme Court decided that the evidence need not be excluded from use in court, despite the fact that it was obtained through a search that was incident to an *unlawful* arrest. As with their other good-faith exceptions, the justices decided that as long as the police did not do anything wrong, then improperly obtained evidence can be used in court. The Court's focus is on police errors or misconduct rather than on whether a constitutional right was violated. If the police did nothing wrong and some other official made the error that created the rights violation, the police can use evidence obtained through a search that violated the Fourth Amendment. Thus rights violations go unremedied. In dissent, Justice John Paul Stevens complained that "The offense to the dignity of the citizen who is arrested, handcuffed, and searched on a public street simply because some bureaucrat has failed to maintain an accurate computer data base strikes me as . . . outrageous."

Special Needs of Law Enforcement

The Supreme Court has approved warrantless searches in several specific contexts, including airports, borders, and roadway sobriety checkpoints to enable officers to detect whether motorists are driving under the influence of alcohol. Although the Court has rejected efforts to create drug interdiction roadblocks outside of international border areas (*City of Indianapolis v. Edmond*, 2000), the approved contexts for checkpoints can also raise issues about rights because officers use their discretion to determine which individuals will be searched. In particular, issues of discrimination arise when officials choose which individuals to subject to questioning and searches that extend beyond the cursory examination applied to everyone at a border or airport. For example, a study in 2000 by the federal government's General Accounting Office found that among passengers passing through U.S. Customs at American airports after traveling back from visits to foreign countries, African-American women were selected more frequently than any other demographic group for strip searches and x-ray examinations. The focus on African-American women occurred despite the fact that the results of searches showed that they were less likely than other people to carry drugs or other contraband. African-American women were nine times more likely than white American women to be x-rayed but less than half as likely to be concealing illegal drugs. X-ray searches found drugs on whites and African-American men almost twice as often as on African-American women.[6] By permitting police officers to stop entire classes of people (e.g., travelers returning from overseas) without individualized suspicion, the Supreme Court has also facilitated intrusive, discriminatory searches of specific individuals who may have done nothing to create any reasonable suspicion of illegal conduct.

Exigent Circumstances

Exigent circumstances provide a potential catch-all justification for many warrantless searches. If officers claim that a warrantless search was justified by an urgent situation, judges may be very reluctant to second-guess the officers' determination after the fact. Judges are sensitive to the fact that police officers face physical dangers and must often make snap decisions in the course of responding to crimes. Thus judges are frequently deferential to officers' claims about exigent circumstances. For example, when Los Angeles police detectives began their investigation of the murders of Nichole Brown Simpson and Ronald Goldman, they arrived at the home of Simpson's ex-husband, Hall of Fame football legend O. J. Simpson, with the claim that they wanted to make sure everyone in Simpson's family was safe. One detective believed he saw a spot of blood on the car parked outside the house. When no one answered after the officers pushed the button on the outer gate, a detective climbed over the fence and, in the course of exploring the backyard, allegedly discovered a bloody glove that was seized and that was used—ineffectively—as evidence in O. J. Simpson's murder trial. Simpson's attorneys challenged the warrantless search of the backyard as unjustified and sought to have the glove excluded from evidence. However, the judge who presided over the evidentiary hearing accepted the officers' claim that exigent circumstances justified their entry and search. The murders occurred at a different location and the officers had little reason to believe that an immediate entry was urgently needed. Yet the judge deferred to the officers' judgment. As illustrated by this example, officers may enjoy substantial freedom to make claims about exigent circumstances that will be accepted by judges if later challenged in court. Indeed, unethical officers can conduct searches whenever they want to and then subsequently create false rationalizations about their perceptions of an urgent situation in order to justify the search to a deferential judge.

Consent

Because people have the ability to waive their rights, it makes sense to permit officers to conduct searches when people voluntarily consent to searches of their persons and property. Several problems arise in the implementation of this rule that effectively diminish the legal protections people are purported to enjoy under the Fourth Amendment. First, officers are not required to inform people of their right to decline a request that they consent to a search (*United States v. Drayton*, 2003). Thus there are risks that people will feel pressured to consent to police requests to conduct searches simply because they are unaware that they have the ability to say "no." Because so many people are ignorant of the law's specific details, unaware of their rights, and fearful of the police, it is no surprise that numerous people have consented to searches while knowing that they have large quantities of illegal narcotics in their clothes, luggage, or vehicles (*Mendenhall v. United States,* 1980). Supreme Court majority opinions on this subject begin with the fictitious presumption that all Americans are knowledgeable about their rights and therefore, in the absence of evidence of explicit coercion such as overt threats of violence by police officers, consents to searches are deemed to be voluntary. This presumption clashes with the principle underlying *Miranda v. Arizona* (1966). *Miranda* is based on the idea that people are not knowledgeable and therefore need to be informed by the police about their constitutional rights with respect to the right to counsel and self-incrimination. By contrast, the Court treats Fourth Amendment rights differently. In reality, it seems very obvious that many people do not know that they are permitted to decline police officers' requests. Otherwise, people carrying ten pounds of cocaine in a suitcase would not agree to let officers search the suitcase. Moreover, many police officers do not follow the rule that they must accept a citizen's refusal to consent and thereby end their effort to gain a consent to search. In fact, newspaper reports have revealed instances of officers sternly ordering people to consent to searches and refusing to permit motorists to continue on their way from stops for traffic citations until they consent to have their vehicles searched.

Another problem occurs when officers claim that a person gave consent but the person claims that he or she never consented to the search (*Florida v. Bostick,* 1991). This "his/her-word-against-mine" situation generally only arises if criminal evidence is discovered during the course of the search. If no such evidence is discovered, the individuals who were subjected to the search go on their way with little recourse concerning their belief that their rights have been violated. If criminal evidence is found and its admissibility is challenged in court, the judge is likely to believe the word of police officers over that of a person who had cocaine, weapons, or other illegal items in his or her possession. The claims of the defendant are easy to label as "self-serving" in order to justify dismissing them. Thus, even if unethical police officers lie, they know that the court is likely to believe that the individual consented if they make that claim after finding criminal evidence—provided there are no respectable witnesses within earshot to contradict the police officers' claims. As with other aspects of the Bill of Rights, the protection of Fourth Amendment rights depends heavily on the honesty and professionalism of the police officers who must implement those rights.

In addition, the Supreme Court permits consent to be given by people who have no authority over the property to be searched. For example, the girlfriend of an apartment dweller used a key to permit police officers to search the apartment. The resident did not know that his girlfriend still had a key, she did not live in the apartment, and her name was not on the lease. Despite her lack of authority to consent to the search, the Supreme Court ruled that the officers acted in good faith by reasonably relying on their belief that the girlfriend possessed the authority to consent (*Illinois v. Rodriguez,* 1990). This decision raises concerns that police officers will not adequately investigate whether a person has authority to consent because they are more interested in conducting the search than in ensuring that they are speaking to the resident. For example, imagine that police officers say to someone standing outside an apartment door that is partially open, "Do you mind if we search this apartment?," and the person replies, "That's fine with me." The police officers could go ahead with the search, even if that person has nothing to do with the apartment in question and just happened to be standing outside. The officers would merely need to claim that they reasonably believed that the person lived in the apartment. The Supreme Court's decision may actually serve to diminish officers' incentives to investigate whether the person has the authority to consent.

Motor Vehicles

Police officers have broad discretionary authority to make traffic stops, even if they are plainclothes officers assigned to specialized units, such as narcotics, who are not supposed to make traffic stops in unmarked cars according to their own department's guidelines (*Whren v. United States,* 1996). Traffic stops are supposed to have a justification and not be based on mere hunches and whims. Officers may not, for example, randomly stop vehicles as a means to check licenses (*Delaware v. Proust,* 1979). Despite these rules, it is not difficult for officers to come up with reasons to stop vehicles. It is relatively easy, for example, for unethical officers to claim that someone failed to use a turn signal when changing lanes, even if the claim is not true. The driver cannot prove otherwise, and an officer's word is likely to be accepted in court if the driver contests the claimed violation. The Supreme Court has said that police officers cannot search a motor vehicle merely because they give the driver a citation for a traffic offense (*Knowles v. Iowa,* 1998). However, the Court has also said that there is no violation of the Fourth Amendment if officers make arrests for minor traffic offenses, even offenses punishable only by fines (*Atwater v. City of Lago Vista,* 2001). Moreover, if drivers are arrested, their vehicles must usually be towed away and impounded while they are in custody. Impounded vehicles are subject to extensive inventory searches because officers are authorized to go through the vehicle to make a record of all the items it contains (*South Dakota v. Opperman,* 1976). Thus an officer intent on undertaking a search can make an arrest for a minor traffic offense and then conduct a search of the vehicle and person incident to that arrest.

Officers can also search an entire vehicle and the containers within the vehicle when probable cause exists. This authority to search is especially broad because the officers are determining probable cause for themselves. There is no neutral judicial officer evaluating the police officer's statement of facts before issuing a warrant. If, for example, drugs are found in the pocket of the driver of a car, the Supreme Court has said that this discovery provides probable cause to search the entire vehicle in all places where other drugs may be found, including the purse and luggage of any passenger, even if there is no specific reason to suspect any wrongdoing by the passenger (*Wyoming v. Houghton,* 1999). Obviously, the Fourth Amendment provides relatively little protection against searches of motor vehicles, especially if police officers are so eager to search that they are willing to be less than honest in justifying traffic stops and the basis for probable cause.

Discretion and Warrantless Searches

The existence of broad discretion provides police officers with many opportunities to undertake warrantless searches. For example, officers use their discretion in determining whether they have reasonable suspicion to justify a stop-and-frisk search, whether exigent circumstances exist, and whether probable cause exists to search a motor vehicle and the containers within it. In the contexts of warrantless searches, the protection of Fourth Amendment rights depends heavily on the honesty and professionalism of police officers. It is relatively easy for them to create justifications for many kinds of searches with the knowledge that judges will be reluctant to second-guess the on-the-spot decisions made by a police officer on the front lines of the battle against crime.

The flexibility and discretion involved in warrantless searches can encourage many police and prosecutors to *not* seek warrants, even if they have the lead time and information necessary for a warrant application. According to a study of one prosecutor's office,

> [P]rosecutors see few advantages in [search warrants] and many liabilities. The prosecutors are reluctant to issue a warrant because of the possible pitfalls of a

specific statement of the facts . . . and the police failure to respect the limits of a search warrant. Therefore, when the police request a warrant, the state's attorneys encourage the police to search in some other way, such as visual inspection. If they see something remiss they may be able to search under the "plain view doctrine" that does not require a search warrant. . . . The prosecutors may elect a [different] alternative—not issuing a search warrant but allowing the police to search. . . . [T]he prosecutors may decide the odds are better if they later try to reconstruct an ambiguous situation rather than prematurely commit themselves to the specifics required by a search warrant.[7]

The quoted study was conducted in the 1970s before the Supreme Court during the Burger Court (1969–1986) and Rehnquist Court (1986–current) eras made many of the decisions that increased police officers' opportunities to undertake and justify warrantless searches. Thus, in the early twenty-first century, even more reasons are available for officers to create after-the-fact justifications for warrantless searches that are later challenged in court. If officers conduct a warrantless search first and then worry later about whether a judge will exclude the evidence for violating someone's Fourth Amendment rights, the officer has time to think through the list of justifications for warrantless searches to develop an excuse, such as exigent circumstances or reasonable suspicion justifying a patdown or probable cause for a car search, that will be accepted by a deferential judge. As Professor David Neubauer has noted, the inclination of some prosecutors to avoid warrants in favor of encouraging warrantless searches for which justifications can later be manufactured demonstrates how the impact of the Supreme Court's decisions is shaped by the implementation process. In Neubauer's words, "The prosecutor's discouragement of search warrants shows how the goals of the upper courts may be deflected by the actions and perceptions of the [criminal justice] officials who make the day to day decisions."[8]

Summary

The words of the Fourth Amendment implicitly focus on the role of the neutral decision maker who will issue warrants only upon a showing of probable cause. In reality, the police officers who seek to conduct searches use their own discretion to decide how and when many searches will occur. The creation of several categories of permissible warrantless searches by the Supreme Court effectively authorized police officers to make their own determinations of reasonable suspicion, probable cause, persons authorized to consent, and exigent circumstances in many situations. Because most judges are reluctant to second-guess police officers' on-the-scene determinations of search justifications, the Fourth Amendment may provide relatively little protection against specific kinds of searches, such as patdowns and automobile searches, especially if police officers are not honest in evaluating the validity of their own justifications prior to conducting searches.

THE SUPREME COURT AND FOURTH AMENDMENT RIGHTS

Conventional Wisdom 16

The Kyllo *case (2001) described in the opening of Chapter 1 shows that the Supreme Court places a priority on protecting Fourth Amendment rights because the justices barred the police from examining a house from the outside with a thermal-imaging device.*

The *Kyllo* decision shows that the Supreme Court has not abandoned the Fourth Amendment. Specific cases arise that lead a majority of justices to support the Fourth Amendment rights of individuals. However, the Court's Fourth Amendment decisions do not indicate that the justices are determined to ensure that Fourth Amendment rights are clear and strong. Instead, the justices struggle with their efforts to strike an appropriate balance between the privacy interests protected by the Fourth Amendment and society's need to enable law enforcement personnel to investigate crimes. In the last quarter of the twentieth century and the beginning of the twenty-first century, the Court's decisions tended to grant increasing discretionary authority to law enforcement officials with respect to searches and arrests. The *Kyllo* case and other decisions supporting individuals receive attention from the news media because they are unusual and inconsistent with the overall trend, not because they represent the Court's dominant orientation.

Any perception that the *Kyllo* decision demonstrates the Court's commitment to the sanctity of people's property and homes against warrantless examinations can be dispelled by a review of the Court's other decisions. In *Oliver v. United States* (1984), the Court found no Fourth Amendment violation when police officers ignored a locked gate, a fence, and "no trespassing" signs to make a warrantless entry on an individual's wooded property in order to look for marijuana. The Court approved similar actions in *United States v. Dunn* (1987) when officers crossed three fences without a warrant in order to look inside a barn for drug-manufacturing equipment. Officers can also look for illegal activity by flying over fenced property in airplanes (*California v. Ciraolo,* 1986) and hovering over a backyard greenhouse in a helicopter (*Florida v. Riley,* 1989). The Court has even permitted a police officer to peer through a gap in the blinds covering an apartment window, although in that case the Court's justification for permitting the seizure of evidence was the fact that the men observed engaging in illegal activity were not residents or overnight guests in the apartment (*Minnesota v. Carter,* 1998). Only a minority of justices concluded that all invited guests inside a private residence should benefit from Fourth Amendment protections, whether or not they spend the night.[9] The *Kyllo* case shows that specific situations arise that attract majority support for Fourth Amendment protections. The *Kyllo* case barely attracted that support because only five justices concluded that the warrantless use of thermal imaging on a home violated the homeowner's constitutional rights.

In another example, the Court declared that the Fourth Amendment includes the common law "knock and announce rule" that generally requires police officers to knock and identify themselves as police officers before executing a warrant by entering the premises (*Wilson v. Arkansas,* 1995). Because of the Court's dominant trend toward giving police officers greater flexibility and discretion for searches and arrests, it was easy for some observers to mistake this decision as one that moved the Court in a new direction toward supporting stronger Fourth Amendment rights. In reality, the decision merely embodied the Court's usual balancing of interests that generally defers to law enforcement interests rather than establishing strong Fourth Amendment principles. As the Court made clear in *Richards v. Wisconsin* (1997), the "knock and announce rule" does not apply in any circumstances in which knocking and announcing might threaten police officers' safety or mission. The "knock and announce rule" does not embody a constitutional right so much as it states a desired policy to be employed when it will not hamper police officers' effectiveness.[10]

Summary

Individual decisions by the Supreme Court interpreting the Fourth Amendment cannot be read in isolation when attempting to evaluate the Court's orientation and impact on constitutional rights. Although the Court has supported the protection of Fourth Amendment rights in specific cases, the trend in decisions since the 1970s has been toward giving police officers greater flexibility and discretion for searches and arrests. The Court's individual decisions protecting rights are counterbalanced by related decisions that demonstrate the justices' desire to preserve and enhance the capability of law enforcement officers to investigate crimes. In striking a balance between this desire and Fourth Amendment interests, the creation and preservation of substantive constitutional rights often seem to be less important priorities.

CONCLUSION

How symbolic or substantive are Fourth Amendment rights? The Supreme Court's expansive definition of "reasonable" searches and seizures gives police officers broad authority to use their discretion to conduct various kinds of warrantless searches. There is nothing to protect a citizen against a stop-and-frisk search by a police officer, except the officer's ethics and professionalism. If the officer conducts such a search without a justification and finds no weapons or criminal evidence, there is little that the victimized citizen can do other than file a complaint with the police department that is not likely to lead anywhere. If the officer finds contraband, the officer may simply seize it and destroy it with the knowledge that a citizen cannot seek to use the law to regain possession of illegal objects. If the officer uses the evidence to arrest and prosecute the individual, the officer will have time before the initial hearing to construct the circumstances and reasons that purportedly provided the necessary reasonable suspicion to justify the search, whether or not the officer had thought of those justifications at the time that the search occurred. The search might actually have been based on a hunch or whim, but the court will not know that unless the officer admits that those factors provided the motivation for the search.

In other search circumstances, officers can claim that exigent circumstances, consent, or the officer's own determination of probable cause, in the case of a vehicle search, provided the necessary justification. Again, those justifications may or may not be accurate, but the deferential judge often has little inclination or ability to ferret out the nature of the officer's knowledge and perceptions at the time that the search occurred.

When warrants are sought prior to searches or arrests, the judicial officers rely on the statements of fact provided by police officers and prosecutors. These judicial officers must apply the vague, flexible concept of "probable cause." Inevitably, they must use their own judgments in determining whether a reasonable person would conclude that it is more likely than not that evidence will be found in a certain location or that a particular individual committed a crime. The vagueness of the concept ensures that different criteria will be applied in different courthouses. The warrant requirement may protect some individuals against searches and arrests when a judge determines that police officers presented insufficiently timely, reliable, and substantial information to constitute probable cause. For other individuals, however, the probable cause and warrant requirements provide little protection. If a judicial officer issues a warrant without sufficient information, police officers can still conduct the search and seize evidence if they claim that they made a good-faith presentation of information to the judicial officer (*United States v. Leon,* 1984). Thus the individual's Fourth Amendment rights are violated by an improper warrant and search, yet the evidence can still be used against the person in court. The result produced by the contemporary Supreme Court's good-faith exception to the warrant requirement directly clashes with the conclusion of the Supreme Court justices of 1914 who wrote in *Weeks v. United States:*

> If letters and private documents can thus be seized [improperly] and held and used in evidence against a citizen accused of an offense, the protection of the [Fourth] Amendment, declaring his right to be secure against such searches and seizures, is of no value, and, so far as those thus placed are concerned, might as well be stricken from the Constitution.

The Supreme Court's creation of exceptions to the exclusionary rule has an especially powerful effect in translating constitutional rights into mere symbols. Three examples of good-faith exceptions were discussed in this chapter: the good-faith exception to the warrant requirement in *United States v. Leon* (1984); the good-faith exception to the requirement that persons with proper authority must consent to searches in *Illinois v. Rodriguez* (1990); and the good-faith exception for relying on erroneous computer records in making searches incident to *unlawful* arrests in *Arizona v. Evans* (1995). In these cases, the Court effectively concedes that people's Fourth Amendment rights were violated, yet it provides no remedy. Evidence obtained from such improper searches is admissible for use against the defendant in court. Moreover, these exceptions reduce the incentives for police officers to be careful in gathering information before proceeding with a search. Indeed, the decisions may even discourage officers from investigating carefully because they know that if a judge issues a warrant based on insufficient evidence or a consent is obtained from a plausibly situated but unauthorized individual, then the officers may proceed to search and obtain evidence anyway—provided that they claim that they were well intentioned and acting in good faith.

In light of the interpretations of the Fourth Amendment produced by the Supreme Court, courts have limited ability to ensure that rights from the amendment are protected. Instead, it rests largely with police officers to determine whether Fourth Amendment rights will be symbols or substance. In order to give substance to Fourth Amendment rights, officers must resist the temptation to use any means available to investigate crimes. Instead, they must recognize that they hold the Constitution in their hands with every decision that they make and every action that they take. They must make the protection of constitutional rights a high priority in their own decisions and actions. In order to do so, they must be knowledgeable, ethical, and professional in conducting investigations and testifying in court. When the actions of individual police officers fall below the ethical standards of law enforcement professionals, then the people affected by the officers' actions will find that their Fourth Amendment rights are largely symbolic.

THE FIFTH AMENDMENT

No person shall be held to answer for a capital or otherwise infamous crime, unless on a presentment or indictment of a Grand Jury, except in cases arising in the land or naval forces, or in the Militia, when in actual service in time of War or public danger; nor shall any person be subject for the same offence to be twice put in jeopardy of life or limb; nor shall be compelled in any criminal case to be a witness against himself, nor be deprived of life, liberty, or property, without due process of law; nor shall private property be taken for public use, without just compensation.

The Fifth Amendment contains a variety of rights focused primarily, but not exclusively, on the criminal justice process. As described in Chapter 2, the first right listed in the amendment has never been incorporated into the Due Process Clause of the Fourteenth Amendment by the Supreme Court. Thus the right to an indictment by a grand jury before being prosecuted for a "capital or otherwise infamous right" applies only for people accused of violating federal criminal statutes, such as bank robbery, kidnapping, counterfeiting, and drug trafficking. The majority of people accused of crimes face charges in state courts so the Fifth Amendment right to a grand jury is not even symbolic for them. They simply do not have it at all unless grand juries are mandated under the laws of the state in which the crime occurred. Obviously, the Supreme Court has treated the Fifth Amendment right to a grand jury as less essential than nearly every other right in the Bill of Rights, since all but a few have been incorporated and applied against the states. The grand jury presumably serves an important function by preventing overzealous, discriminatory, and vindictive prosecutions. A body of citizens can hear preliminary evidence about a case and then decide whether there is sufficient justification for prosecuting a suspect. Because the grand jury is absent from cases in many states, the dominant presumption seems to be that the trial process will guard against improper prosecution through the decisions of trial judges and trial juries.

The other rights in the Fifth Amendment have been incorporated for application throughout the United States. From the perspective of judicial interpretation, the most difficult-to-define phrase in the amendment is the right to "due process." The phrase also appears in the Fourteenth Amendment where it is specifically intended to provide legal protections against actions by state and local governments. Historically, "due process" has been used by the Supreme Court as a "catch-all" right. If the Court wanted to declare that a right exists but the literal language of the Constitution did not provide a sufficient basis to justify the recognition of the right, then the Court simply said that the legal protection came from the constitutional right to due process. For example, the Court used the right to due process from the Fourteenth Amendment (state) and the Fifth Amendment (federal) in the early twentieth century to say that people have a right to economic freedom that precludes the government from enacting minimum wage laws or laws regulating working hours and conditions (*Lochner v. New York,* 1905). This constitutional "freedom" to work for less than minimum wage and to work long hours under dangerous, unregulated conditions served the interests of corporations and the ideology of capitalism, but it provided few advantages for the supposed beneficiaries of the constitutional right—American workers. The right to due process from the Fourteenth Amendment was also used to prevent some abusive practices in the criminal justice system, such as torturing criminal suspects until they confessed (*Brown v. Mississippi,* 1936). However, the incorporation of most of the rights in the Bill of Rights reduced the Court's reliance on interpreting the phrase "due process" and shifted the focus of most criminal decisions to other specific provisions of the Constitution.

DOUBLE JEOPARDY

Conventional Wisdom 17

The constitutional right against double jeopardy prevents people from being tried twice for the same offense. If they are acquitted in their first trial, they cannot be tried again unless they commit a new offense.

The constitutional right against double jeopardy is intended to prevent the government from trying again and again to convict someone of a crime. The right is supposed to force the prosecution to put its best foot forward in the first trial because there will not be a second chance. Thus the defendant can get on with his or her life if there is an acquittal. The government cannot use criminal prosecution as a means to tie up people's lives and money repeatedly for an indefinite period of time. If, however, the defendant appeals a conviction and wins the appeal, the defendant may be retried. The defendant, by pursuing the appeal, keeps his or her own first trial from becoming final; thus, there is no double jeopardy when the second trial occurs (*Green v. United States,* 1957).

Despite the general understanding of the purposes of the Double Jeopardy Clause, the Supreme Court's interpretation of the constitutional right against double jeopardy creates opportunities for multiple prosecutions against a person for a single criminal act or event. For example, when Los Angeles police officers were videotaped from an apartment window in 1991 as they beat motorist Rodney King while he lay on the ground after a police chase, several officers were charged with crimes in state court. The trial conducted in Simi Valley, California, resulted in the officers being acquitted of criminal charges.[1] However, the officers could not necessarily get on with their lives. Two officers were subsequently charged with crimes under federal civil rights statutes. Based on the same acts—striking Rodney King—that produced their acquittals in the first trial, the two officers were later convicted in U.S. district court in Los Angeles on the federal charges. Some critics argue that the officers were subjected to double jeopardy because they faced two trials for the same allegedly criminal actions. However, the Supreme Court's interpretation of the Fifth Amendment permits such successive proceedings on the grounds that the two trials concerned alleged violations of two different sets of laws, one state and the other federal. Thus, contrary to conventional beliefs about the Fifth Amendment, the right against double jeopardy does not prevent successive trials from occurring when those trials concern separate state and federal charges arising from the same criminal behavior.

Offenders can also be retried after conviction if a different state charges them with crimes arising out of the same criminal conduct. In *Heath v. Alabama* (1985), the defendant financed and orchestrated a crime in which a woman was kidnapped in one state and then taken across the state line to be murdered. After the defendant pleaded guilty in one state in order to accept a life sentence and avoid capital punishment, the Supreme Court permitted the second state to try him on its own charges in order to seek the death penalty.[2]

As these examples illustrate, the definition of the right to double jeopardy is more complicated than the simple notion drawn from the amendment's words that people cannot be tried twice for the same offense. Within a single jurisdiction, the Supreme Court would permit someone to be tried more than once on different charges arising out of the same criminal act (*United States v. Dixon,* 1993). In the *Dixon* case, a man was convicted of criminal contempt for violating a court order that barred him from assaulting or threatening his wife. Although his assaultive actions in violation of the court order had already produced a criminal conviction for contempt of court, the Supreme Court said those same actions could be the basis for a second prosecution on assault charges. Dissenting justices were concerned that the Court's interpretation of the Fifth Amendment would permit the government to try an individual multiple times for the same criminal conduct as long as each prosecution involved a different charge that required different elements of proof. Thus the dissenters' concern amounts to a fear that, contrary to the apparent purposes of the Fifth Amendment, a prosecutor might be permitted to say, "Since we weren't able to persuade a jury to convict him of assault when he got into a fight outside of the movie theater, why don't we see if we can convict him of disorderly conduct for that fight when we prosecute him a second time?"

Summary

The right to double jeopardy does, indeed, bar a second trial on the same charge when a person has been acquitted in the initial trial. Beyond that specific situation, however, the meaning of double jeopardy becomes complicated and the constitutional right provides less protection than is commonly assumed. Additional prosecutions can occur, for example, from charges pursued by different jurisdictions or by different charges arising out of the same incident in one jurisdiction. In this instance, the limitations of the constitutional right flow directly from the Supreme Court's interpretations rather than from the vagaries of implementation that cause some other rights to develop symbolic aspects at odds with common understandings and assumptions.

MIRANDA WARNINGS AND SELF-INCRIMINATION

Conventional Wisdom 18

Police officers must inform people of their Miranda *rights immediately upon arresting them.*

In 1966, the Supreme Court issued its landmark decision in *Miranda v. Arizona.* The decision was intended to protect both the Fifth Amendment privilege against compelled self-incrimination as well as the right to counsel. The Court required police officers to inform people of their rights before they were questioned while in custody. The *Miranda* warnings include notice to arrestees that they have a right to remain silent, that anything they say can be used against them, that they are entitled to have a defense attorney present during questioning, and that an attorney will be appointed to represent them if they cannot afford to hire one. Chief Justice Earl Warren's majority opinion in *Miranda* made clear that the majority of justices were very concerned about abusive police interrogation practices that coerced people into confessing. The opinion was especially concerned about **incommunicado interrogation:** questioning that takes place behind closed doors where the suspect is alone with police officers without any witnesses or any contact with the outside world. In the *Miranda* case itself, two detectives went into a room with the suspect and later emerged with a signed confession. How does anyone know what was said or done to such a suspect in order to gain the confession? Warren's words provide a clear indication of the harms that the *Miranda* warnings were intended to prevent:

> In a series of cases decided by this Court[,] . . . the police resorted to physical brutality—beatings, hanging, whipping—and to sustained and protracted questioning incommunicado in order to extort confessions. . . . Even without employing brutality, the "third degree" or the specific [psychological strategies taught to officers in interrogation training manuals], the very fact of custodial interrogation exacts a heavy toll on the weakness of individuals. . . . It is obvious that such an interrogation environment is created for no purpose other than to subjugate the individual to the will of the examiner. This atmosphere carries its own badge of intimidation. To be sure, this is not physical intimidation, but it is equally destructive of human dignity. The current practice of incommunicado interrogation is at odds with one of our Nation's most cherished principles—that the individual may not be compelled to incriminate himself. Unless adequate protective devices are employed to dispel the compulsion inherent in custodial surroundings, no statement obtained from the defendant can truly be the product of his free choice.

Many Americans gained familiarity with *Miranda* warnings through crime dramas on television in which police officers inform suspects of their rights upon arrest. "Read him his rights" is a commonly heard portion of dialogue in such shows as the superior officers instruct their subordinates to fulfill the requirements of *Miranda*. Many actual police departments instruct their officers to read *Miranda* warnings from a printed card when a suspect is taken into custody. This standard procedure helps to ensure that the warnings are given properly and consistently. However, other police departments and individual officers have adapted their questioning techniques in order gain incriminating information from suspects without providing *Miranda* warnings.

How can officers ask questions without first providing *Miranda* warnings? Easy. The *Miranda* decision required officers to inform suspects of their rights *before they were questioned while in custody.* If officers ask questions before they take suspects into custody, then no warnings are required. Also, if officers use techniques to elicit confessions from suspects that do not involve directly questioning the suspects, then *Miranda* warnings are not required for suspects who are in custody but are not asked questions.

Officers can avoid the risk that *Miranda* warnings will hinder their ability to gain damaging admissions by questioning suspects before making an arrest. For example, officers may ring the front doorbell at the suspect's home and then ask questions while standing on the porch. The situation does not fit Chief Justice Warren's description of the inherently coercive environment of an interrogation room. Moreover, many people do not realize that they can decline to answer questions posed to them by the police. Some suspects feel obligated to answer. Others are overly confident about their ability to deceive the police. But their answers are often inconsistent and contradictory, thus giving police officers further clues about evidence that should be explored. Similarly, officers may ask questions to people on the street or in a shopping mall, including people whom they plan to arrest momentarily because they have observed the person engaged in criminal activity such as shoplifting.

After they have arrested a suspect, officers may delay providing the *Miranda* warnings with the hope that the suspect will make a damaging statement. For example, officers may drive around town with the handcuffed suspect in the back of the car. Some suspects initiate conversations and, in so doing, provide incriminating information. A nervous suspect being driven by silent police officers may suddenly say, "I know that you think I did it. But I didn't do it. I was at my uncle's house when the robbery happened. That gun you found—that was one I found in the street when I was walking home." In the course of providing an informative monologue of excuses, a guilty suspect may provide important information, such as information that could be known only to the robber or information that reveals the alibi is phony.

Police officers may also ask someone to come to the police station to talk to them. If the person comes to the station, his presence is regarded as voluntary and he is free to leave at any time—even if he does not know it. Thus they are not in custody and the police are not required to provide *Miranda* warnings (*Oregon v. Mathiason*, 1977).

Officers may also talk to each other while driving the suspect to the police station. In *Rhode Island v. Innis* (1980), the police officers in the front seat talked to each other about the potential for tragedy if a child found the shotgun that they believed the robbery suspect had hidden near a school for handicapped children. As the officers spoke, the suspect suddenly interrupted and directed the officers to the location where he had hidden the gun. The Supreme Court ruled that the gun could be used in evidence against him because the officers had not directed questions at the suspect in violation of *Miranda*. Although the dissenters expressed their belief that the officers' "conversation" was actually a calculated effort to gain a confession without providing *Miranda* warnings, the majority declared that the officers had merely been talking to each other.

In *Oregon v. Elstad* (1985), police arrested a suspect in his home and questioned him without providing him with his *Miranda* warnings. He made incriminating statements. After he was taken to the police station, he was given his *Miranda* warnings and asked to repeat the incriminating statements. The majority of justices decided that the statements made after the *Miranda* warnings at the station were admissible against him. The dissenters claimed that those statements were tainted by the earlier illegal interrogation because the suspect would be led to believe that "the cat is out of the bag." Therefore he would see no point in asserting a right to silence after being given the belated warnings. This decision provided police officers with an additional strategic technique to reduce the effect of *Miranda*. The Court, in effect, told officers that they may be able to wipe away *Miranda* violations by providing belated warnings and then inducing the suspect to confess again.

Summary

Contrary to popular entertainment media portrayals, police officers are not obligated to inform suspects of their rights immediately upon arrest. Officers have developed techniques to question and otherwise gain information from suspects without being hindered by the Miranda *requirement that warnings be provided before questioning a suspect being held in custody. These techniques include questioning of suspects who are not yet in custody and creating situations to induce confessions without formal questioning.*

Conventional Wisdom 19

Miranda *warnings protect criminal suspects from the pressure to confess that police officers applied during interrogations in earlier decades of American history.*

When the Supreme Court issued its decision in *Miranda v. Arizona,* many politicians and police chiefs complained that officers would no longer be able to solve crimes because suspects would not confess anymore. The complaints were, in part, overstatements because many crimes are solved based on evidence other than confessions, such as witness testimony and physical evidence. Although a few studies suggest that *Miranda* warnings reduced the number of confessions in some jurisdictions,[3] *Miranda* warnings became much less controversial as many police officers saw that confessions continued to occur and as officers adapted their practices to obtain confessions while obeying *Miranda.*

Miranda warnings have become so familiar to much of the television-viewing public that many suspects can probably chant the warnings along in unison with the police officers. How many hundreds of times does one need to see the warnings delivered on *Dragnet, Hawaii Five-O, Law and Order, NYPD Blue,* and hundreds of other police shows before *Miranda* warnings become like the Pledge of Allegiance—something recited reflexively without any thought to what the words mean? Many new police officers express surprise at the number of arrestees who make damaging admissions immediately after being informed of their *Miranda* rights. For many Americans, *Miranda* warnings may have become too familiar so that they no longer listen to and think about what the police officers are telling them. Moreover, when the warnings are given in the immediate aftermath of an arrest, people may be too worried, distracted, and confused to think carefully about the meaning of their rights.

The Supreme Court has also permitted police officers to change *Miranda* warnings in ways that may confuse suspects. In *Duckworth v. Eagan* (1989), the police added to the usual *Miranda* warnings the statement that an attorney could be appointed for the suspect "if and when you go to court." In fact, *Miranda* requires that the suspect be provided with an attorney during questioning if he or she requests one. The dissenters argued that such a statement could mislead a suspect into believing that there was no point in asking for a defense attorney to be provided during questioning since the police had already indicated that an attorney would only be available at a later date. The majority, however, asserted that the *Miranda* precedent did not require that the warnings be given in a precise manner and that police practices are satisfactory if they provide the defendant with the essential information. Critics of such decisions fear that they encourage the police to experiment with the form and content of *Miranda* warnings in order to diminish suspects' understanding of the warnings and to increase the likelihood of eliciting incriminating admissions.

Police officers have also adapted their strategies to the *Miranda* requirements. They seek to gain confessions despite having provided warnings to arrestees about Fifth Amendment rights. Scholars who have studied police interrogation have identified a number of interrogation techniques used by officers to elicit admissions.[4] Officers may pretend to be sympathetic to the suspect. They may minimize the seriousness of the crime and act as if they are just gathering matter-of-fact information rather than seeking evidence to be used to convict the suspect of a serious crime. When delivering the *Miranda* warnings, the officers may use various strategies to encourage the suspect to waive the right to counsel and speak to officers immediately.

> Detectives will use subtle psychological strategies to predispose a suspect toward voluntarily waiving his or her *Miranda* warnings. For example, the detective may precede the reading of the *Miranda* warnings with a discussion of the importance of truth-telling. . . . Or the detective may subtly nod his head up and down as he reads to the suspect the waiver statement that follows the warnings. . . . Or the detective may lightly refer to the warnings as a formality that the suspect is well aware of from television and can probably recite better than the investigator. . . . Or the detective may inform the suspect that this is going to be his one and only chance to tell the police his side of the story. . . . Or . . . the detective may explicitly tell the suspect that the police will no longer be able to help him if he calls for a lawyer.[5]

An instructional article published by the American Prosecutors Research Institute in 1998 provides an illustration of the training given to law enforcement personnel about how to elicit confessions despite *Miranda* warnings. In an article entitled "Interviewing the Child Molester: Ten Tips for Eliciting Incriminating Statements," the author presents and discusses ten strategies:[6]

1. Never give up. The officer should assume that a lengthy interrogation will be necessary. Also, the questioning should occur where it can be

observed via closed-circuit television so that other officers can give advice and comments during breaks in the questioning.

2. Confront each denial. The officer should confront each denial with evidence or with arguments about the implausibility of the denial.
3. Emphasize the child's love of the perpetrator.
4. Emphasize the perpetrator's love of the child.
5. Explore the possibility the suspect was abused as a child.
6. Offer support for the perpetrator. Tips numbered three through six all relate to developing rapport with the suspect and providing the illusion of support and understanding.
7. Corroborate the victim's version. One of the primary goals of the questioning is to develop evidence that will enhance the child victim's credibility and increase the likelihood that a jury will believe the child's accusations rather than the suspect's denials.
8. Give the suspect an out. The officer should allow the suspect to rationalize and blame alcohol and other people for his problems because this may increase his willingness to admit to the alleged acts.
9. Consider using a polygraph examination. Although the examination is likely to be inadmissible as evidence, the suspect may make admissions as the officer continues to express disbelief about the suspect's statements.
10. Consider having the victim make a controlled and recorded telephone call to the perpetrator to discuss the assault. If the victim is old enough and sufficiently sophisticated, he or she may be able to help police elicit incriminating statements.

One of the most striking aspects of police officers' adaptation to *Miranda* and the formal training provided to elicit incriminating statements is the manner in which it mirrors the techniques used in 1966 that led Chief Justice Earl Warren and the majority of Supreme Court justices to conclude that warnings are necessary to protect suspects. Compare Warren's description of police training manuals in 1966 with the post-*Miranda* advice presented in 1998 about interviewing child molestation suspects.

According to Warren's opinion in *Miranda*,

> A valuable source of information about present police practices, . . . may be found in various police manuals and texts which document procedures employed with success in the past, and which recommend various other effective tactics. These texts are used by law enforcement agencies as guides. . . .
>
> To highlight the isolation and unfamiliar surroundings, the manuals instruct the police to display an air of confidence in the suspect's guilt and from outward appearance to maintain an interest in confirming certain details. The guilt of the subject is to be posited as a fact. The interrogator should direct his comments toward the reasons why the subject committed the act, rather than court failure by asking the subject whether he did it. Like other men, perhaps the subject has

had a bad family life, had an unhappy childhood, had too much to drink, had an unrequited desire for women. The officers are instructed to minimize the moral seriousness of the offense, to place blame on the victim or on society. These tactics are designed to put the subject in a psychological state where his story is but an elaboration of what the police purport to know already—that he is guilty. Explanations to the contrary are dismissed and discouraged.

Apparently, contemporary police practices do not merely make *Miranda* warnings ineffective for some suspects; these practices also replicate the very techniques that the Warren Court justices believed would be diminished by requiring *Miranda* warnings. One might be tempted to ask, as do some critics of the *Miranda* warnings, whether the warnings should simply be abolished if they do not accomplish any purpose. In effect, this can be seen as an argument in favor of removing the illusion of a constitutional protection when the protection is, in fact, very ineffective. Other critics of the warnings concede that many suspects utilize their *Miranda* rights by remaining silent or requesting an attorney.[7] However, these critics believe that the Supreme Court interpreted the Constitution improperly when it required officers to give warnings that are not mandated by the words of the Fifth Amendment.[8]

Defenders of *Miranda* would counter with the claim that the *Miranda* warnings have helped to professionalize law enforcement by making officers sensitive to the fact that they must follow rules and procedures. Moreover, it reminds officers that courts may subsequently evaluate their actions and thereby rule that confessions are inadmissible if they were obtained improperly. In addition, the alternative for and predecessor to *Miranda* was a "voluntariness rule" under which suspects had to prove that their admissions were involuntarily obtained through improper physical or psychological coercion in order to have statements excluded from evidence. When police officers can question suspects alone behind closed doors, it is practically impossible for suspects to prove that they were subjected to threats and coercion, even if such improper actions occurred. This point is illustrated by the film, *In the Name of the Father* (1993), portraying the true story of several men from Northern Ireland who were convicted for a bombing in England that they did not commit. In the film, the police obtained a confession by sticking a gun into the mouth of the suspect and threatening to pull the trigger if he did not admit that he planted the bomb. When the police subsequently denied that they had done such a thing, how could the suspect prove otherwise, especially after signing a confession at gunpoint stating that he made admissions of his own free will?

The problem of abusive police practices remains real in some American cities. In Prince Georges County, Maryland, police officers questioned a man for twenty-eight hours without an attorney present before the exhausted man finally confessed to a murder that he did not commit. DNA evidence later proved that he was innocent of the crime, and the real killer sexually assaulted seven more victims while the police kept the wrong man in jail.[9] In other cases within the same county, detectives subjected teenagers and people with disabilities, among others, to similar lengthy interrogations while refusing to permit them to speak with attorneys. In at least three other cases, innocent people confessed to homicides for which they were later exonerated.[10] In Georgia, a mentally retarded man with an IQ of 59 was convicted of murder, sentenced to death, and executed after signing a confession written out for him by the police, despite the fact that he could not read. In fact, his ability level was so low that he could not even count to ten.[11] Obviously, this raises a significant question about whether he could have possibly understood the confession that he signed.

Summary

Miranda warnings were created to permit suspects to protect their Fifth Amendment privilege against compelled self-incrimination as well as their right to counsel. Although some suspects make use of these rights, many others do not, in part, because the police have adapted their strategies to the require-ments of Miranda *and developed techniques for eliciting confessions despite informing suspects of their rights. These techniques involve many of the same psychological ploys and deceptions that motivated the Supreme Court's deci-sion in the original* Miranda *case. In light of continuing problems of abusive police interrogation practices in some places, it is clear that* Miranda *warnings cannot prevent improper questioning from occurring. However, defenders of the* Miranda *decision, including many police officers, believe that the Supreme Court's requirement of providing warnings to suspects has helped to profes-sionalize the police, sensitize them to the importance of rights, and provide a mechanism for holding police accountable for improper conduct in some cases.*

Conventional Wisdom 20

> *When police officers violate suspects'* Miranda *rights, the evidence obtained cannot be used against the suspects.*

When the Supreme Court mandated that officers provide warnings to suspects, they also applied the exclusionary rule to violations of *Miranda*. If defense attorneys could establish that the police failed to inform suspects of their rights prior to custodial questioning, denied suspects' requests for an attorney during questioning, or improperly coerced suspects into confessing, any incriminating statements would be excluded from evidence in court. Thus the threat of the exclusionary rule provided the original "teeth" in the *Miranda* rules that purported to force the police to comply with the Supreme Court's decision. However, as the Supreme Court's composition changed during the 1970s and 1980s, the Court produced new decisions that weakened the enforcement of *Miranda* by creating exceptions to the exclusionary rule.

In *Harris v. New York* (1971), the Supreme Court said that voluntary statements obtained in violation of *Miranda* could be used to **impeach testimony** presented by the defendant in court. In other words, the improperly obtained statements could be used to show that the defendant's court testimony was inconsistent with statements made to the police immediately after arrest. Thus, the prosecution can cast doubt on the defendant's testimony by showing that the jury should not believe what the defendant has to say. The improperly obtained statements cannot be presented to prove the guilt of the defendant. However, if the statements were incriminating, even if they were just presented for impeachment purposes, the jurors may remember those statements as part of the evidence and include them in their consideration of the defendant's possible guilt.

The Court created an **inevitable discovery rule** to the exclusionary rule that can be applicable to Fourth Amendment searches and to Fifth Amendment interrogation issues. The exception was created in a case concerning the Fifth Amendment. In *Nix v. Williams* (1984), the Des Moines police drove along an Iowa highway after picking up a kidnapping suspect in another city. Although the officers knew that the suspect was represented by an attorney in Des Moines who was waiting to be present when any questioning occurred, the officers spoke to the suspect in the car. Their statements to the suspect about the need for the kidnap victim to get a Christian burial were based on their knowledge of the suspect's mental illness and religious fixations. When the suspect confessed and directed the officers to the victim's body, the Supreme Court initially excluded the confession as obtained in the violation of *Miranda* and excluded the body from evidence because it was the product of the rights violation (*Brewer v. Williams*, 1977). The prosecution, however, retried the defendant on the theory that they would have found the body inevitably anyway—even without the *Miranda* violation—because they had search teams moving across the Iowa countryside. In their second consideration of the case, the Supreme Court affirmed the conviction and endorsed Iowa's theory as an exception to the exclusionary rule. The inevitable discovery rule is more flexible and uncertain than it may appear because it is difficult to say if the police would necessarily have found something merely because they were looking for it. Judges must use their judgment to determine whether they believe something would have been found anyway without the rights violation that actually led to its discovery. As with other rights issues, many judges are likely to be deferential to the police and prosecutor, especially because the situation only arises in cases in which evidence has been found that tends to support the defendant's guilt.

The **public safety exception** is an even broader exception to the exclusionary rule. This exception gives police officers significant discretion to determine whether circumstances constitute such a threat to public safety that the protection of the public must take priority over the reading of *Miranda* rights to a suspect. The Court created the exception in *New York v. Quarles* (1984). In *Quarles,* police pursued an armed assault suspect into a grocery store. When they apprehended the suspect, they found an empty shoulder holster under his jacket. After they handcuffed him, they immediately asked "Where's the gun?" without first taking the time to read him his *Miranda* warnings. He showed the officers where the gun was hidden, and the weapon was used in evidence against him along with his incriminating response to the question that indicated he had knowledge of the gun's location. The defendant sought to have the weapon and the statement excluded from evidence because they were obtained in violation of *Miranda.* However, a majority of justices used this case to establish the public safety exception to the exclusionary rule. It is not clear how many different kinds of situations might qualify for application of the exception. The Court would never try to define all such situations for fear that they would omit a dangerous situation in which the police would need to act quickly without taking the time to worry about constitutional rights. Thus the public safety exception is potentially broad and creates the opportunity for officers to provide after-the-fact justifications for situations in which they failed to obey the dictates of *Miranda.* Moreover, this is precisely the type of exception that is likely to lead to deferential decisions by judges who are asked to review the police officers' actions and determine the admissibility of evidence. Many judges are extremely reluctant to decide that an urgent, dangerous situation did not exist when a police officer who was on the scene said that it did.

Another Supreme Court decision created an avenue to ignore Fifth Amendment violations, although it did not create an exception to the exclusionary rule. In *Arizona v. Fulminante* (1991), a government agent posing as an incarcerated organized crime figure told another prisoner, Fulminante, that he would provide protection against threats from other prisoners, but only if Fulminante told him everything about rumors that Fulminante had murdered a child. Fulminante confessed to the murder and was prosecuted as a result of the confession given to the "fellow prisoner." The Supreme Court determined that the confession was coerced in violation of the Fifth Amendment's privilege against self-incrimination. A majority of justices found that Fulminante's fear of violence at the hands of other prisoners had been exploited by the police agent in a manner that violated the Fifth Amendment prohibition on coercing confessions. However, a majority of justices also determined that a coerced confession can be regarded as a **harmless error** that does not automatically require that a conviction be overturned. In the context of constitutional rights, harmless errors are rights violations that are sufficiently minor or inconsequential that they need not be remedied and need not invalidate a criminal conviction. Usually, a coerced confession based on a threat or physical mistreatment by police officers will lead to the reversal of a conviction. However, the fact that a coerced confession in *Fulminante* could be regarded as a harmless error opens the possibility of specific contexts in which Fifth Amendment rights for some individuals will be completely symbolic because a violation of the right will not be remedied when the improper coercion is less direct or less physically abusive than traditional overt threats.

Despite the debates about the propriety and effectiveness of *Miranda* warnings, the Supreme Court has endorsed the continuation of *Miranda* as a requirement of the Constitution (*Dickerson v. United States,* 2000). A federal court of appeals had ruled that *Miranda* warnings were not required by the Constitution but were merely a rule created by judges. Therefore, the appellate court said that Congress could enact a statute that permitted federal law enforcement officers to omit *Miranda* warnings prior to questioning suspects in custody. The Supreme Court overturned the lower court's decision. The Court's 7-to-2 decision relied heavily on *stare decisis,* the importance of case precedent, as a justification for the decision. Moreover, the majority opinion indicated that *Miranda* remains desirable, even in the eyes of many conservative justices who do not favor broad rights for criminal defendants. According to Chief Justice Rehnquist's opinion,

> Whether or not we would agree with *Miranda*'s reasoning and resulting rule, were we addressing the issue in the first instance, the principles of *stare decisis* weigh heavily against overruling it now. . . . *Miranda* has become embedded in routine police practice to the point where the warnings have become part of our national culture. . . . [O]ur subsequent cases [after *Miranda*] have reduced the impact of the *Miranda* rule on legitimate law enforcement while reaffirming the decision's core ruling that unwarned statements may not be used as evidence in the prosecution's case in chief. . . . In sum, we conclude that *Miranda* announced a constitutional rule that Congress may not supercede legislatively. Following the rule of *stare decisis,* we decline to overrule *Miranda* ourselves.

Summary

Many possible situations exist in which evidence can be used against a defendant despite the fact that it was obtained in violation of Miranda *rights. The Supreme Court has created several exceptions to the exclusionary rule, including a potentially broad public safety exception that permits police officers to make discretionary judgments about when to omit* Miranda *warnings.*

NONTESTIMONIAL EVIDENCE

Conventional Wisdom 21

The Fifth Amendment right against being compelled to be a witness against one's self prevents the police from forcing a person to provide self-incriminating evidence.

In *Rochin v. California* (1952), police officers entered a man's house without a warrant. As they reached the doorway to his bedroom, they saw him grab and swallow pills on the nightstand that they wanted to seize for testing as possible illegal narcotics. After failing to extract the pills from the man's throat, they took him to the hospital and ordered doctors to pump his stomach. The pills came back up when the man was forced by doctors to vomit, and tests revealed that the pills were, in fact, illegal drugs. In deciding that the pills must be excluded from evidence, Justice Felix Frankfurter's majority opinion characterized the police officers' actions as "shock[ing] the conscious" and comparable to torture. In concurring opinions by Justices Hugo Black and William O. Douglas, the police officers' conduct was characterized as a direct violation of the Fifth Amendment privilege against compelled self-incrimination. According to Black, "I think a person is compelled to be a witness against himself not only when he is compelled to testify, but also when as here, incriminating evidence is forcibly taken from him by a contrivance of modern science."

The *Rochin* case illustrated the question of whether the government can force people to produce evidence against themselves when that evidence is not in the form of words. The views of Black and Douglas did not prevail, however, as the Court examined more cases. Indeed, the Supreme Court came to define the Fifth Amendment protection solely in terms of **testimonial evidence.** People can be compelled to produce other kinds of evidence against themselves as long as that evidence is not testimony.

In various cases, the Supreme Court approved requiring people to submit to blood tests, wear clothing like that of the perpetrator of a crime, participate in identification lineups, and provide writing and voice samples.[12] The Court's interpretation of what it means to "be a witness against" one's self under the Fifth Amendment is more literal than its interpretation of many other constitutional rights. There is nothing inconsistent or implausible about the Court's interpretation, but the effect of the Court's decision is to make the Fifth Amendment right relatively narrow. The right could have been interpreted as if its purpose was to require the prosecution to gather and present evidence without compelled contributions from the defendant's body. Instead, the right focuses on avoiding coercion in inducing the defendant to provide testimonial evidence. The Court's interpretation facilitates the use of new technologies, such as DNA testing and hair analysis, by limiting the Fifth Amendment's focus on the pre-technological concerns of its eighteenth-century authors rather than viewing this constitutional right as one that should adapt its protections to the developments of science.

The Court's interpretive approach to the Fifth Amendment raises questions about whether any future scientific techniques will violate the justices' perceptions of what constitutes excessive intrusiveness or unwarranted pressure to convict one's self. For example, one scientist has developed an electronic headband that detects people's brain-wave responses to words and pictures. In theory, if the person demonstrates a brain-wave response to words or pictures that would only be familiar to the witness or perpetrator of a crime, the brain-wave response would provide evidence of guilt.[13] The evidence produced would not be "testimony," but it would involve permitting criminal justice officials to delve into one of the most intimate possessions of any human beings—their thoughts. Would the Supreme Court find that such techniques violate the Fifth Amendment? Will other scientific techniques be developed that can actually read people's thoughts? It is difficult to predict what scientific developments will occur, but the Supreme Court's interpretation of the Fifth Amendment has left the door open for such devices to be built, tested, and then challenged in court.

Summary

Despite arguments from some justices that the compelled extraction or production of evidence from a suspect's body constitutes a violation of the Fifth Amendment, the Supreme Court has adopted a narrower view. The Court's definition of the privilege against compelled self-incrimination focuses solely on testmonial evidence. Suspects can be forced to produce other kinds of evidence, such as samples of blood and handwriting, that can be used against them in court.

CONCLUSION

Fifth Amendment rights do not provide as much protection as many people may believe. The limited protection provided by the Double Jeopardy Clause and the privilege against compelled self-incrimination stem from the Supreme Court's interpretations of those constitutional provisions. The Court has opened the possibility for subsequent prosecutions of many defendants for different charges or for charges applied by the federal government or another state. The definition of what it means to "be a witness against" one's self protects only against coerced testimony and not other forms of evidence produced from a suspect. By contrast, the effectiveness, or lack thereof, of *Miranda* warnings stems largely from the discretionary decisions and actions of police officers who must implement the Supreme Court's mandate. Police officers adapted their practices to *Miranda's* requirements at the same time that the Supreme Court weakened *Miranda* by creating exceptions to the Fifth Amendment exclusionary rule. As a result, *Miranda* does not have the impact sought by its creators on the Warren Court and its protective effects fall short of popular beliefs and expectations.

THE SIXTH AMENDMENT

In all criminal prosecutions, the accused shall enjoy the right to a speedy and public trial, by an impartial jury of the State and district wherein the crime shall have been committed, which district shall have been previously ascertained by law, and to be informed of the nature and cause of the accusation; to be confronted with the witnesses against him; to have compulsory process for obtaining witnesses in his favor, and to have the Assistance of Counsel for his defence.

The Sixth Amendment focuses on trial rights. The emphasis of the right to counsel and the other Sixth Amendment rights is the preparation and conduct of adversarial judicial processes. The defense attorney is a key figure in the process. The attorney is responsible for ensuring that the other Sixth Amendment rights, as well as such Fifth Amendment rights as the privilege against compelled self-incrimination, are protected. If the defendant lacks the Sixth Amendment rights to a speedy trial, a jury trial, confrontation of adverse witnesses, and compulsory process for obtaining witnesses, then the prosecution presumably gains unfair advantages in the adversarial process.

In many ways, the interpretation and the implementation of Sixth Amendment rights are a test of the American justice system's commitment to the ideal of the adversary process. The American system is based on the assumption that the truth about criminal cases can best be revealed through a clash of skilled advocates who present opposing arguments and evidence to a group of citizen-jurors who determine whether the defendant is guilty. Sixth Amendment rights attempt to prevent the prosecution from gaining an unfair advantage. If defendants have no effective right to confront adverse witnesses and call witnesses to support the defense, there are risks that the prosecution could obtain automatic convictions in one-sided proceedings in which only the prosecution witnesses are presented to the decision makers. Similarly, the right to a speedy trial seeks, in part, to prevent prosecutors from gaining an advantage by delaying cases in the hope that witnesses for the defense will die or move away before a trial occurs. The right to a jury trial is the democratic feature of the Sixth Amendment that attempts to give citizens the opportunity to speak on behalf of the community in determining who is subjected to criminal punishment. Unlike legal systems in which professional decision makers (i.e., judges and lawyers) possess authority to determine the outcomes in every case, the use of juries permits citizens to ensure that prosecutors have not engaged in vindictive or otherwise unfair prosecutions. Obviously, the right to counsel also plays an important role. If defendants are not represented effectively by professional advocates, then the prosecution could enjoy a huge advantage, especially because the prosecutor can rely on the police to handle investigation and evidence gathering in each case. Without a professional advocate to handle investigation and presentation of evidence, an unrepresented defendant has little hope of matching the resources, experience, knowledge, and effectiveness of the prosecution in the typical criminal case. Ideally, the goal of the American system is to convict people of crimes because the system's truth-seeking processes determine that they are guilty. The system should not produce convictions of people simply because they have no attorney, no opportunity to present witnesses, or suffer other significant disadvantages in the adversary process that prevent them from effectively countering the prosecution's arguments and evidence.

Speedy Trial

Conventional Wisdom 22

The right to a speedy trial means that a defendant is entitled to have the case resolved in less than one year and that the prosecution cannot cause delays.

The time period for the Sixth Amendment right to a speedy trial runs from the moment of arrest or indictment, whichever comes first, until the beginning of the trial to determine whether the defendant is guilty. The right to a speedy trial attempts to serve several purposes. One purpose is to prevent the prosecution from hanging a cloud of suspicion over people's heads for a prolonged period of time. When people are charged with crimes, they usually suffer adverse consequences until those charges are resolved. The defendants may lose their jobs and be shunned by the people in their community. They may suffer heavy psychological costs with worries about being convicted and sent to prison. In addition, if they are unable to make bail, they suffer the loss of liberty until a verdict is produced or the charges are dropped. The loss of liberty prior to conviction should be a special concern for the American justice system because it burdens people whose guilt has not been proven and who are supposed to enjoy the **presumption of innocence** until conviction. In reality, the families of presumptively innocent people suffer severe economic and personal consequences when loved ones are in jail, especially when those loved ones are parents or family breadwinners. Long delays before trials, especially in cases that produce **acquittals,** are especially painful and unfortunate. The right to a speedy trial is intended to limit these potential harms by moving cases forward toward decision at an appropriate pace.

Another purpose of the right to a speedy trial is to prevent the prosecution from delaying a case with the hope that the defendant's evidence will become lost. For example, witnesses for the defense can die or move away. Available witnesses' memories of events may begin to fade. Documents may become misplaced. Defense attorneys begin to forget details of their investigations as they focus on other cases while waiting for a particular case to move forward. Delays may decrease the accuracy of truth seeking in the adversary process and give unfair advantages to the prosecution. Of course, delay may also create similar disadvantages for the prosecution if, for example, its witnesses die or disappear. However, the constitutional right to a speedy trial is granted to the defendant for his or her protection. Like other rights, it is for the benefit of the individual and not for the benefit of the government. Thus, presumably the interpretation and definition developed by the Supreme Court should seek to ensure that the individual's interests are protected.

Obviously, the major interpretive challenge is to provide a definition for the word *speedy.* Like other ambiguous terms in the Constitution, this is a concept that invites disagreements about its meaning. Should any trial that occurs after a set time limit, such as one year, be considered insufficiently "speedy"? Should there be a time period longer than one year or a shorter deadline? Should the definition of the term vary depending on the nature of the case? Some cases involve minor crimes and relatively straightforward evidence. For example, a case may rest on a police officer's testimony that "I saw the defendant sneak up behind the victim, strike the victim on the head with a brick, and then run away with the victim's purse." Other cases are much more complicated, such as when the government must gather records and witnesses from several countries in order to piece together complex financial transactions to prove money laundering or fraud. Defining violations of the right to a speedy trial according to a universal time limit may be unrealistic, unless a lengthy time period is permitted, such as two years. On the other hand, such a lengthy time limit may be unfair to defendants whose cases are more straightforward and simple.

The Supreme Court gave its most complete interpretation of the right to a speedy trial in *Barker v. Wingo* (1972). In the *Barker* case, two men were charged with a murder. The prosecution sought to move ahead with one man's case because the evidence against him was stronger. The prosecution believed it needed this man's testimony in order to convict Barker of the crime, and it thought that it could pressure the first defendant to testify against Barker in exchange for a lighter sentence after the first defendant had been convicted of the crime. Unfortunately for the prosecution, it took a long time to gain the first conviction. Thus the prosecution requested sixteen **continuances** or court-approved delays before undertaking Barker's prosecution more than five years after he was indicted by the grand jury.

The first trial of Barker's co-defendant, Manning, ended in a **hung jury,** a situation in which the jurors become hopelessly deadlocked and cannot reach an agreement on a verdict. The second trial resulted in a conviction, but the conviction was overturned on appeal because of the admission of evidence obtained through an illegal search. The third trial again produced a conviction, which was again overturned on appeal because of an error by the trial judge. The fourth trial resulted in a hung jury. Manning was finally convicted in the fifth trial, which occurred three and one-half years after he was indicted. After Manning's conviction, the prosecution asked for additional continuances for Barker's case because of the illness of a key prosecution witness. When Barker's trial finally occurred, Manning served as the chief prosecution witness. Barker was convicted and given a life sentence. He filed an appeal claiming that his right to a speedy trial had been violated.

When the case reached the U.S. Supreme Court, the justices rejected the prosecution's argument that defendants in all cases waive their right to a speedy trial if they do not object to the prosecution's requests for continuances and demand an immediate trial. Throughout the processing of the case against Manning, Barker had never objected to the prosecution's requests for delays and thus, according to the prosecution's theory, he had lost his right to claim that his entitlement to a speedy trial had been violated.

Barker's attorney, on the other hand, argued that the Supreme Court should define the right to a speedy trial according to a definite, specified time period, such as one year or two years. Under this definition of a speedy trial, the five-year delay in Barker's trial would require that the charges against him be dismissed. Unfortunately for Barker, the justices also rejected this argument.

Instead of adopting any arguments in favor of a clear rule for the fulfillment of the right to a speedy trial, the Supreme Court created a vague and flexible balancing test. The Court said that in each case raising the issue of a speedy trial, judges must balance four factors: the length of the delay, the reason for the delay, the defendant's actions in demanding or failing to demand a speedy trial, and whether the accused's defense was harmed as a result of the delay. In legal terms, the final factor was stated as examining the extent of "**prejudice** to the defendant" as a result of the delay. The creation of such a test places discretionary decision-making responsibilities in the hands of judges who must weigh and balance these factors. Without a clear rule for each case, the Supreme Court created the likelihood that the right to a speedy trial will be defined differently in different defendants' cases.

How would a judge balance these factors? Clearly, a long delay would raise the likelihood that the right is considered violated unless the defendant caused the delay or the defendant never objected to the delay or the delay had no adverse impact on the defendant and the presentation of defense evidence. On the other hand, a shorter delay might be judged a violation if it was caused by the prosecution, was objected to by the defense, and was the source of disadvantages for the defense, such as the death of a key witness in the interim. Obviously, when these four factors are combined in other ways, the decision about a rights violation is more complex. In Barker's case, for example, there was a very long delay caused by the prosecution. However, Barker did not object to the delay for the first several years and the Court believed that there were no adverse impacts on the defense as a result of the delay. In balancing these factors together, the Court concluded that Barker's right was not violated. Thus, although it may seem shocking that a trial that occurs more than five years after indictment fulfills the constitutional right to a speedy trial, the Court's interpretation of the right permits very long delays when judges find that the balance of factors places some responsibility but only minor disadvantages on the defendant.

Is the right to a speedy trial a substantive right or is it merely symbolic? The fact that long delays are permitted between indictment and trial makes the actual right less clear and powerful than it would appear to be from the words of the Sixth Amendment. Moreover, defendants have no guarantee about what the right to a speedy trial will mean for them because the use of a balancing test gives judges significant freedom to determine how the four factors weigh against each other. What if the delay in Barker's case had lasted more than seven years? Would the length of that delay outweigh the Court's evaluation of his failure to object and the lack of harm to his case? It is impossible to answer that question. However, it is instructive to note that the Court found that no violation of the right to a speedy trial had occurred when delays were as long as seven and one-half years (*United States v. Loud Hawk*, 1986), so Barker could have no confidence that a delay of additional years in his case would have resulted in the recognition of a violation of his right to a speedy trial.

In the *Loud Hawk* case, a major portion of the delay resulted because it took a court of appeals five years to hear two appeals. Dissenting justices argued that delays caused by courts should count against the government and not against the defendant, but the majority of justices declined to weigh that factor in the defendant's favor, even though the defense had consistently objected to the delays. Because the four factors that comprise the balancing test created in *Barker v. Wingo* are so malleable, some observers suspect that judges' actual definitions of violations of the right to a speedy trial are influenced by the judges' assessments of the seriousness of the offense and the defendant's dangerousness.[1] Thus an accused murderer is much less likely to have a court find that the speedy trial right was violated than is someone without a prior record who is accused of theft. For example, in *Doggett v. United States* (1992), the Court found a violation of the right to a speedy trial when someone was indicted for a marijuana offense while out of the country. He subsequently moved back to the United States and lived a law-abiding life openly under his own name for six years before he was arrested and tried. As Charles Whitebread and Christopher Slobogin have observed, "[I]n *Doggett,* . . . the Court was willing to assume prejudice after an eight and one-half year delay, six years of which was attributable to government negligence. But *Doggett* involved a relatively minor crime and a sympathetic defendant (who had lived a law-abiding life during the six years)."[2] Because fallible human beings wear the black robes of judicial office and make decisions about the right to speedy trial and other constitutional rights, it would not be surprising to observe that their decisions are not made consistently and that courts treat defendants more harshly, even for the purpose of defining rights, when these defendants are charged with the most serious crimes. However, if this is true, it raises important questions about the nature of constitutional rights. Are some rights more symbolic for the defendants that society fears most? The Constitution does not distinguish between defendants in pronouncing the entitlement to constitutional rights, but judicial decision makers may create distinctions between defendants, especially when interpreting and applying flexible definitions for rights.

Summary

The words of the Sixth Amendment do not provide guidance about the meaning of the right to a speedy trial. The Supreme Court used its interpretive powers to provide a definition for the right. The Court rejected suggestions that it give a clear definition based on a specific, maximum time period. Instead, the Court produced a flexible balancing test that requires judges to consider the length of the delay, the reason for the delay, the defendant's reaction to the delay, and the effect of the delay on the defendant's case. This flexible standard means that judges must use their judgment in determining when the right is violated. Moreover, the Supreme Court's own applications of the standard have permitted delays as long as seven and one-half years before trial without any violation of the constitutional right. The flexibility of the right's definition and the tolerance of lengthy delays provide support for the conclusion that the right is less substantive than one might believe from reading the words of the Sixth Amendment.

THE RIGHT TO TRIAL BY JURY

Conventional Wisdom 23

The Constitution clearly gives criminal defendants the right to a jury trial.

The Constitution addresses the right to trial by jury in two places. Article III, section 2, clause 3 of the Constitution says, "The Trial of all Crimes, except in Cases of Impeachment, shall be by Jury. . . ." In addition, the Sixth Amendment says "In all criminal prosecutions, the accused shall enjoy the right to a speedy and public trial, by an impartial jury. . . ." Unlike the ambiguous, interpretable phrases in other parts of the Constitution and Bill of Rights, there is nothing ambiguous about the phrases "trial of all crimes . . . shall be by jury" and "in all criminal prosecutions, the accused shall enjoy the right to a . . . trial, by an impartial jury." The use of the word *all* seems to make the literal meaning as clear as it can be. However, the language of Article III applies only to federal cases. Article III does not purport to define how state judicial processes must operate. The Sixth Amendment phrase, by contrast, applied solely to federal court processes only until 1968. In that year, the Supreme Court incorporated the right to trial by jury into the Due Process Clause of the Fourteenth Amendment in *Duncan v. Louisiana*. Ever since that decision, the constitutional right to trial by jury has also applied to criminal cases in state and local courts.

The *Duncan* decision justified incorporating the right to a jury trial and applying it to the states because it characterized jury trials as fundamental to the American system of justice. The use of juries helps to prevent abusive prosecutions. By permitting citizens drawn from the community to make determinations of guilt, the democratic governing system provides a check against prosecutors and judges who might attempt to exceed their powers by punishing people without sufficient evidence of guilt. The jury is an important element of the English legal system that the people of the United States adopted in order to limit governmental power, prevent the possible mistreatment of individuals, and guard against the abuse of their rights.

A case in 1996 (*Lewis v. United States*) provided greater clarity about the Supreme Court's interpretation of the right to trial by jury. A postal worker was charged with two counts of obstructing the mail for opening and stealing money from letters at the post office. Each charge was punishable by a possible sentence of six months of incarceration. Thus he faced a maximum possible sentence of one year in prison. He requested a jury trial, but the presiding judicial officer denied his request for a jury. The judge said that she would decide the case in a **bench trial,** meaning a trial with a judge and not a jury. In denying the request for the jury, she also assured the defendant that, if convicted, he would not receive a sentence of more than six months in prison, even if he were convicted of both charges. The defendant challenged the judge's ruling on appeal and claimed that she had violated his constitutional right to have a jury trial.

The Supreme Court ruled that there was no violation of the defendant's constitutional right. According to the majority opinion, the right to trial by jury only exists for **serious offenses,** those for which the potential punishment is more than six months in prison. In this case, because he was only charged with **petty offenses,** he was not entitled to a jury. As a practical matter, however, this defendant could have been sentenced to more than six months in prison if convictions on both charges would have drawn a separate six-month sentence for each offense. If a judge ordered that he serve **consecutive sentences** with the second six-month sentence beginning at the conclusion of the first six-month sentence, then the defendant could have received a year in prison for the two offenses. The problem would not arise if he was ordered to serve **concurrent sentences,** incarceration for multiple offenses that are served simultaneously. The Supreme Court's decision focused on the nature of the offenses charged rather than the possible time served. Thus there is no right to trial by jury, even if someone is charged with multiple petty offenses that could lead to a cumulative punishment of many years in prison. For example, if the postal worker had been charged with individual counts for opening forty letters, the total cumulative sentence, if consecutive rather than concurrent, could be twenty years in prison. For one hundred letters, the punishment could even be fifty years in prison. Yet even with the possibility of such long sentences, the Supreme Court's decision in *Lewis v. United States* declares that there is no right to a jury trial because the crimes charged are petty offenses.

Summary

On its face, the Lewis *decision clashes with the words of both Article III and the Sixth Amendment. Unlike state and local cases, for which only the Sixth Amendment applies, the* Lewis *case was a federal prosecution; therefore, both sections of the Constitution clearly applied. Yet, despite the Constitution's language mandating jury trials in "The trial of all criminal cases" (Article III) and "In all criminal prosecutions" (Sixth Amendment), the Supreme Court has decided that there is no right to trial by jury in cases of petty offenses, even if the possible cumulative sentence could total many years in prison.*

THE RIGHT TO COUNSEL

Conventional Wisdom 24

The Sixth Amendment right to counsel guarantees that individuals whose rights and liberty are placed at risk in the criminal justice system will receive representation from an attorney.

In order for the adversary system to be effective, individuals must be able to counteract the government's evidence and arguments with evidence and arguments of their own. The government is virtually always represented by professional attorneys from trial-level prosecutions through appeals. Prosecutors at the local and federal levels are attorneys. Assistant state attorneys general who handle many appeals and other post-conviction processes on behalf of the state government are also attorneys. These individuals have been trained in law. They know the rules of evidence and procedure. They can conduct research to discover the most recent judicial interpretations of statutes and constitutional rights. If individuals do not have professional representation in the criminal justice process, they are at a significant disadvantage and they are unlikely to be able to fulfill the adversary system's ideal of revealing the truth through the clash of skilled advocates. Without representation by attorneys, there are grave risks that defendants will present their own evidence ineffectively and they will be unable to protect their own constitutional rights. As a result, innocent people may be erroneously convicted of crimes or defendants may receive more severe sentences than they otherwise would have received.

For most of American history, the right to counsel merely meant that defendants in *federal* cases could not be prevented from hiring attorneys if they had enough money to do so. The Sixth Amendment was not initially interpreted to place any affirmative obligation on the government to provide attorneys for **indigent defendants,** those who were too poor to hire their own attorneys. Moreover, the Supreme Court did not incorporate the right to counsel and apply it to the states until the 1960s. Thus most trials throughout American history were quick proceedings in which the police and prosecutor presented evidence and the defendant said very little or made an ineffective attempt to present arguments and evidence on his own behalf. However, without knowledge of the rules of evidence and procedure, defendants would have little hope of making proper presentations or making objections to improper statements and inadmissible evidence by the prosecution.

In the 1930s, the Supreme Court gradually began to require that the government provide attorneys for poor defendants in certain kinds of cases. In *Powell v. Alabama* (1932), the Court used the Fourteenth Amendment's Due Process Clause to require states to provide attorneys for poor defendants in death penalty cases who were incapable of representing themselves. In 1938, the Court required the federal government to provide attorneys for indigent defendants charged with serious federal crimes that could draw sentences of six months or more in prison (*Johnson v. Zerbst*). By the mid-1940s, the Court required states to provide attorneys to indigent defendants in serious state cases who were unable to represent themselves because of illiteracy, mental retardation, mental illness, or some other detectable disabling condition (*Betts v. Brady*, 1942). The Court's rule still left literate defendants of average intelligence to fend for themselves through the 1950s and into the early 1960s, despite the fact that even a college graduate who lacked training in law would have great difficulty effectively challenging prosecutors' arguments and evidence. However, during this same period, most states beat the Supreme Court to the punch by developing their own rules for providing attorneys for indigent defendants in criminal trials.[3] Yet, a few states continued to provide no attorneys in noncapital cases.

The Supreme Court incorporated the Sixth Amendment right to counsel in the famous case of *Gideon v. Wainwright* (1963). The Court ruled that states must provide attorneys for indigent defendants facing serious charges in state court. Gideon's case provides a good example of the problems faced by defendants who must represent themselves. Gideon was charged in Florida with breaking into a pool hall and stealing coins, cigarettes, and beer. At his trial, he made an effort to question witnesses, but he was very ineffective. Because he had dropped out of school before reaching high school, Gideon had limited knowledge of law and little sense of strategy in formulating questions that would reveal the facts in the case. Gideon was sentenced to five years in prison. He set the landmark precedent in motion while sitting in his prison cell by drafting a handwritten petition for the Supreme Court that asserted his Sixth Amendment right to counsel. The justices appointed one of the nation's most prominent attorneys, Abe Fortas, a future Supreme Court justice, to represent Gideon in the high court. After Fortas won the case, Gideon received a new trial in Florida. This time, however, he was represented by an attorney. His attorney's investigation and presentation of the case revealed that the government's star witness, who claimed to have seen Gideon at the scene of the crime, was actually the person who was most likely to have committed the crime.[4]

On the day that it issued the decision in *Gideon*, the Supreme Court also issued a decision expanding the right to appointed counsel to appeals in state criminal cases (*Douglas v. California*, 1963). A few years later, the Court expanded the right to counsel to every criminal trial in which the defendant faced incarceration, even if the possible sentence was less than the six-month threshold of serious offenses (*Argersinger v. Hamlin*, 1972). This proved to be the final expansion, however, because the Court began to move in different directions when its composition changed in the early 1970s. Thus in 1974, the Court declared that there is no right to appointed counsel for indigents who carry their appeals beyond their first appeal of right (*Ross v. Moffitt,* 1974). Thus if someone loses an initial appeal in a state court of appeals, there is no constitutional right to counsel for a subsequent appeal to a state supreme court. Unless the state provides an attorney under its own laws, the individual must fend for him- or herself in attempting to prepare an appeal for the state's highest court.

In addition, the Court also decided that there is no right to appointed counsel when a defendant faces trial for a minor offense with a penalty less than incarceration, such as a charge that carries only a small fine as punishment (*Scott v. Illinois,* 1979). Justice Rehnquist's opinion minimized the risks and harms from being unrepresented in such cases and expressed concern about the costs that would be imposed on state and local governments if they were required to provide attorneys in all minor cases. However, the lack of an attorney can increase the risks that an erroneous conviction may occur. Even in minor cases, an erroneous conviction can have significant consequences. A minor conviction is still a criminal conviction that may affect a person's employment options and other opportunities in life. In addition, a criminal conviction carries with it social stigma that may cause others to shun or avoid a convicted offender. This would be especially harmful for an innocent person who was wrongly convicted.

When people convicted of crimes have appealed unsuccessfully, federal law provides an additional opportunity to gain judicial review of alleged constitutional violations in the investigation and prosecution of their cases. The *habeas corpus* process permits state prisoners to have their cases considered by federal judges for the limited purpose of determining whether any federal constitutional rights were violated that remained uncorrected by state trial and appellate judges. Although very few federal *habeas corpus* petitions result in individuals gaining their release from prison, it is an important mechanism for making sure that state courts protect rights under the U.S. Constitution. Moreover, there are some cases in which the *habeas* process permits federal judges to correct errors by state courts that sent innocent people to prison or that left constitutional rights violations unremedied. In 2001, for example, a federal judge in New York City ordered the release of a man who had served thirteen years in prison for murder. The judge found that state courts had mistakenly refused to admit into evidence testimony about a confession made by another man who claimed responsibility for the murder.[5] The man in New York was lucky because he had attorneys representing him in his *habeas corpus* action. Most other people are not so fortunate because the Supreme Court has said that there is no right to counsel in *habeas corpus* proceedings, not even for people on death row who must use the *habeas* process as their final hope for demonstrating that there were constitutional errors in their cases (*Murray v. Giarratano,* 1989). Because many criminal cases reach the

U.S. Supreme Court through *habeas corpus* actions, this rule effectively requires criminal defendants to prepare their own petitions for the U.S. Supreme Court, just as *Gideon* did in the early 1960s, unless they can afford to hire an attorney or an attorney volunteers to present the case to the Court. The Court will only appoint an attorney to represent indigents in criminal cases *after* the justices have decided to accept a case. This practice naturally raises questions about whether some convicted offenders might have had their cases accepted for hearing by the high court if only they had benefited from the assistance of an attorney while preparing their initial petitions. The odds of having a case accepted are very slim because the Supreme Court only accepts approximately eighty cases per year for full hearings out of nearly seven thousand petitions submitted annually.

There is also no right to counsel for individuals who wish to file civil rights lawsuits against law enforcement officials. If police officers undertake illegal searches or arrests in violation of the Fourth Amendment that do not result in criminal charges being filed against an individual, there is no way to seek a remedy for those rights violations other than filing a lawsuit against the officers and agencies involved. The Sixth Amendment focuses on criminal cases, but civil rights lawsuits are civil cases, even when they involve criminal justice officials. Therefore the Sixth Amendment does not apply to such cases. For convicted offenders in prison, the lack of attorneys for civil rights lawsuits poses special problems because prisoners must use litigation as the means to enforce rights that affect their daily living conditions. If prisoners are being denied humane living conditions, being physically abused, or being denied their right to freedom of religion, they must use litigation to seek court orders that vindicate the limited constitutional rights that they continue to possess in prison. Without attorneys, it can be especially difficult for prisoners to protect their rights effectively and present evidence demonstrating impermissible practices and conditions because so many prisoners are school dropouts, illiterate, mentally ill, or otherwise unable to even attempt to study and utilize law and legal processes.[6] Although many Americans show little concern about the protection of rights for convicted offenders, contemporary prisons regularly have problems with deprivations of medical care that lead to serious injuries and deaths for prisoners as well as incidents of violence inflicted on prisoners by corrections officers.[7] In order to prevent and remedy such constitutional violations, prisoners need to be able to bring their claims to the attention of courts. This can be very difficult to accomplish effectively without the assistance of attorneys.

Summary

Over the course of the twentieth century, the Supreme Court expanded the right to counsel by requiring appointed counsel for indigent defendants in state and federal courts. However, this right is limited to individuals facing incarceration or pursuing an initial appeal. Beginning in the 1970s, decisions by the Supreme Court limited the right to counsel. There is no right to counsel for trials of minor charges that do not carry sentences of incarceration. There is also no right to counsel for appeals beyond the first appeal to an intermediate appellate court. Thus there is no right to counsel for appeals to state supreme courts or for actions filed in the U.S. Supreme Court. In addition, there is also no right to counsel for habeas corpus *petitions or for civil rights lawsuits concerning the criminal justice system, even though these actions are the primary means available for convicted offenders to seek protection of their constitutional rights.*

Conventional Wisdom 25

When defendants are represented by attorneys, they are assured of receiving the representation necessary to fulfill the objectives of the adversary system or else their Sixth Amendment rights will be considered to have been violated and they will receive a new trial.

The Supreme Court's decisions defined the right to counsel but did not guarantee how that right would be implemented. Implementation was left to state and local governments. As a result, these governments made different choices about how to provide attorneys for indigent defendants. In addition, individual county governments must often pay for defense attorneys without financial assistance from the state or federal governments. Poor counties have great difficulty finding sufficient funds to provide high-quality representation for indigent criminal defendants.[8]

Some cities and counties hire **public defenders** who are full-time, salaried criminal defense attorneys. Many observers consider public defenders to be the best mechanism for providing defense attorneys because these attorneys devote themselves to criminal law. They have demonstrated an interest in criminal defense through their career choice, and their constant attention to criminal cases provides them with knowledge, experience, and skill. The major drawbacks of using public defenders stem from the limited financial resources devoted to indigent criminal defense. Public defenders' salaries may be so low that they regularly leave for better-paying positions elsewhere in the legal profession. As a result, these offices may be continually hiring new, inexperienced defenders. In addition, public defenders' caseloads may be too large to permit adequate attention to each case. Public defenders may be asked to handle more than one hundred cases simultaneously. Such large caseloads may create pressures toward encouraging clients to submit quick guilty pleas in order to permit the attorney to move ahead to the next case.

The most prevalent form of indigent defense representation is through the use of **appointed counsel.** Appointed counsel are attorneys in private practice who agree to handle criminal cases for indigents as part of their law practice. Appointed counsel systems can save money for local governments, but they do not ensure that defendants will receive high-quality representation. The hourly pay for appointed counsel may be too low. Thus experienced, skilled attorneys may decline to handle such cases. In these circumstances, indigent defendants may find themselves represented by inexperienced or unsuccessful attorneys who need to generate income but who have little knowledge or interest in criminal law. One scholar accused many appointed counsel of serving as "double agents" who actually work in the interests of the court system by pressuring their clients to enter quick guilty pleas. The attorneys want to pocket their fees quickly rather than do the extensive work required for genuine adversarial representation that might lead to a lengthy and unprofitable trial.[9] Even scholars who take a more sympathetic view of appointed attorneys' difficult circumstances in working with uncooperative clients for very low pay have characterized these attorneys as "beleaguered dealers" who are pressured by the system to seek speedy plea bargains for their clients.[10]

The third mechanism for providing defense attorneys is the use of **contract counsel,** attorneys who bid on an annual contract to provide representation for all indigent defendants in a county or city. Depending on the structure of the contract, the attorneys may have an incentive to spend as little time as possible on each client's case in order to maintain a profitable income. These attorneys may also feel pressured by judges to avoid representing their clients too enthusiastically or else they might lose the contract the following year. In one study, contract attorneys lost their contract because local judges did not want them to file motions and assert the defendants' rights to have a preliminary hearing in each case. The judges preferred to have defense attorneys who would cooperate with the system rather than actually mount a vigorous, adversarial defense on behalf of the indigent defendants.[11]

Obviously, the quality of representation provided for each defendant may vary from attorney to attorney and court to court. A defendant whose attorney is a knowledgeable, dedicated public defender may receive better representation and greater protection of constitutional rights than someone represented by an appointed counsel who is only interested in collecting fees as quickly as possible. Several prominent lawyers in Georgia proposed reforms in 2001, including increased funding, because of problems with the quality of indigent representation within the state. A study of representation within the state "found that in many rural Georgia counties, poor defendants spend months with no legal representation, then meet their lawyers about ten minutes before trial. The court-appointed lawyers, often paid $50 or less per case, routinely persuade their clients to plead guilty to avoid a trial, and in some counties, rates of guilty pleas are as high as 98 percent."[12]

The federal court system and some localities use more than one indigent defense system. The federal courts use public defenders for 65 percent of indigents' cases and appointed counsel for the other 35 percent. Interviews with federal judges in 1997 and 1998 found that over 90 percent of these judges rated the federal public defenders as "very good" or "excellent" but only 65 percent of judges rated the appointed attorneys as "very good" or "excellent."[13] Federal judges attribute the poorer quality of representation to the low hourly rates paid to appointed counsel. According to the chairperson of the federal judiciary's Committee on Defender Services, "The degree of specialization required by federal criminal law has reduced the pool of available, qualified attorneys, and many of those attorneys whose experience is needed in federal court simply are not willing to accept appointments, particularly in protracted and complex cases, at the current rates of compensation."[14]

The varied implementation of indigent defense systems and the inadequate funds devoted to those systems set the stage for inconsistent and, sometimes, inadequate representation of criminal defendants. If the quality of an attorney's representation falls below standards set by the Supreme Court, then the defendant's Sixth Amendment right to counsel has been violated because the defendant received **ineffective assistance of counsel.** Thus the Supreme Court has a role in ensuring that the right to counsel remains substantive rather than symbolic within these varied systems for providing defense attorneys. However, the criteria established by the Supreme Court for demonstrating ineffective assistance of counsel are so difficult to meet that extremely poor efforts and performances by attorneys can be deemed adequate for Sixth Amendment purposes.

The Supreme Court and other appellate courts have regularly examined cases in which attorneys did little preparation; did not raise appropriate objections to evidence; failed to assert their clients' rights; and had inadequate time, expertise, and resources to effectively counter the prosecution's case. If an attorney fails to object to improper evidence, it may be because of a strategic decision to avoid appearing hostile or unfriendly in front of the jury. It is sometimes difficult to tell the difference between attorneys' strategic decisions and their negligent failures to take action. The justices are extremely reluctant to second-guess attorneys' strategic decisions; thus their negligent performances also escape scrutiny. This reluctance to establish clear performance standards leads to Supreme Court decisions that make it very difficult for defendants to prove that they had ineffective assistance of counsel. Defendants must show that their attorneys made specific errors that affected the outcome of the case and produced an unfair result (*Strickland v. Washington,* 1984). Although it is possible to argue that specific decisions, actions, or failures to act by an attorney constitute errors, it is extremely difficult to show that the defendant might have been acquitted if these errors had not occurred. To the defendant, this process can seem as if they are being required to prove their innocence although the system is supposed to put the burden of proof on the prosecution, not on defendants. A defendant can argue that without the attorney's errors the jury would have had reasonable doubts about the defendant's guilt. However, because appellate judges are so reluctant to second-guess trial attorneys, those judges may not be willing to accept such arguments except in the most compelling cases. As a result, there are significant risks that indigent defendants will receive inadequate representation by counsel without any hope that an appellate court will actually pass judgment on the ineffective defense attorney's performance.

When the varied mechanisms for representing indigent defendants are combined with the Supreme Court's weak and vague standards for judging ineffective assistance of counsel, many cases emerge in which defense attorneys' performances were shockingly poor. One attorney was so drunk during a death penalty case that the judge delayed the trial one day so the attorney could be held in jail to sober up. Not surprisingly, the defendant, a woman accused of murdering her husband, was convicted when the attorney neglected to gather any available medical records and other evidence about her claims that she feared for her life because her husband beat her. Such evidence might have helped establish a claim of self-defense or mitigated the punishment for the killing. Instead, she received the death penalty.[15] A court-appointed attorney in Texas who handled many death penalty cases bragged about spending little time on legal research and not taking notes in court. He became well known for moving his clients' cases quickly through trial to a steady stream of convictions and death sentences.[16] In other cases, appointed attorneys handled capital cases without ever reading their state's death penalty statutes, failed to cite any cases in appellate briefs, and failed to talk to their clients.[17] The problem is well illustrated by a case in 2000 in which a federal appellate court considered whether a defendant in a capital murder trial was denied effective assistance of counsel when his attorney *slept through portions of the trial (Burdine v. Johnson*, 2000). The three-judge appellate court panel did not make a clear-cut declaration about the adverse impact of sleeping attorneys but instead debated whether one could presume that the attorney's slumber adversely affected the outcome of the case without knowing whether the attorney was asleep during "important" moments in the trial. Subsequently, the case was reargued before all fourteen judges on the Fifth Circuit U.S. Court of Appeals. A majority of the entire court ruled that the Sixth Amendment "compels the presumption that counsel's unconsciousness prejudiced the defendant," yet six judges dissented against that conclusion (*Burdine v. Johnson*, 2001). Clearly, there is no consensus among federal judges that the Sixth Amendment demands high standards of performance, let alone consciousness, on the part of criminal defense attorneys.

Summary

The Sixth Amendment right to counsel for indigent defendants has been implemented differently in various cities and counties. The organization and funding of indigent defendants' representation raise serious questions about whether all defense attorneys are sufficiently knowledgeable and dedicated when handling cases. The problems of inconsistent and inadequate criminal defense representation

are compounded by the Supreme Court's vague and weak criteria for judging inef-
fective assistance of counsel. When appellate courts are open to the possibility that
a defense attorney who fell asleep repeatedly during a death penalty trial may not
have caused enough harm to the client's case to constitute ineffective assistance of
counsel, then the right to counsel does not guarantee much for criminal defendants.
Does the right to counsel mean anything more than an entitlement to have an attor-
ney present while a guilty plea is entered or a trial is conducted? For many defen-
dants, the right does not mean much more than that.

THE RIGHT TO CONFRONTATION

Conventional Wisdom 26

*The right to confront witnesses against you means that you have a
right to be face-to-face with your accusers in the courtroom if you are
charged with a crime.*

The right to confrontation is intended to prevent secret trials or the use of evidence that is not presented in open court. The adversary process presumes
that each side will be able to test the other's evidence by, for example, cross
examining witnesses or inspecting physical evidence and documents. If the
government were permitted to present evidence by merely saying, "A witness
told us that the defendant is guilty," then there would be no way to test the
accuracy of the information or the reliability of the witness. At the time that
the Sixth Amendment was written, there was no way to confront accusers
except in face-to-face encounters in the courtroom. However, as society has
developed, new issues and technologies have emerged to provide both the
means and justification to alter the tradition of face-to-face confrontation.

One problem that has generated experimentation with the means of
confrontation is the desire to spare child victims and sex crime victims from
the trauma of seeing their abusers in court. There is a fear that the sight of the
perpetrator may cause the victim to become fearful, emotional, and unable to
testify clearly. Moreover, there are fears that the victims will suffer further
psychological harm from being forced to see the individual who was the source
of their life's major traumatic event.

In order to address these problems, the state of Iowa experimented with the
use of a large, wooden screen in the courtroom. The screen stood between the
witness stand and the defense table. It kept the victim and the defendant from
seeing each other, although the defendant could hear what the victim said and
the jurors, defense attorney, prosecutor, and judge could all see the victim and
the defendant. In *Coy v. Iowa* (1988), the Court ruled that the use of the screen
violated the defendant's Sixth Amendment right to confrontation. The decision

did not prevent further experimentation. Indeed, because the justices were so divided in *Coy*, there was reason to believe that an alternative mechanism to protect victims might be acceptable to enough justices to produce a supportive decision. Thus Maryland employed a closed-circuit television system through which the defendant and everyone in the courtroom could see and hear the child victims testifying in another room, but the victims could not see the defendant. When the Supreme Court considered the Maryland approach, a majority of justices approved the use of closed-circuit television (*Maryland v. Craig*, 1990). As a result, it is clear that the Supreme Court's interpretation of the right to confrontation does not require face-to-face confrontation in the courtroom.

The Court's decision in *Maryland v. Craig* (1990) sought to preserve the purpose of the confrontation right while also protecting the victims' interests in avoiding further trauma. Such efforts to balance competing interests do not necessarily avoid reducing the scope of the constitutional right in question. For example, if a dishonest witness would have squirmed and looked nervous while giving false testimony in front of the person who would be harmed by the lies, then the Court's decision has reduced the protective nature of the confrontation right and hindered the truth-seeking mechanisms of the adversary process. Under such circumstances, the untruthful witness testifying via closed-circuit television will have an easier time giving false testimony and the defendant's ability to challenge that testimony will have been reduced.

Summary

The right to confront one's accusers was written into the Sixth Amendment at a time when the only form of confrontation was the face-to-face encounter in the courtroom as testimony was being presented. In an effort to accommodate a separate objective concerning the protection of psychologically vulnerable witnesses, states experimented with mechanisms to permit the defendant to hear live testimony but keep the witness from seeing the defendant in person. Although the Supreme Court has not passively accepted all such experiments, a majority of justices approved the use of closed-circuit television to protect child victims while they gave testimony. This accommodation changes the original, literal meaning of the Confrontation Clause and may have reduced the scope of the right's protection.

COMPULSORY PROCESS

Conventional Wisdom 27

The right to compulsory process guarantees that defendants can summon to court and call as witnesses any persons with knowledge relevant to the case.

The right to compulsory process seeks to ensure that defendants can attempt to present a complete and effective defense. If prosecutors possessed the sole authority to summon witnesses to court, defendants would be at a significant disadvantage and would have little hope of contesting the prosecutor's case in the adversarial process. The Supreme Court does not, however, treat the right as absolute. Indeed, the Court's decision in *Taylor v. Illinois* (1988) revealed where the right to compulsory process stands on the justices' list of priorities.

In *Taylor,* the defense attorney in an attempted murder trial submitted a witness list prior to trial as required by court rules so that the prosecutor would have the opportunity to interview the defense witnesses. It is important for attorneys to be able to interview opposing witnesses so that they can plan the questions that they will ask during cross examination. The defense attorney submitted an amended witness list on the first day of the trial. Then, on the second day of the trial, the defense attorney asked to amend the witness list again in order to add Mr. Wormley as a witness. The attorney said that he had previously been unable to locate Mr. Wormley and that was why the name was not listed on the earlier lists. However, prior to permitting the new witness to testify, the judge questioned Mr. Wormley and learned that he had actually met with the defense attorney two weeks prior to the trial. In other words, the defense attorney deliberately violated court rules about providing prior notice of witnesses because he apparently wanted to spring a surprise witness on the prosecution. As a result of this discovery, the judge decided that Mr. Wormley would not be permitted to testify.

The exclusion of Mr. Wormley as a witness was a potentially significant blow to the defense. The attempted murder charges arose out of a shooting that occurred during a fight between two sets of brothers. Mr. Wormley was going to testify that he was sitting on his front porch when he saw the victim and his brother walking toward the confrontation. According to Mr. Wormley, he saw the victim's brother carrying a gun. Thus Mr. Wormley's testimony would have substantiated the testimony presented by two friends of the defendant who said that the victim was actually shot accidently by his own brother. Instead, the testimony was excluded and the defendant was convicted of attempted murder. As described by one justice's opinion,

> We may never know for certain whether the defendant or [the victim's] brother fired the shot for which the defendant was convicted. We do know, however, that the jury that convicted the defendant was not permitted to hear evidence that would have both placed a gun in [the victim's] brother's hands and contradicted the testimony of [the victim] and his brother that they possessed no weapons that evening—and that, because of the defense counsel's five-day delay in identifying a witness, an innocent man may be serving ten years in prison.

Unfortunately for the defendant, this sympathetic description of the case was written by a dissenting justice.

The defendant challenged his conviction by claiming that the exclusion of Mr. Wormley as a witness violated his Sixth Amendment right to compulsory process. However, a slim majority of justices on the Supreme Court rejected the rights violation claim. According to the majority opinion, the willful misconduct by the attorney in violating court rules justified the imposition of the most severe sanction. The five justices in the majority also rejected the argument that the defendant should not be punished for the attorney's misconduct. The Court said that "it would be highly impracticable to require an investigation of th[e] relative responsibilit[y] [of the defendant and the attorney for the misconduct] before applying the sanction of preclusion [of the witness]."

Is it fair that the defendant should be punished for the attorney's misdeed? The exclusion of a defense witness could very well be the factor that ends up leading the defendant to be convicted and sent to prison. By contrast, the attorney who actually committed the violation of the court rules suffers no sanction at all. The majority opinion paid lip service to the importance of the right to compulsory process by saying, "Few rights are more fundamental than that of an accused to present witnesses in his own defense. . . . Indeed, this right is an essential attribute of the adversary system." However, if the justices really considered the compulsory process right to be a high priority, they could have upheld the right and directed the lower courts to initiate disciplinary action against the attorney. If attorneys were threatened with suspension or loss of their law licenses, that would serve as a significant deterrent to misbehavior. Is the exclusion of witness testimony really a deterrent to attorney misconduct? To what extent does the attorney really care whether the client is convicted and sentenced to prison? Private attorneys require their criminal defendant clients to pay the complete legal fees and court costs prior to trial. Thus they suffer no financial loss if a client is sent to prison. Public defenders and appointed counsel receive the same pay no matter how the case turns out. In reality, it appears that exclusion of evidence will deter attorney misconduct only if the attorney has a genuine personal friendship with the client. In most cases, such relationships are not likely to exist. The attorney–client relationship is usually strictly professional. Typically, after the case is over, the attorney simply puts that client aside and moves ahead to the next client's case.

In a dissenting opinion, Justice William Brennan called it "particularly ironic" that most of the justices who agreed that the witness testimony should be excluded in *Taylor* are also justices who have been critical of the exclusionary rule. These justices raised concerns about the exclusion of evidence in Fourth and Fifth Amendment cases when the prosecutor's case will be disadvantaged, yet they expressed no reservations about excluding evidence that was beneficial to the defense.

Summary

What does the Taylor decision indicate about the Supreme Court's priorities? The justices sent a clear message that they believe enforcement of procedural court rules is more important than an individual's Sixth Amendment right to compulsory process. How substantive is a right if it can be pushed aside in favor of adherence to court procedures? According to Justice Brennan's opinion in Taylor, *"The Court today thus sacrifices the paramount values of the criminal justice system in a misguided and unnecessary effort to preserve the sanctity of [court rules]."*

CONCLUSION

The substance of rights in the Sixth Amendment has been affected by both the Supreme Court's interpretations of the amendment and by implementation issues. The right to trial by jury is one of the most clearly expressed and absolute rights contained in the Constitution. Yet, despite language mandating jury trials in "all prosecutions," the Supreme Court's interpretation of the right creates opportunities for defendants who are charged with petty offenses to be sentenced to potentially long prison terms without any opportunity for citizen jurors to determine whether the evidence proved guilt beyond a reasonable doubt. The Supreme Court limited the scope of the right because of concerns about imposing excessive costs upon trial courts throughout the country. In advancing the system's administrative goals, however, the Court has diminished the nature of the right to a jury trial and moved the right's definition away from the expectations and understandings that are naturally produced by the Constitution's clear, emphatic words on the subject.

In the example of the right to compulsory process, the Court demonstrated a willingness to set aside a defendant's constitutional right in order to protect the integrity of court rules that one would normally assume to be less important than a command of the Constitution. With respect to the right to confront adverse witnesses, the Court's interpretation of the right accommodated states' efforts to implement the right in a manner that would also protect the interests of vulnerable child victims. Again, the Court's interpretation of a right seems to differ from the intentions of the Constitution's words and, in limited circumstances, alters the nature of the right when certain kinds of witnesses testify in a case.

The right to counsel eventually applied throughout the nation's court systems, but the Court limited its applicability to trials and initial appeals in cases that could produce sentences of incarceration. As a result, there is no constitutional right to counsel for trials of minor offenses punishable by fines, appeals to state supreme courts, petitions to the U.S. Supreme Court, *habeas corpus* petitions, and civil rights lawsuits to remedy rights violations by criminal justice officials. The substance of the right is further affected by the implementation of the right through varied mechanisms, including public defenders, appointed counsel, and contract counsel. Each approach raises its own risks that the right will be largely symbolic for defendants represented by inexperienced, unenthusiastic, or unethical attorneys. These risks are compounded by the Supreme Court's vague criteria for determining ineffective assistance of counsel that discourage judges from second-guessing decisions by defense attorneys and that tolerate disappointingly poor performances in planning and presenting cases on behalf of defendants. The right to counsel, as much as any other right, can be largely symbolic if defense attorneys do not fulfill their ethical responsibilities to provide zealous, professional efforts on behalf of their clients. Moreover, when attorneys fail to provide the substance of the Sixth Amendment right, they are likely to diminish the substance of the other criminal justice rights that they are expected to protect in the course of providing a vigorous defense.

THE EIGHTH AMENDMENT

Excessive bail shall not be required, nor excessive fines imposed, nor cruel and unusual punishments inflicted.

In Chapter 2, we encountered the Eighth Amendment in several examples that explained the nature of constitutional rights and the interpretation of the Constitution's words. The Eighth Amendment contains three provisions, two of which concern the imposition of punishment on criminal offenders. These two prohibit "excessive fines" and "cruel and unusual punishments." The third provision focuses on the possibility that people suspected of crimes will be placed in jail and deprived of their liberty, even though they are presumptively innocent until proven guilty or until they enter a guilty plea. The prohibition on "excessive bail" seeks to prevent the government from setting a bail amount that is so high that it needlessly keeps someone in jail who could otherwise live safely in the community until his or her case is processed in court. All three provisions obviously intend to place limits on government's treatment of people drawn into the criminal justice system, but each provision's precise meaning is unclear. The term *excessive* is inherently ambiguous and thereby invites judges to define the acceptable limits of fines and bail by interpreting the Eighth Amendment. Similarly, the words *cruel and unusual punishments* have no inherent meaning. Judges must give meaning to any constitutional amendments that they interpret, but the Eighth Amendment, in particular, invites judicial interpretation because none of its terms have any arguably clear definitions implied by the authors' choice of words.

EXCESSIVE BAIL

Conventional Wisdom 28

Because people are presumed to be innocent when they have not yet been convicted of crimes, the Eighth Amendment protection against excessive bail protects individuals against the possibility that the government will seek an unreasonably high bail merely to hold someone in jail for a long period of time before trial.

The purpose of bail is to ensure that people return to court for their hearings and trials when they have been charged with crimes. Simultaneously, it is intended to spare presumptively innocent people from being deprived of their liberty while they wait for their cases to be processed. Thus bail should be set at an amount that will be sufficient to induce the accused person to return to court by making him or her fear the thought of forfeiting that money or property by fleeing. If bail is set too high, presumptively innocent people will lose their freedom unnecessarily.

Obviously, it is difficult to know what amount of money or property to require from an accused in order to fulfill the historic purposes of bail. In addition, some accused persons are so poor that any amount of money required as bail will be more than they can afford to pay and therefore force them to sit in jail awaiting the processing of their cases. The right against "excessive bail" in the Eighth Amendment appears to serve two functions. First, it warns trial judges that some undefined bail amount may be so high as to violate the Constitution. Second, it also provides a basis for appellate courts to assert supervisory authority over trial judges' decisions by declaring that particular bail amounts that have been challenged by jailed defendants are, in fact, too high.

The U.S. Supreme Court exercised this supervisory authority in *Stack v. Boyle* (1951). During the era in which Americans were especially fearful of the threat of Communism, several individuals were charged with conspiring against the government. The trial judge set bail for each defendant at $50,000, which was an even more significant sum at the dawn of the 1950s than it is today. However, the Supreme Court found that this amount violated the Excessive Bail Clause of the Eighth Amendment. According to Chief Justice Fred Vinson,

> Upon final judgment of convictions, the petitioners face imprisonment of not more than five years and a fine of not more than $10,000. It is not denied that bail for each petitioner is fixed in a sum much higher than that usually imposed for offenses with like penalties and yet there has been no factual showing to justify such action in this case. The Government asks the courts to depart from the norm by assuming without introduction of evidence that each petitioner is a pawn in a conspiracy and will, in obedience to a superior, flee the jurisdiction. To infer from the fact of indictment alone a need for bail in an unusually high amount is an arbitrary act. Such conduct would inject into our own system of government the very principles of totalitarianism which Congress was seeking to guard against in passing the statute under which the petitioners have been indicted.[1]

Chief Justice Vinson's statement implies that a bail amount that exceeds the ultimate potential punishment for the crime or that exceeds the amount usually applied for similar offenses may violate the Constitution. The decision also acknowledges, however, that the government may seek a high bail if it provides specific justifications. The Court did not purport to provide any clear definition for when a bail amount is "excessive." The Court indicated that excessiveness can be revealed by comparing the bail amount with other bail amounts and with any fines that may ultimately be imposed as punishment. Although these indicators provide guidance for some nonviolent offenses, bail amounts have often been extremely high for people accused of violent offenses because of the implicit intention of ensuring that they could not gain release and endanger the community. As a result, there is virtually no guidance about what would constitute "excessive bail" for a violent offense. Moreover, appellate judges seem extremely reluctant to second-guess bail decisions by trial judges and thereby assume the risk of blame if a newly released defendant disappears or commits another crime while out on bail. Thus it is extraordinarily rare for an appellate court to find any Eighth Amendment violations in the bail process.

Under the **Bail Reform Act of 1984,** Congress made it quite clear that federal judges were not obligated to set any bail at all if they concluded that specific defendants posed a danger to the community or that no amount of money as bail could ensure that the defendant would return to court. The Supreme Court endorsed judicial authority to decline to set bail in *United States v. Salerno* (1987). Clearly, the right against excessive bail has not been interpreted to require that bail be set in every case. Indeed, the Eighth Amendment is treated as if it says, "*If* bail is set for a defendant, then the bail cannot be excessive."

Summary

The Eighth Amendment prohibition against excessive bail does not constitute a right to have bail set. Presumptively innocent defendants can be kept in jail pending trial without ever having the opportunity to put forward an amount of money or property to provide assurance of appearing at hearings and trials. Although the Supreme Court has enforced the Eighth Amendment provision in a case with a bail amount that exceeded bail amounts for similar crimes and the fines that might be imposed upon conviction for the crime, the Court has not provided any definition of the word excessive. *Moreover, appellate judges are extremely reluctant to second-guess bail decisions by trial court judges. Thus the right against excessive bail is applied only on rare occasions when a specific appellate court uses its discretion to overrule a decision by a trial judge. In general, however, whatever bail is set by a trial judge, even if it is an amount that ensures that a presumptively innocent defendant will be forced to remain in jail, will remain unreviewed and undisturbed by appellate courts.*

Excessive Fines

Conventional Wisdom 29

The Eighth Amendment's prohibition against excessive fines prevents judges from imposing financial penalties that are disproportionate to the crime or otherwise unfair.

For most of American history, the U.S. Supreme Court paid little attention to the constitutional protection against excessive fines. As part of the federal government's "War on Drugs" policies in the 1980s, law enforcement officials at all levels of government made increased use of **forfeiture** as a means to combat drug trafficking. Forfeiture laws permit officials to seize money, property, and other assets that may have been gained as a result of illegal activities. Governmental forfeiture laws were often sufficiently broad to permit the seizure of property before the suspect's guilt had been proven. Forfeiture laws were also applied against people who broke no law but whose property was used by others to commit crimes. If a man used his wife's car to sell drugs, hire a prostitute, or engage in other illegal activities without her knowledge, her car could potentially be seized by the government despite her innocence (*Bennis v. Michigan,* 1996).

In two cases in the early 1990s, the U.S. Supreme Court raised the possibility that property forfeitures could be considered as excessive fines in violation of the Eighth Amendment. In *Austin v. United States* (1993), the Court said it might be an unconstitutionally excessive fine when officials seized an offender's mobile home and auto body shop after he was convicted of possessing a small amount of cocaine. *Alexander v. United States* (1993) concerned the forfeiture of a bookstore and millions of dollars in assets after a conviction for racketeering and selling pornographic materials. The Supreme Court did not define the meaning of an "excessive" fine in either case. Instead, it sent the cases back to the lower courts with the instruction that they should reexamine the cases to determine if an Eighth Amendment violation had occurred.

The Supreme Court finally took action in 1998 to identify the existence of an unconstitutionally excessive fine. In *United States v. Bajakajian,* a law enforcement dog trained to sniff for cash detected money in a man's suitcases at a Los Angeles airport. Officers informed the man that if he was transporting more than $10,000 in cash outside the country, he was required to fill out a form that would inform the government of that fact. The man may have erroneously believed that it was illegal to carry that amount of cash, because he denied having more than $8,000. In reality, it is permissible to carry cash out of the country. The law merely requires that a form be filed to notify the government. When the officers opened the man's suitcases, they found $357,144 in cash. If he were to be convicted of violating the currency disclosure law, his punishment could be a maximum of six months imprisonment and a maximum fine of $5,500. However, the law also permitted the government to seize any cash that they found when apprehending someone in violation of the disclosure statute. Thus the government seized the entire $357,144.

In a 5-to-4 split decision, the Supreme Court ruled that the government's action violated the Eighth Amendment's Excessive Fines Clause. According to Justice Clarence Thomas's majority opinion,

> Comparing the gravity of the respondent's crime with the $357,144 forfeiture the Government seeks, we conclude that such a forfeiture would be grossly disproportional to the gravity of the offense. It is larger than the $5,000 fine imposed [as punishment on the offender] by the District Court by many orders of magnitude, and it bears no articulable correlation to any injury suffered by the Government.

Summary

The Supreme Court's decision in the Bajakajian *case indicates that the Eighth Amendment protection against excessive fines may be applied to protect individuals in cases in which fines are grossly disproportionate to the punishment for the offense. In that case, the offender's loss from forfeiture of property was seventy-one times greater than the actual criminal fine imposed in the case. Although this case demonstrated that the Eighth Amendment may be used to protect individuals, it provided little guidance for judges throughout the country about the precise meaning of the term* excessive. *The case does not indicate that appellate courts will provide close supervision of fines and forfeitures handled in lower courts. It merely shows that appellate courts may act in extraordinary instances of grossly disproportionate financial penalties. It is also uncertain whether this limited protection will remain meaningful for an extended period of time because the 5-to-4 judicial precedent upon which it is based could be overturned if the Supreme Court's composition changes.*

CRUEL AND UNUSUAL PUNISHMENTS

Conventional Wisdom 30

The prohibition on cruel and unusual punishments prevents government officials from using violence against American citizens in any situations other than self-defense or circumstances requiring the protection of the public against the threat of violence.

During its first century, the Eighth Amendment's prohibition on cruel and unusual punishments was regarded as prohibiting only those punishments that could be equated with torture. The Cruel and Unusual Punishments Clause had little applicability, however, because it applied only against the federal government and the federal government had relatively little involvement in criminal justice other than a few federal criminal statutes and the enforcement of laws in sparsely settled territories of the West. For example, the U.S. Supreme Court rejected a claim that execution by firing squad violated the Eighth Amendment when a condemned offender in the Utah territories raised the issue in federal court (*Wilkerson v. Utah,* 1879). The incorporation of the clause did not occur until 1962 (*Robinson v. California*), but most states had their own prohibitions on cruel and unusual punishments so lawyers could pursue such claims in state court during the pre-incorporation era. The extent to which state constitutional provisions provided actual protection against actions by state and local criminal justice officials depended on the interpretation of those provisions by state judges.

During the twentieth century, the U.S. Supreme Court began to see a larger number of cases concerning Eighth Amendment claims. In *Weems v. United States* (1910), the Court expanded the coverage of the Cruel and Unusual Punishments Clause by deciding that it prohibited disproportionate punishments as well as torturous punishments. Mr. Weems had been sentenced to loss of citizenship as well as a term of imprisonment at hard labor for embezzling a small amount of money from a U.S. government agency that was overseeing the administration of the Philippines in the aftermath of the Spanish-American War. The Court found that the punishment was far too severe for the crime committed by the defendant. This decision expanded the range of possible claims that could be brought under the Eighth Amendment. Several decades later, the Court provided a definition for "cruel and unusual punishments" that continues to guide federal judges in the interpretation of the Eighth Amendment.

The case of *Trop v. Dulles* (1958) also concerned the loss of citizenship as punishment for a crime, but this time the punishment had been mandated by Congress as a penalty for military deserters during World War II. In deciding that the loss of citizenship was too severe as a punishment, the Court provided a test for determining when punishments violate the Eighth Amendment by being "cruel and unusual." According to Chief Justice Earl Warren's majority opinion, the Cruel and Unusual Punishments Clause must be defined according to "the evolving standards of decency that mark the progress of a maturing society." In other words, the definition of "cruel and unusual punishments" evolves and changes as society changes. Governmental actions that are acceptable under society's values in one era may no longer be acceptable in later decades as values change. Because the test is so vague, its application rests on judges' perceptions of evolving society values.

Federal judges applied this test during the 1960s to ban the use of whipping in prisons (*Jackson v. Bishop,* 1968). Previously, officials in many prisons had broad discretion to use violence as a means to punish and control prisoners, even if prisoners had not done anything wrong. The use of violence created the risk of abuse, especially because many prisons in southern states gave whips and guns to selected prisoners and told them to make sure that their fellow convicts worked hard in planting and harvesting crops on prison farms. The supervising prisoners were often selected for their jobs because of their brutality, not because they showed leadership qualities or good behavior. The qualifications—or lack thereof—of one supervising prisoner were highlighted in an opinion that found constitutional problems with the application of whippings in Arkansas prisons:

> The evidence also discloses that on two occasions, Talley [the victimized prisoner,] has been assaulted and beaten by James Pike, the [trusty prisoner] assigned to Talley's [work detail]. Pike, an illiterate, is a convicted murderer serving a sentence for beating to death a warden at the Mississippi County Penal Farm where Pike was formerly confined on a misdemeanor charge. . . .[2]

It does not seem surprising that abusive violence occurred when prisoners who murdered corrections officials were placed in charge of the discipline of other prisoners. Whippings were administered by corrections officials as well as by supervisory inmates. The use of violent punishments in prisons was barred after 1968 when Judge (and later U.S. Supreme Court Justice) Harry Blackmun of the U.S. Court of Appeals for the Eighth Circuit wrote, "[T]estimony of two expert penologists [prison specialists] clearly demonstrates that the use of the strap in this day is unusual and we encounter no difficulty in holding that its use is cruel."[3] It is worth noting that the courts did not lead the movement toward the abolition of punitive violence in prisons. Nearly all states had eliminated the use of whippings on their own by 1968, and the federal courts merely forced the remaining states to adopt the prevailing practice of using loss of privileges, isolation cells, and other nonviolent means for punishing prisoners' misbehavior.

The courts' abolition of violent punishments in prisons did not prevent prison officials from using force, when needed, to control prisoners and maintain safety. Prison officials can use appropriate levels of force in self-defense, for the defense of visitors and other prisoners, to prevent crimes by prisoners, to maintain order, and to prevent escapes.[4] Prison officials cannot be sued for violating the Eighth Amendment in their use of force unless they use force "maliciously and sadistically for the very purpose of causing harm."[5] Thus, even if prison officials mistakenly shoot an innocent prisoner while trying to quell a violent disturbance within a prison, their actions do not violate the Eighth Amendment unless they intentionally sought to hurt the prisoner without any justification (*Whitley v. Albers,* 1986).

As indicated by the prison cases, conventional wisdom holds true with respect to the Eighth Amendment's prohibition on punitive violence against prisoners. It is not true, however, that the Eighth Amendment bars violent actions by government officials in other settings. The U.S. Supreme Court has limited the application of the Cruel and Unusual Punishments Clause by declaring that the word *punishments* in the Eighth Amendment only refers to actions taken against people who have been convicted of crimes. The clause does not apply to other people in society. This point was illustrated most clearly in *Ingraham v. Wright* (1977), a case concerning the administration of corporal punishment to students in public schools. When the case arose, public school officials in Dade County, Florida, were authorized to "paddl[e] recalcitrant student[s] on the buttocks with a flat wooden paddle measuring less than two feet long, three to four inches wide, and about one-half inch thick."[6] The case arose because a student was sent to the hospital due to the severity of the paddling that he received for being "slow to respond to his teacher's instructions":

> Ingraham was subjected to more than 20 licks with a paddle while being held over a table in the principal's office. The paddling was so severe that he suffered a hematoma [i.e., the consequence of an injury in which a local mass of blood and discoloration exists within the tissue at the site of the injury] requiring medical attention and keeping him out of school for several days. Andrews was paddled on several occasions for minor infractions. On two occasions he was struck on his arms, once depriving him of the full use of his arm for a week. . . .[7]

Justice Lewis Powell's majority opinion concluded that "the Eighth Amendment does not apply to the paddling of children as a means of maintaining discipline."[8] Powell's opinion acknowledged that "schoolchildren could be beaten without constitutional redress, while hardened criminals suffering the same beatings at the hands of their jailers might have a valid constitutional claim under the Eighth Amendment."[9] Yet, the Court still limited the application of the Eighth Amendment to corrections and not to other inflictions of violence upon citizens by government officials in other settings. Although many states have banned the paddling of students within their own schools, corporal punishment is still applied, often in an arbitrary and discriminatory manner, to thousands of American schoolchildren each year in states that permit such actions by school officials.[10]

In some other settings, the Supreme Court applies amendments other than the Eighth Amendment to protect people against violence from government officials. For example, people who are arrested and placed in jail do not receive the protection of the Cruel and Unusual Punishments Clause until they have been convicted of a crime. They are not covered by the Eighth Amendment during the time period, which can potentially last for many months, that they are held in jail awaiting trial. During this period, they are presumptively innocent and therefore not being "punished" by the government. In order to protect unconvicted pretrial detainees against abusive violence by jail personnel, the Supreme Court has interpreted the Due Process Clauses of the Fifth and Fourteenth Amendments as providing protection against official violence. This due process right is parallel to the protections provided for convicted offenders by the Eighth Amendment (*Bell v. Wolfish*, 1979). In cases of violent actions administered by the police against citizens, the Supreme Court identifies the Fourth Amendment as providing necessary protections (*Tennessee v. Garner*, 1985). If police officers hit or shoot someone without an appropriate justification, such as self-defense, it is considered a violation of the Fourth Amendment right against "unreasonable . . . seizures." In such situations, the victims may be able to sue the police officers and seek compensation for their injuries and for the violation of their rights.

Summary

Judicial interpretation of the Cruel and Unusual Punishments Clause of the Eighth Amendment led to the abolition of whippings and other violent punishments applied to prisoners. Because the Court limits the application of the clause to convicted criminal offenders, it has used other amendments to protect people from official violence in some other contexts. However, the Court has not completely barred the use of violence for intentional infliction of pain and injury by government officials as illustrated by its unwillingness to recognize constitutional violations when public school officials beat schoolchildren, even when severe paddlings occur for such minor offenses as being "slow to respond to teachers' instructions."

Conventional Wisdom 31

Federal judges have distorted the protection against "cruel and unusual punishments" to force prison officials to make correctional institutions as cushy and comfortable as hotels for the convicted offenders who reside there.

For most of American history, prison officials used violence and threats of violence as the means to control the behavior of incarcerated offenders. Depending on the rules and supervision applied by wardens in specific institutions, there were risks that this violence could be applied without any justification or limits. If a corrections official wanted to administer a beating to a prisoner, there might be little to prevent this violence from occurring unless higher authorities within the institution limited the actions of their subordinates. As discussed in the preceding section on corporal punishment, prisons in southern states gave specific prisoners the authority to use violence against their fellow prisoners. Often there was little concern about whether this violence was employed in response to actual instances of misbehavior or whether this violence caused serious injuries and deaths. In such institutions, prison officials were primarily concerned with ensuring that prisoners did not escape, fail to work dawn to dusk in agricultural fields, or cause disturbances. They were not concerned with humane conditions; the fairness of punishments; or the infliction of unnecessary pain, injuries, and deaths upon convicted offenders. Judge Frank Johnson's opinion concerning Alabama's prisons in *Pugh v. Locke* (1976) illuminated the kinds of problems being addressed by judges through their interpretations of the Eight Amendment:

> Old and filthy cotton mattresses lead to the spread of contagious diseases and body lice. Nearly all inmates' living quarters are inadequately heated and ventilated. The electrical systems are totally inadequate, exposed wiring poses a constant danger to inmates. . . . There was repeated testimony at trial that they are overrun with roaches, flies, mosquitoes, and other vermin. . . . This gross infestation is due in part to inadequate maintenance and housekeeping procedures. . . . In one [cellblock], housing well over 200 men, there is one functioning toilet. Many toilets will not flush and are overflowing. . . . Witnesses repeatedly commented on the overpowering odor emanating from these facilities. . . . Personal hygiene is an insurmountable problem in the circumstances. The parties stipulated that the state supplies prisoners only with razor blades and soap. It was further stipulated that the state furnished no toothpaste, toothbrushes, shampoo, shaving cream, razors, or combs. . . . Food service conditions are equally unsanitary. Food is improperly stored in dirty storage units, and is often infested with insects. . . . [A] United States public health officer. . . . testified at trial that he found these facilities wholly unfit for human habitation according to virtually every criterion used by public health inspectors. . . . Violent inmates are not isolated from those who are young, passive, or weak. Consequently, the latter inmates are repeatedly victimized by those who are stronger and more aggressive. Testimony shows that robbery, rape, extortion, theft, and assault are everyday occurrences. . . . [Handicapped and elderly inmates] are left without supervision in second-floor quarters that are accessible only by stairway, with no means of evacuation in the event of fire or other physical emergency, and utterly helpless in the event of the sort of medical emergency to which the elderly are susceptible. . . . Guards rarely enter the cell blocks and dormitories, especially at night when their presence is most needed. . . . One 20-year-old inmate, after relating that he has been told by medical experts that he has the mind of a five year old, testified that he was raped by a group of inmates on the first night he spent in an Alabama prison. On the second night he was almost strangled by two other inmates who decided instead that they could use him to make a profit, selling his body to other inmates. . . .[11]

Many Americans may read such descriptions and say, "So what? They're criminals. They deserve what they get." Obviously, people are entitled to their own opinions, but there may be additional factors to consider before reaching such conclusions. For example, the use of incarceration is supposed to punish people by depriving them of their liberty. That deprivation is considered to be a significant sanction in a society that values individual liberty above all else. Incarceration is not intended to be deprivation of liberty *plus* the infliction of any additional life-threatening harms that authorities wish to impose. Remember that people can end up in prison for a variety of reasons. All prisoners are not murderers or other violent offenders. Young people can go to prison for stealing a car. College students could go to prison for possessing marijuana or even lying on their financial aid forms. Someone could even go to prison if a small child runs in the street in front of a car and the jury disagrees with the driver's heartfelt belief that it was impossible to stop the vehicle in time to avoid hitting the child, even while traveling safely within the speed limit. If the courts sentence such people to a one-, two-, or five-year term of incarceration as the punishment for their crimes, should they be forced, in effect, to actually suffer the death penalty by dying from poor sanitation, contagious diseases, or violence? If there are no standards for correctional institutions, what will prevent such deaths from occurring?

For example, one of the issues mentioned in the Alabama case and discussed in other cases is the existence of plans for safely evacuating offenders in case of a fire or other emergency. In May 2002, eight jail inmates died in a fire in Mitchell County, North Carolina, when the jailer could not reach their second-floor cells. Each cell in the fifty-year-old jail had to be opened individually by hand with a key, and there was no fire-prevention sprinkler system. A twenty-year-old inmate who was one week away from his college graduation died while serving a weekend sentence for drunk driving. Another twenty-year-old was serving a sentence for driving with a revoked license. The other victims also had short sentences for minor offenses.[12] Without standards for living conditions in correctional institutions, there are serious risks that incarcerated offenders, even those incarcerated briefly for minor offenses, may suffer grave and permanent harms.

Court decisions during the 1960s that abolished the use of whipping in prisons were at the leading edge of a wave of judicial cases throughout the country that called upon federal judges to evaluate whether prison conditions violated the Eighth Amendment protection against cruel and unusual punishments. Judges throughout the United States, both Republicans and Democrats, began to examine whether living conditions in prisons violated the *Trop v. Dulles* standard that evaluated "cruel and unusual punishments" in light of contemporary societal values. In judicial decisions throughout the 1970s and 1980s, federal judges issued orders concerning food, shelter, sanitation, working conditions, and medical care in prisons through their interpretations of the Cruel and Unusual Punishments Clause. Such decisions affected prisons in every state. In *Hutto v. Finney* (1978), the U.S. Supreme Court endorsed the authority of lower court judges to use the Eighth Amendment to order remedies in deficient prison conditions. Even if a prison did not receive a direct judicial order to change its living conditions and policies, it might adapt its practices to comply with the standards emerging in judicial orders applied to other institutions. These decisions had their greatest impact on southern prisons, which were forced to change from plantation-style institutions that used prisoners for dawn-to-dusk labor under the supervision of violent offenders to custodial institutions with professional staff in accordance with the model employed by correctional institutions elsewhere in the United States.[13] The judicial decisions concerning the Eighth Amendment had the effect of creating national minimum standards for living conditions in correctional institutions.

What is the nature of the rights developed for prisoners under the Eighth Amendment? The right to medical care provides an instructive example. In *Estelle v. Gamble* (1976), the U.S. Supreme Court declared that prisoners have a limited right to medical care. According to Justice Thurgood Marshall's majority opinion, there is a violation of the Cruel and Unusual Punishments Clause when prison officials demonstrate "deliberate indifference to [prisoners'] serious medical needs." This is not a right to the best medical care. It is not even a right to good medical care. As Justice Marshall noted, "A complaint that a physician has been negligent in diagnosing or treating a medical condition does not state a valid claim of medical mistreatment under the Eighth Amendment." Mere negligence or poor treatment does not constitute a rights violation. Instead, the prisoner must show "deliberate indifference" on the part of officials. If a prisoner is experiencing pain and officials are responsive by providing aspirin, there may be no rights violation even if the officials missed an underlying serious condition that worsens over time from lack of appropriate treatment.

Many of the amenities in prisons that the public views as "unnecessary luxuries" are, in fact, not provided because of orders from federal judges. There is no constitutional right for prisoners to have televisions, radios, basketball courts, and weightlifting equipment. As part of their right to humane conditions of confinement, prisoners have a right to nutritious food, appropriate shelter, opportunities to walk around in order to maintain minimum levels of physical fitness, and limited medical care. Televisions, basketball courts, and other extra amenities are provided by the choice of prison officials, not by requirements imposed by federal judges. These amenities are ***privileges,*** not *constitutional rights.* Additional amenities are not provided because corrections officials wish to coddle convicted offenders. They are provided because they advance the goals of the corrections officials. In particular, they help to keep prisons running smoothly because they keep prisoners busy and thereby reduce the risk that bored prisoners will fight with each other or cause disturbances that endanger prison personnel. The existence of privileges also provides corrections officials with tools that they can use to gain prisoners' cooperation. Officials can offer privileges as an incentive to gain prisoners' cooperation, and they can also threaten to take privileges away as a means to keep prisoners from misbehaving. Thus it is important to recognize that all items and opportunities possessed by prisoners are not based on judges' orders concerning constitutional rights. Many of them are privileges granted by corrections officials in pursuit of their goal of creating incentives for cooperative behavior.

Beginning in the 1980s, the U.S. Supreme Court reduced the extent of constitutional rights for prisoners. In *Wilson v. Seiter* (1991), the Supreme Court applied the "deliberate indifference" standard from *Estelle v. Gamble* to all claims of unconstitutional prison conditions rather than just to medical care claims. In *Wilson,* a prisoner in Ohio had made various allegations concerning deficiencies in a prison's ventilation, food services, and overcrowded cell blocks. Justice Antonin Scalia's majority opinion drew from the *Estelle v. Gamble* decision to impose clear limits on prisoners' ability to prove Eighth Amendment violations. The "deliberate indifference" standard requires prisoners to prove not merely that the actual conditions are deficient for humane living but also that prison officials knew about the conditions and failed to take any actions. As noted in a separate opinion by Justice Byron White, the *Wilson* rule invites prison officials to defeat constitutional claims concerning "inhumane prison conditions simply by showing that the conditions are caused by insufficient funding from the state legislature, rather than by any deliberate indifference on the part of prison officials."[14] Thus, although court decisions have pushed corrections officials to meet minimum standards for food, housing, and medical care, prisoners cannot easily prove violations of these standards and they have virtually no ability to persuade judges to expand entitlements related to the quality of living conditions. As far back as 1982, the U.S. Supreme Court indicated that lower court judges had gone far enough in applying the Eighth Amendment for the purposes of developing standards for prison conditions. In the words of Justice Lewis Powell, "In discharging this oversight responsibility [over prison conditions], however, courts cannot assume that state legislatures and prison officials are insensitive to the requirements of the Constitution or to the perplexing sociological problems of how best to achieve the goals of the penal function in the criminal justice system" (*Rhodes v. Chapman*).[15] Many observers interpreted this statement as advising judges to show greater deference to prison officials by being reluctant to identify new violations and by permitting officials to develop their own remedies for proven constitutional violations.

Although judicial decisions interpreting the Eighth Amendment helped to professionalize prison administration and diminish the existence of inhumane conditions and practices, the standards developed by judges are not easily enforceable by prisoners. Prisoners who believe that unconstitutional conditions exist within their institutions, such as overt deprivations of medical care or access to bathroom facilities, face further hurdles in addition to those imposed by the *Wilson* requirement of proving "deliberate indifference." There is no right to counsel for prisoners in lawsuits concerning possible constitutional violations in conditions of confinement. If a prisoner cannot afford to hire his or her own attorney and no attorney volunteers to take the case, then the prisoner must pursue the case through self-representation. Serving as one's own attorney would be extremely difficult for college-educated people who lack formal training and experience in law; it is even more difficult for convicted offenders, most of whom never came close to attending college. For many prisoners, problems with basic literacy, mental illness, or the fact that English is not their native language create insurmountable barriers to the pursuit of legal cases.

Because prisoners must use the courts in order to obtain protection for their constitutional rights, the Supreme Court ruled in *Bounds v. Smith* (1977) that correctional institutions must provide prisoners with resources that will permit them to file legal cases in court. Most prisons fulfill this obligation by establishing prison law libraries that prisoners can use to conduct their own research. In practice, according to one federal judge, this approach does very little to help prisoners make sure that their rights are protected:

> In this court's view, access to the fullest law library anywhere is a useless and meaningless gesture in terms of the great mass of prisoners. . . . To expect untrained laymen to work with entirely unfamiliar books, whose content they cannot understand, may be worthy of Lewis Carroll['s *Alice in Wonderland*], but hardly satisfies the substance of constitutional duty. Access to full law libraries makes about as much sense as furnishing medical services through books like: "Brain Surgery Self-Taught," or "How to Remove Your Own Appendix," along with scalpels, drills, hemostats, sponges, and sutures.[16]

Uneducated prisoners have little hope of understanding court procedures, identifying recognizable legal issues, drafting legal documents effectively, and citing appropriate legal precedents, even if they have a valid claim against the prison.

Despite these difficulties, the U.S. Supreme Court has restricted the ability of federal judges to order prisons to provide legal assistance to prisoners beyond merely making books available. In *Lewis v. Casey* (1996), Justice Antonin Scalia's majority opinion insisted that prisoners prove to a judge that they were incapable of utilizing court processes before a judge could even consider ordering corrections officials to provide additional assistance through law-trained advisors (e.g., lawyers, paralegals, or law students). Although Scalia's rule may sound sensible, it presents a problem when applied in practice. If prisoners come to court to attempt to prove they are incapable of presenting issues effectively in court, the mere fact that they managed to file papers in court can be used as proof that they *do not* need legal assistance. Prisoners who are high school dropouts, illiterate, mentally retarded, mentally ill, or native speakers of foreign languages are not likely to discover on their own how to file a claim to request that a judge order needed legal assistance. Thus many prisoners have no realistic hope of seeking remedies if their Eighth Amendment or other constitutional rights are violated.

Congress imposed further restrictions on prisoners' ability to file lawsuits concerning constitutional rights with passage of the Prison Litigation Reform Act of 1996. The act had two primary purposes. First, it imposed barriers to prisoners' lawsuits by, for example, imposing greater obligations on prisoners to pay their own court fees, even if they have very little money, and requiring that prisoners be barred from having court fees waived if they have previously had three cases dismissed for failing to state a proper legal claim.[17] In effect, a prisoner who had previously had three cases dismissed because of ineffective presentations of legal issues could only seek waiver of court fees in future cases concerning "imminent danger of physical injury."[18] Such a prisoner, if penniless, would have no opportunity to file claims concerning other constitutional rights violations. The second purpose of the Prison Litigation Reform Act was to limit the authority of federal judges to order remedies for constitutional violations. These limitations include strict rules about potential remedies for prison overcrowding and a "sunset" provision that permits corrections officials to demand the termination of judicial orders after a specified time period.[19] Despite the fact that the number of offenders incarcerated in American prisons reached an all-time high of 1.4 million at the beginning of the twenty-first century,[20] the number of constitutional rights lawsuits filed by prisoners in federal courts dropped from 68,235 in 1996 to 25,504 in 2000.[21] It seems clear that the Prison Litigation Reform Act has significantly reduced prisoners' constitutional claims. As many scholars have observed, there are two ways to curtail rights under the law. One way is through new judicial interpretations that restrict the definitions of rights. The other way is through the creation of barriers to litigation that might have been used to identify and remedy rights violations.[22] Thus most prisoners face serious difficulties if they wish to seek enforcement of their limited Eighth Amendment rights through the judicial process.

Summary

Judges' decisions interpreting the Eighth Amendment played an important role in reducing inhumane practices in American prisons and pushing all correctional institutions toward a model of professional administration. The Eighth Amendment provides limited rights to medical care, nutrition, shelter, and other aspects of living conditions. Many of the amenities enjoyed by prisoners and viewed as objectionable by the public, such as televisions, basketball courts, and weightlifting equipment, are actually privileges voluntarily supplied by prison officials rather than requirements imposed by federal judges as a component of constitutional rights. Despite the existence of limited rights for prisoners under the Eighth Amendment, these rights are very difficult to enforce when violations occur. Prisoners must prove not merely that conditions fall below Eighth Amendment standards but also that violations were caused by prison officials' "deliberate indifference." It is difficult to prove such intentions on the part of prison administrators and staff. Because prisoners have no right to counsel in cases concerning Eighth Amendment rights, it is extremely difficult for most prisoners to seek judicial remedies when rights are violated. The Supreme Court's decisions have limited judges' ability to provide legal assistance for prisoners, and the Prison Litigation Reform Act provides further limitations on judges' authority and prisoners' opportunities to litigate. Thus violations of prisoners' limited Eighth Amendment rights can easily go unremedied.

CAPITAL PUNISHMENT

Conventional Wisdom 32

The prohibition against cruel and unusual punishments places careful restrictions on the death penalty to ensure that is applied in a fair and humane fashion.

The U.S. Supreme Court has interpreted the Cruel and Unusual Punishments Clause to limit the applicability of the death penalty. In *Coker v. Georgia* (1977), the Court determined that capital punishment is a disproportionate penalty for raping an adult. In *Atkins v. Virginia* (2002), the Court declared that it is cruel and unusual to apply the death penalty to mentally retarded offenders. With respect to another category of offenders whose executions are generally barred in other countries, however, the Supreme Court has not interpreted the Eighth Amendment to limit the death penalty. The United States is one of only seven countries in the world known to have executed people for offenses they committed as juveniles. Seventeen American states permit imposition of capital punishment to teenagers for crimes that they committed at age sixteen, and five other states use seventeen as the minimum age. The other countries that have executed juveniles for capital offenses are those that the United States frequently criticizes for human rights violations: Democratic Republic of Congo, Iran, Nigeria, Pakistan, Saudi Arabia, and Yemen. None of these countries are among those to which the United States typically compares itself as a democracy with constitutional rights for individuals. Yet, several of these countries changed their laws and practices in recent years to limit execution of juvenile offenders. Pakistan and Yemen changed their laws to apply capital punishment only to those who commit crimes at age eighteen or over, and the Democratic Republic of Congo imposed a moratorium on the execution of juvenile offenders.[23] The application of the death penalty to teenagers is highly "unusual" in looking at countries around the world, yet the Eighth Amendment has not been applied to prevent capital punishment for American juveniles over the age of fifteen (*Stanford v. Kentucky,* 1989).

Eighth Amendment questions also linger about the methods used for executions. In earlier decades, the Supreme Court rejected challenges to execution methods. In 1890, the Court turned back a challenge to the newly invented electric chair by the prisoner who was slated to be the first person executed through the device (*In re Kemmler*). Despite the inherently "unusual" nature of a new invention, the Court endorsed the new device as representing the advancement of humane treatment through science. Later, a closely divided Court rejected a challenge to a second execution when a malfunctioning electric chair merely severely shocked but did not kill a condemned man in the first attempt (*Louisiana ex rel. Francis v. Resweber,* 1947). Ten states permit the use of the electric chair, a method that U.S. Supreme Court Justice William Brennan described as "nothing less than the contemporary technological equivalent of burning people at the stake." Brennan described such executions in *Glass v. Louisiana* (1985):

> Th[e] evidence suggests that death by electrical current is extremely violent and inflicts pain and indignities far beyond the "mere extinguishment of life." Witnesses routinely report that, when the switch is thrown, the condemned prisoner "cringes," "leaps," and "fights the straps with amazing strength." The hands turn red, then white, and the cords of the neck stand out like steel bands. The prisoner's limbs, fingers, toes, and face are severely contorted. The force of the electrical current is so powerful that the prisoner's eyeballs sometimes pop out and "rest on [his] cheeks." The prisoner often defecates, urinates, and vomits blood and drool.

The Georgia Supreme Court found that the use of the electric chair violated the prohibition on cruel and unusual punishments in its *state* constitution, and various state legislatures switched to lethal injection as the means of execution due to fears that the U.S. Supreme Court or other courts might decide that the electric chair violates federal or state constitutional provisions.[24]

The gas chamber, which is available as a means of execution in only five states, has been supplanted by lethal injection for the same reasons. It has been declared unconstitutional by lower federal courts in California,[25] but the U.S. Supreme Court has not determined the gas chamber to be unconstitutional under the Eighth Amendment despite effects that can be characterized as akin to physical torture. As described by a federal district judge (*Fierro v. Gomez,* 1994):

> [A]n inmate probably remains conscious anywhere from 15 seconds to one minute, and . . . there is a substantial likelihood that consciousness, or waxing and waning of consciousness, persists for several additional minutes. During this time, . . . inmates suffer intense, visceral pain, primarily as a result of a lack of oxygen to the cells. The experience of "air hunger" is akin to the experience of a major heart attack, or to being held under water. Other possible effects of the cyanide gas include tetany, an exquisitely painful contraction of muscles, and painful build-up of lactic acid and adrenaline. Cyanide-induced cellular suffocation causes anxiety, panic, terror, and pain.

Lethal injection is not necessarily, however, a smooth and painless method for imposing death. There have been numerous botched executions in which technicians spent long periods of time attempting to find veins suitable for the various needles; the needles popped out of the condemned person's veins during the administration of the drugs; or the condemned person had a reaction to the drugs that caused convulsions, violent gagging sounds, and other extended physical reactions prior to death.[26] Despite concerns raised by execution witnesses about whether this method is, indeed, humane, it is unlikely to be scrutinized closely by courts unless other, less troubling methods of execution are developed.

Another potential issue is whether the execution of an innocent person would violate the prohibition on cruel and unusual punishments. Justice Harry Blackmun, on behalf of Justices John Paul Stevens and David Souter, argued that condemned people's Eighth Amendment right against cruel and unusual punishments would be violated if courts ignored newly discovered evidence of innocence and permitted an execution to proceed (*Herrera v. Collins,* 1993). However, this argument was made in a dissenting opinion and has never been endorsed by a majority of the Supreme Court's justices. Justice Scalia, a member of the majority in that case, argued that there is no right to have new evidence considered in court after a person has been convicted of a crime, even if that evidence shows that the person is innocent. In effect, the current position of the Court is that criminal defendants have a right to a fair trial under the Sixth Amendment, but they have no Eighth Amendment right that prevents them from being executed if their fair trial produces an incorrect result. This is an important issue because as of 2003 more than 100 people sentenced to death in the United States since 1973 were later discovered to be innocent and released from death row. There is strong evidence that some innocent people have been executed, but limitations in the appeals process prevented them from presenting their cases for reconsideration or the evidence of innocence was discovered after the execution.[27] Despite the evident extent of erroneous convictions, the Supreme Court has not moved closer to interpreting the Cruel and Unusual Punishments Clause to bar the execution of innocent people. Indeed, prosecutors continue to use the absence of such an interpretation as a justification for speeding cases toward execution despite questions about guilt. For example, during oral arguments before the Missouri Supreme Court in February 2003, a state supreme court justice specifically asked an assistant attorney general whether the right against cruel and unusual punishments would be violated if an innocent person was executed despite new DNA evidence that clearly proved that the defendant was not guilty of the crime. The assistant attorney general replied that the execution must move forward, in spite of the person's innocence, unless some separate right, such as the Sixth Amendment right to counsel, had been violated because there is no Eighth Amendment violation when an innocent person is executed.[28] Although the assistant attorney general's words seemed to shock some members of the state supreme court, his statement appears to be an accurate characterization of the U.S. Supreme Court's interpretations of the Eighth Amendment.

Justice Scalia claims that evidence of innocence will inevitably lead a governor to pardon the death row inmate in question so that the courts do not need to address the issue (*Herrera v. Collins,* 1993). Scalia's confident prediction has proven to be less-than-completely accurate. DNA tests exonerated a Virginia death row inmate named Earl Washington, yet the governor of Virginia kept the test results secret and merely commuted Washington's sentence to life in prison. Commentators speculated that the governor was interested in running for election to the U.S. Senate and did not want to be accused of freeing people from prison. Only after a PBS documentary revealed the facts of Washington's case to a national television audience was a pardon issued eighteen months later by a new governor.[29] In Washington's case, he was freed through the attention of a documentary filmmaker, not merely through the discovery of evidence of his innocence.

There are other possible applications of the Cruel and Unusual Punishments Clause to capital punishment. For example, Justice John Paul Stevens has argued:

> Delay in the execution of judgments imposing the death penalty frustrates the public interest in deterrence and eviscerates the only rational justification for that type of punishment. From the standpoint of the defendant, the delay can become so excessive as to constitute cruel and unusual punishment prohibited by the Eighth Amendment.[30]

The Supreme Court has not, however, explored this aspect of capital punishment.

Summary

The Cruel and Unusual Punishments Clause places some limitations on capital punishment, such as prohibitions on executions of rapists and mentally retarded offenders. The Supreme Court has not, however, interpreted the Eighth Amendment to bar a category of executions that is forbidden nearly everywhere else in the world, namely executions of juveniles. The Supreme Court has not used the Eighth Amendment to limit methods of execution, even when those methods cause severe physical pain and suffering that are arguably comparable to torture. The Court also has not interpreted the clause to prevent the execution of innocent people. Under the Supreme Court's interpretations of the Eighth Amendment, it would not be unconstitutionally "cruel and unusual" to execute a person who was convicted after a fair trial but whose innocence was later definitively established through DNA tests or other newly discovered evidence. In other words, there is no constitutional right to be free from execution for a crime that you did not commit, even under circumstances in which you can clearly prove your innocence after your trial has been completed.

Conclusion

The words of the three protective provisions of the Eighth Amendment are especially vague. There is no inherent meaning to the word *excessive* in the Excessive Fines Clause and the Excessive Bail Clause. Moreover, the prohibition on "cruel and unusual" punishments has no evident meaning. All three provisions must be given meaning through judicial interpretation, and none of them have been interpreted to provide the specific protections that Americans may presume to exist. With respect to the provisions concerning fines and bail, the Supreme Court has made isolated case decisions that convey the message that there are some unusual circumstances in which violations of the clauses may occur. However, the Court has provided no specific guidance about the meaning of the word *excessive* and has rarely provided oversight for the discretionary decisions about bail and fines made by lower court judges. Thus these provisions do not provide specific, identifiable protections for individuals. They serve primarily as a warning to lower court judges that there may be some, undefined outer limit to judicial authority in setting fines and bail. Yet these judges know perfectly well from experience that their decisions are unlikely to be second-guessed even when suspects and offenders seek to appeal trial court decisions.

The Eighth Amendment prohibition on cruel and unusual punishments has been interpreted more frequently to provide specific protections for individuals. Judicial interpretations of this clause provided the basis for reforming prisons and diminishing widespread violent practices and inhumane conditions. Although the Eighth Amendment prevents the application of corporal punishment against convicted offenders, it does not protect citizens generally against governmental violence. Because the Eighth Amendment only protects people after they have been convicted of crimes, the amendment does not protect children in public schools who may be subjected to painful, injury-causing beatings in states that still permit such punishments. These beatings may be applied upon quick, reactive, discretionary decisions by school officials, without any requirements that the offense at issue be serious or that evidence be presented to be certain that the child is, in fact, guilty of the offense.

In the prison setting, the Eighth Amendment provides the basis for limited rights to medical care and humane conditions of confinement. Prison officials may not show "deliberate indifference" to prisoners' "serious medical needs"; and they must provide food, shelter, and sanitation that meet public health standards. Other amenities of prison life, such as television, education programs, and recreation equipment, are usually removable privileges provided voluntarily by state officials to keep the prisoners from causing trouble rather than through Eighth Amendment mandates from judges. The limited Eighth Amendment protections promised to prisoners are increasingly difficult to enforce because of Supreme Court decisions imposing a high standard of proof ("deliberate indifference") to establish violations as well as judicial and statutory actions that make it extremely difficult for most prisoners to make use of the judicial process. Because prisoners have no right to counsel for civil rights lawsuits, Eighth Amendment rights are unenforceable promises for most prisoners if corrections officials' decisions and actions make rights merely symbolic by failing to fulfill constitutional standards. Fortunately, many corrections officials are educated professionals who make efforts to ensure that their institutions comply with constitutional standards even when it is highly uncertain if their inmates could effectively use the courts to force them to remedy Eighth Amendment violations.

The Cruel and Unusual Punishments Clause has been applied to capital punishment to limit the scope of the death penalty. Although the Supreme Court bars the execution of rapists and mentally retarded offenders, the United States continues to accept the application of the death penalty for teenage offenders even as nearly every other country finds such a policy to be inhumane. The execution of teenage offenders is clearly "unusual" in the context of criminal justice throughout the world, but it has not been judged by the Supreme Court to fit the meaning of prohibited "cruel and unusual" punishments under the Eighth Amendment. Although the original intention of the Cruel and Unusual Punishments Clause was to prevent punishments that were comparable to torture,[31] the Eighth Amendment has not been applied by the U.S. Supreme Court to limit the methods of execution used by the states, even when those methods inflict physical pain and suffering that seem akin to torture. The electric chair and the gas chamber, in particular, provide particularly prolonged and painful death experiences when used as methods of execution. More striking still is the Supreme Court's disinclination to declare that it is unconstitutionally "cruel and unusual" for innocent people to be executed for crimes that they did not commit, even when there is newly discovered evidence that demonstrates their innocence. For such people, notions of justice as well as constitutional rights are entirely symbolic if judges turn a blind eye to evidence of innocence and demonstrate a narrow-minded preoccupation with the lesser issue of whether the trial process was fair, despite its flaws and inaccuracy.

THE FOURTEENTH AMENDMENT

All persons born or naturalized in the United States, and subject to the jurisdiction thereof, are citizens of the United States and of the State wherein they reside. No State shall make or enforce any law which shall abridge the privileges or immunities of citizens of the United States; nor shall any State deprive any person of life, liberty, or property, without due process of law; nor deny to any person within its jurisdiction the equal protection of the laws. . . .

Unlike the Bill of Rights, the Fourteenth Amendment explicitly provides rights for individuals against actions by state and local governments. The specific rights-granting phrases applicable to criminal justice are the Due Process Clause and the Equal Protection Clause. These phrases are more vague than much of the language in the Bill of Rights. How does one know when the right to "due process" has been violated? What does the right to "equal protection" mean? Because the meaning of these phrases is not clear from the language itself, the Supreme Court must obviously use its interpretive powers to provide definitions for these rights. As discussed in prior chapters, the Supreme Court's interpretations defined the Due Process Clause as the vehicle through which specific rights from the Bill of Rights could be applied against state and local governments. With respect to criminal justice, the Supreme Court incorporated most of the specific rights in the First, Fourth, Fifth, Sixth, and Eighth Amendments into the Due Process Clause of the Fourteenth Amendment. Although the incorporation decisions of the mid-twentieth century had a profound impact on criminal justice by requiring state and local officials to respect the same constitutional rights applicable in the federal justice system, they were not the only Supreme Court interpretations of the Due Process Clause to impact criminal justice. The Court also uses the clause to identify circumstances in which officials' actions violate a general right to due process.

The historical purpose of the Equal Protection Clause was to limit the ability of states to engage in racial discrimination. The language of the clause is general, and thus it could also apply to prohibit other forms of governmental discrimination. However, the Supreme Court has applied the right to equal protection in limited ways. In addition to racial discrimination, the Court has also applied the right to prohibit certain forms of gender discrimination as well as specific instances of discrimination by nationality. The clause does not protect against discrimination based on wealth and other categories. There is no constitutional right to be free from governmental discrimination for these other categories. However, the Fourteenth Amendment is not the sole source of legal protections against discrimination. There are statutes that bar discrimination by religion, age, and disability in employment contexts and certain government programs. In addition, statutes provide protection against certain kinds of discrimination by businesses and private citizens. The Equal Protection Clause applies only against discrimination by state and local governments.

EQUAL PROTECTION

Conventional Wisdom 33

The Equal Protection Clause prohibits criminal justice officials from engaging in racial discrimination in their treatment of suspects, defendants, and convicted offenders.

The time period from the Supreme Court's landmark decision outlawing racial segregation in schools (*Brown v. Board of Education,* 1954) through congressional enactment of the Civil Rights Acts and the Voting Rights Acts of the mid-1960s saw American law change from a facilitator of racial discrimination to a weapon against it. Law is not always an effective weapon in eliminating discrimination, but it is a weapon nonetheless. Thus, since the 1960s, courts have used the right to equal protection to eliminate official policies of racial discrimination. In the context of criminal justice, the Supreme Court said that prisons could not have explicit policies that imposed racial segregation within prisons (*Lee v. Washington,* 1968). Courts have also examined and rejected informal policies that led to racial segregation in prison housing units. For example, a jail was barred from permitting detainees to choose their own cells when it led African-Americans to live on one side of the jail and whites to live separately on the other side (*Jones v. Diamond,* 1981). A court also stopped the practice of assigning whites to "honor housing blocks" in one prison while assigning African-Americans to regular housing, thus producing racial segregation in the institution (*Santiago v. Miles,* 1991).

The fact that courts use the right to equal protection to prohibit official policies of racial discrimination does not mean that the right prevents discrimination from occurring. Such formal policies are openly stated and easy to see. By contrast, discretionary decision making is pervasive throughout the criminal justice system, yet not usually exercised in public view. Police officers make their own judgments about whom to stop, search, and arrest. Prosecutors use discretion in deciding whom to charge, what the charges will be, what plea agreements will be offered, and what sentences will be recommended. Many judges have discretion in making decisions about sentencing. When these officials use discretion to treat people differently because of their race, it can be very difficult for the discrimination victim to prove that the decision was based on race. An official policy of racial discrimination is relatively easy to attack by making an equal protection claim. Discretionary decisions are far more difficult to address because it is almost impossible to prove that discrimination is racially motivated unless the criminal justice official is foolish enough to make a derogatory racial comment in front of witnesses. A criminal justice official could make a racially biased statement while deciding to arrest someone. For example, an unethical white officer could say, "I don't like your attitude, you black so-and-so. I'm putting you in jail to teach you to show some respect to white people." Without witnesses present, however, the officer could deny making the statement and the discrimination victim would find it virtually impossible to prove that the arrest was racially motivated.

Racially biased statements are not the only possible form of evidence that could be used to prove the existence of improper racial discrimination. Under employment discrimination law, victims of alleged racial discrimination are permitted to present statistics showing hiring and promotion practices that diverge significantly from the racial composition of an employer's applicant pool and workforce. The statistics can raise an inference of illegal racial discrimination and thereby force the employer to provide an adequate explanation for how hiring and promotion patterns produced the racial disparities for reasons other than racial discrimination. There have been efforts to use statistics in a similar fashion to prove the existence of racial discrimination in discretionary decision making in the criminal justice system, but the Supreme Court has not been receptive to such evidence in the criminal justice context.

Led by Professor David Baldus of the University of Iowa College of Law, a team of researchers studied murder cases in Georgia. They were well aware that one cannot infer the existence of discrimination simply because more African-Americans than whites (or vice versa) were sentenced to death. Under such circumstances, what appear to be racial disparities could actually be caused by differences in the nature of the crimes, such as if more African-Americans committed homicides in the course of robberies or burglaries and therefore the homicides were considered more serious. It could also be the case that killers from one racial group were more likely to have prior criminal records, thus increasing the severity of their punishments. In order to control for these and other factors, the researchers carefully analyzed the factors within each murder case, including prior records and other factors. The study analyzed 230 factors that could have explained any disparities on nonracial grounds. Such factors are called "variables" in statistical analysis. After analyzing factors in more than 2,000 murder cases, the Baldus study found that race emerged as an inescapable factor in producing disparities in the imposition of the death penalty. The role of race was not a matter of simple discrimination against African-American defendants. Instead, the effect of race was seen by looking at the racial classification of both the victim and the defendant. African-Americans convicted of killing whites were much more likely to receive death sentences than were white killers or African-Americans who killed other African-Americans. African-Americans who killed whites were sentenced to death at twenty-two times the rate of African-Americans who killed other African-Americans and more than seven times the rate of whites who killed African-Americans. The analysis controlled for the impact of other factors and found that race was a determining factor in deciding who would receive the death penalty in Georgia.

The results of the Baldus study were presented in court by Warren McCleskey, an African-American man convicted of killing a police officer during a robbery at a furniture store. McCleskey's lawyers argued that the statistics demonstrated that Georgia's capital punishment process was infected with racial discrimination in violation of the Equal Protection Clause and therefore Georgia should be barred from carrying out executions unless and until the discriminatory processes were corrected. Unfortunately for McCleskey, a narrow majority on the Supreme Court rejected the use of statistics to prove the existence of racial discrimination in death penalty sentencing (*McCleskey v. Kemp*, 1987). Justice Lewis Powell's majority opinion acknowledged that the Court accepts statistics as evidence of racial discrimination in employment discrimination cases, but he said that death penalty cases are different because judges and juries make a unique decision in each case. In effect, Powell's opinion required that defendants prove that there was specific evidence of racial discrimination in a particular trial. The Court would not recognize evidence of pervasive discrimination throughout a state's criminal justice system. Thus defendants are virtually unprotected against racially discriminatory processes unless a prosecutor or judge makes an explicitly biased statement during the course of a trial.

The Court's rejection of statistical evidence ignores the nature of decision making in the criminal justice system and effectively permits forms of racial discrimination to continue without remedy. Outcomes in criminal cases are the product of cumulative discretionary decisions. Discrimination can affect decisions in the process without ever producing proof of explicit discrimination in a single decision. For example, prosecutors must decide to seek the death penalty against specific defendants. This discretionary decision could be infected with unseen discrimination if, for example, the prosecutor subconsciously values white victims' lives more than African-American victims' lives in determining which defendants deserve capital punishment. Studies in various jurisdictions confirm the existence of disparities that appear to be related to discrimination. In a study in North Carolina, 11.6 percent of non-white defendants charged with murdering whites were sentenced to death but only 6.1 percent of whites who murdered whites and 4.7 of nonwhites whose victims were nonwhite faced a similar fate.[1] In Philadelphia, African-Americans were found to be four times as likely to be sentenced to death as whites in similar cases.[2] A related example emerged in a study of capital prosecutions in Nebraska, which found that prosecutors were more likely to seek the death penalty and judges were more likely to impose it when the victims were affluent.[3] A prosecutor may simply react to each case depending on how "horrible" it makes him or her feel. For example, most county prosecutors are white and they may feel a greater sense of empathy and identification with white victims and their families.[4] Thus the prosecutor may not recognize that a racial bias exists in reacting more strongly against the killings of whites. These factors can also affect the discretionary decisions of jurors and judges that follow the prosecutor's decisions in ultimately determining who receives the death penalty:

> Prosecutors make subjective decisions, based on a complex variety of factors, about whether to seek the death penalty. Likewise, jurors make comparable subjective decisions about whether to apply the death penalty. If they deliberately apply discriminatory criteria, the defendant cannot challenge their decision unless the decision makers openly express their biases. Moreover, in this complex, multistep decisional process, decision makers may *unconsciously* apply their prejudices, thus precluding any possibility of proving the existence of discrimination. As numerous studies of jury deliberations indicate, people apply their prejudices and biases to reach decisions adverse to members of particular social groups, including ethnic groups.[5]

One of the most troubling aspects of the Court's decision in *McCleskey v. Kemp* emerged years later when the late Justice Thurgood Marshall's papers became available in the Library of Congress. Marshall's papers included internal memoranda that justices wrote to each other as they developed decisions and opinions in many cases. In leaving their personal papers to university libraries or the Library of Congress, Supreme Court justices generally do not permit such internal documents to become available to the public until decades after their own deaths when they feel certain that everyone at the Supreme Court associated with a particular case has long since passed away. Marshall, however, declared that his papers would become available after his own death, without any apparent concern that the contents of the papers might embarrass living justices still serving on the Court.

In the Marshall papers, Professor Dennis Dorin discovered a memorandum written by Justice Antonin Scalia in the *McCleskey* case. In the memorandum, Scalia indicated that he saw no problems with the findings from the Baldus study but that he was hesitant to provide any remedy for racial discrimination:

> I disagree with the argument that inferences that can be drawn from the Baldus study are weakened by the fact that each jury and each trial are unique, or by the large number of variables at issue. And I do not share the view, implicit in [Powell's draft opinion], that an effect of racial factors upon sentencing, if it could be shown by sufficiently strong statistical evidence, would require reversal. Since it is my view that the unconscious operation of irrational sympathies and antipathies, including racial, upon jury decisions and (hence) prosecutorial [ones] is real, acknowledged by the [cases] of this court and ineradicable, I cannot honestly say that all I need is more proof. I expect to write separately on these points, but not until I see the dissent.[6]

Scalia never wrote an opinion to explain his views. He merely provided the decisive fifth vote against McCleskey's claim without providing any explanation. Based on his memorandum, Scalia apparently agreed that the Baldus study demonstrated the existence of racial discrimination. Yet, because Scalia views racial discrimination in the criminal justice system as pervasive and incurable, he did not care to take any action to prevent such discrimination. In the words of Professor Dorin, Scalia "trivializ[ed] [discriminatory practices] by saying, in a single-paragraph memo, that they were merely an unavoidable and legally unassailable, part of life for African-Americans. . . . Apparently for Scalia, the capital punishment system's valuing of a white life significantly above a black one did not implicate any constitutional provisions."[7] In light of Scalia's memorandum, we need to ask ourselves an important question: How substantive is the right to equal protection if Supreme Court justices recognize the existence of racial discrimination but refuse to do anything to correct it because they believe such discrimination is inevitable?

In a dissenting opinion in *McCleskey*, Justice John Paul Stevens voiced his suspicion that the justices in the majority were afraid to acknowledge the pervasiveness of racial discrimination because they did not want to order Georgia and other states to stop sentencing people to death. In the words of Stevens,

> The Court's decision appears to be based on a fear that the acceptance of McCleskey's claim would sound the death knell for capital punishment in Georgia. If society were indeed forced to choose between a racially discriminatory death penalty (one that provides heightened protection against murder "for whites only") and no death penalty at all, the choice mandated by the Constitution would be plain (*McCleskey v. Kemp*, 1987).

The hypothesis presented by Stevens may explain Scalia's actions if Scalia places a higher value on permitting states to impose the death penalty than on making sure that criminal justice officials do not engage in racial discrimination. The problem with this perspective is that it makes the right to equal protection entirely symbolic and ineffective for those victims of racial discrimination whose rights are left unremedied in the interest of advancing a policy preference for preserving capital punishment.

Noncapital cases also can be affected by discretionary decisions based on racial bias that conflict with the purposes of the Equal Protection Clause. In these cases, victims of discrimination face problems demonstrating violations of the right to equal protection. In *United States v. Armstrong* (1996), African-American defendants charged with selling crack cocaine claimed that the prosecutor singled them out for prosecution because of their race. They presented **affidavits,** statements written under oath, by people asserting that all defendants prosecuted for crack cocaine in Los Angeles federal court were African-American despite the fact that many crack cocaine users in Los Angeles are white and that whites are prosecuted for crack cocaine in California state courts. In effect, the defendants asserted that they had **anecdotal evidence** that whites in Los Angeles were involved in crack cocaine but the U.S. Attorney engaged in discrimination by prosecuting only African-Americans in federal court. Anecdotal evidence is nonsystematic evidence based on observations by a few people. The defendants sought to gain access to records in the U.S. Attorney's office to verify the existence of racial discrimination in the prosecution of drug cases.

The issue was particularly important because federal law punishes crack cocaine offenses much more severely than powder cocaine offenses despite the fact that they are the same chemical substance. One gram of crack cocaine is treated as the equivalent of 100 grams of powder cocaine. The distribution of fifty grams of crack is punishable by the same mandatory minimum sentence of ten years in prison that applies to the distribution of 5,000 grams of powder cocaine.[8] Because African-Americans are prosecuted more frequently for crack cocaine offenses, they have been disproportionately affected by longer prison sentences. Indeed, Professor Michael Tonry's analysis of drug laws and their enforcement led to the conclusion that the federal government's emphasis on crack cocaine rather than powder cocaine represented an intentional scapegoating and targeting of minorities in American society:

> Given what we know about past periods of intolerance of drug use and their tendencies to scapegoat minority groups, and that disadvantaged urban blacks are the archetypal users of crack cocaine—and therefore are the principal possessors, sellers, and low-level distributors—anyone who knew the history of American drug policy could have foreseen that this war on drugs would target and mostly engage young disadvantaged members of minority groups as the enemy. And it has.[9]

If the Supreme Court will not permit the use of statistical evidence on racial disparities to demonstrate violations of equal protections, then defendants who believe that they are victims of racial discrimination must look for other evidence. Thus the *Armstrong* case represented an effort to gather concrete evidence of discrimination based on observations about racial disparities in cocaine prosecutions.

In the Court's *Armstrong* decision, Chief Justice Rehnquist rejected the defendants' request to obtain additional information. According to Rehnquist's opinion, the anecdotal evidence comprised of statements by a lawyer, a paralegal, and a drug counselor about the use of crack cocaine by whites and the prosecution's failure to pursue white defendants was not sufficient for the purposes of an equal protection claim. The Court's decision reinforced the apparent message that proof of an equal protection violation would require evidence of an explicitly racist statement by a criminal justice official. As indicated in the prior discussion of *McCleskey,* such evidence is unlikely to arise. Moreover, many instances of racial discrimination can occur without such evidence being produced. In a dissenting opinion, Justice Stevens noted that federal prosecutions and sentencing for crack cocaine raised concerns about unfair racial impacts in the criminal justice process:

> Finally, it is undisputed that the brunt of the elevated federal penalties falls heavily on blacks. While 65 percent of the persons who have used crack are white, in 1993 they represented only 4 percent of the federal offenders convicted of trafficking in crack. Eighty-eight percent of such defendants were black. . . . During the first eighteen months of full [sentencing] guideline implementation, the sentencing disparity between black and white defendants grew from preguideline levels: blacks on average received sentences over 40 percent longer than whites. . . . Those figures represent a major threat to the integrity of federal sentencing reform. . . . The extraordinary severity of the imposed penalties and the troubling racial patterns of enforcement give rise to a special concern about the fairness of charging practices for crack offenses.

Racial disparities are also evident in police decisions, especially with respect to choices about whom to stop and search. Data collected by the Washington State Patrol indicated that African-Americans, Hispanics, and Native Americans are two and one-half times as likely as whites to be forced to submit to a search during a traffic stop.[10] In San Diego, both African-Americans and Hispanics had a 10 percent chance of being searched during a traffic stop, but whites had only a 3 percent chance. Yet, contraband was found in about 13 percent of seraches of whites and African-Americans but only in 5 percent of searches of Hispanics.[11] Studies of police actions on highways in Illinois and Maryland found that minority group members were disproportionately stopped and searched. African-Americans and Hispanics sometimes constituted the majority of drivers searched although their demographic group comprised less than one-quarter of the drivers on the highway.[12] A study by the federal government's General Accounting Office found that African-American women were nine times more likely to be subjected to x-ray searches by U.S. Customs officers at international airports than were their white counterparts, even though African-American women were less than half as likely to be found carrying contraband as white women.[13] These studies and others indicate that many police officers use their discretion to stop and search racial minorities more than whites. These practices reflect, in part, the prevalence of **profiling** as part of the war on drugs. Officers look for certain characteristics that supposedly constitute typical patterns for people involved in the drug trade, such as traveling from Florida or driving below the speed limit to avoid attracting the attention of police. Unfortunately, many officers seem to have included race as an element of the profiles they use to determine whom to investigate. As a result, many African-American and Hispanic people feel as if the police stop and search them without any reasonable justification.

When police officers treat African-American and Hispanic people differently than they treat white people, they are denying those individuals their right to the equal protection of the law under the Fourteenth Amendment. Despite the apparent denial of equal protection, profiling and disproportionate searches aimed at minorities continue because it is so difficult to prove racial discrimination to the satisfaction of the Supreme Court. The Court has endorsed broad discretionary power for police officers to make traffic stops whenever they claim a violation occurred, no matter how minor that violation may be (*Whren v. United States,* 1995). The Court has rejected the use of statistics to prove violations of the right to equal protection, so individual drivers who are stopped must seek other evidence to establish the existence of discrimination. As indicated by the Court's decision in *Armstrong,* the Court is not inclined to let people who feel victimized by discriminatory actions hunt through criminal justice officials' records for evidence of biased policies and practices. Thus individual victims of unequal treatment are left hoping that the officer will say something biased in front of a witness in order to provide evidence for an equal protection claim. If unethical officers conduct an improper search, mistreat someone physically, or make an illegal arrest, the victim may file a civil rights lawsuit against the officers for violating his or her Fourth Amendment rights. However, there is little hope of successfully pursuing a similar lawsuit for an equal protection violation unless the courts eventually begin to accept statistical evidence for proof of racial discrimination in criminal justice.

Summary

The right to equal protection forbids the government from engaging in racial discrimination. If government agencies have formal policies that discriminate by race, such as rules for maintaining racial segregation in prisons, the courts will strike down those policies. However, if criminal justice officials engage in practices that produce racial disparities, the Court has made it very difficult for discrimination victims to prove violations of the right to equal protection. Practices that produce racial disparities stem from the broad discretionary authority possessed by criminal justice officials.

The Court rejected the use of statistics as evidence to demonstrate the existence of racial discrimination in the death penalty. Unfortunately, there are indications that this decision was based on some justices' concerns about preserving the death penalty rather than genuine attention to the issue of racial discrimination. The Supreme Court's requirement of providing clear proof of discrimination in each individual case in order to show a violation of equal protection and its continued endorsement of broad discretion for criminal justice actors effectively facilitate the continuation of racial disparities and discrimination in the justice system.

JURY DISCRIMINATION

Conventional Wisdom 34

The right to equal protection guarantees that racial discrimination will not be used to exclude people from participating in trials as jurors.

Like other decision makers in the criminal justice system, jurors bring their values, attitudes, and biases with them when they make decisions about the guilt of defendants. Wealthy criminal defendants and civil litigants can afford to hire jury consultants who analyze public opinion surveys and people's attitudes associated with certain demographic groups within a community in order to make recommendations about the types of people who are likely to be most sympathetic to a particular defendant or litigant. For many criminal defendants, it is desirable to have the jury include members of racial minority groups, young people, and less affluent people. Many of these people are more likely than white, middle-class suburbanites to have had negative encounters with the police. They may be less likely to automatically believe that all police officers tell the truth. In addition, their assessments of social circumstances may affect their interpretation of facts. To a wealthy person in the suburbs, the fact that a defendant left home in the morning with a knife in his pocket may provide evidence that the defendant planned to cause harm with that knife. By contrast, a less affluent person may see carrying a knife as normal, noncriminal behavior in a neighborhood in which people never know if they will need to defend themselves.[14] Thus the composition of the jury can be very important to a defendant's chances of having the decision makers understand and accept the defense attorney's explanation of the events that led to the arrest and prosecution.

Although Americans are accustomed to hearing the expression "a jury of one's peers," the Sixth Amendment does not contain that phrase. There is no guarantee for a defendant that the jury will be composed of his or her "peers," if that word is taken to mean individuals who share demographic characteristics (e.g., age, gender, race, social class, etc.) with the defendant. The Supreme Court's interpretations of the Sixth Amendment produced the conclusion that defendants are entitled to a jury drawn from a fair cross section of the community. They are not entitled to have a jury that represents the demographic composition of the community, but they are entitled to have the jurors drawn from a pool that reflects the community's composition. A jury could end up all white, all male, or otherwise demographically skewed and this would not violate the Constitution—as long as the jury was drawn from a pool of potential jurors that reflected the diversity (or lack thereof) in the community. Local courts face challenges in creating jury pools that represent the diversity in a community, especially when potential jurors are called from voting lists because poor urban dwellers and members of racial minority groups often register to vote at lower rates than middle-class, white suburbanites.

Jurors are selected for a trial through the *voir dire* process in which jurors are questioned about their potential biases that might affect their ability to make fair decisions. If a juror indicates a clear bias, then attorneys for either side can make a **challenge for cause** to ask the judge to excuse the potential juror. For example, if a juror was recently the victim of a robbery, a defense attorney may ask that the juror be excused from serving in a robbery trial because of concerns that the juror's recent experience would prevent him or her from listening to the evidence and making a decision with an open mind. Even more clearly, if a juror said "most crime is caused by Hispanic youths," the defense attorney for a Hispanic defendant would ask the judge to excuse the person from the jury for the clear expression of a biased belief. Both the prosecutor and the defense attorney can make an unlimited number of challenges for cause. If the judge agrees with the attorney's argument, then the juror is excused.

Jurors can also be excluded through **peremptory challenges.** Each attorney is given a specific number of peremptory challenges, which traditionally permitted the prosecutor and the defense attorney to use their discretion to exclude potential jurors without giving any reason. The attorneys use hunches and assumptions about the attitudes possessed by specific individuals and members of demographic groups in order to exclude jurors who they believe will be sympathetic to the opposing side. Peremptory challenges provide an opportunity for attorneys to attempt to manipulate the jury's composition in a manner favorable to their own case. It is through the use of peremptory challenges that prosecutors in some states often exclude African-American jurors in cases involving African-American defendants and Hispanic jurors in the cases of Hispanic defendants. Prosecutors want to win their cases, and some of them fear that jurors of the same ethnicity as the defendant will be sympathetic to the defendant's arguments.

When examining defendants' claims about racial discrimination in prosecutors' use of peremptory challenges during jury selection, the Court turned away from the Sixth Amendment right to a fair jury trial and instead focused on the Equal Protection Clause. The justices viewed the issue as concerning the right of citizens to have equal opportunities to participate in juries rather than the right of defendants to have any specific demographic composition on juries. The Court determined that race-based exclusions by prosecutors violate the equal protection rights of the juror being excluded rather than the Sixth Amendment rights of the defendant. During the 1980s and 1990s, the Court made a series of decisions reinforcing the importance of eliminating racial discrimination in jury selection. In *Batson v. Kentucky* (1986), the Court declared that an individual defendant could raise a constitutional claim if it appeared that prosecutors were systematically excluding people of a certain race. If such exclusions appeared to be happening, the defense attorney could point out this fact to the judge. If the judge agreed that there was an appearance of discrimination, then the prosecutor would be required to provide a nondiscriminatory justification for the exclusions.

Subsequently, the Supreme Court expanded the right to equal protection for potential jurors by limiting the ability of other attorneys to use racial discrimination in applying peremptory challenges during jury selection. In *Powers v. Ohio* (1991), the Court said that defendants can challenge the race-based exclusion of jurors from racial groups other than their own. Previously, many people believed that white defendants could not complain if African-Americans were excluded from their juries. However, since the right at issue concerns the rights of the potential jurors rather than the rights of the defendants, the Court opened the possibility of any defendant raising the issue of racial discrimination. The Court also barred attorneys in civil lawsuits from using racial discrimination in peremptory challenges (*Edmonson v. Leesville Concrete Co.*, 1991). In 1992, the Court further expanded the reach of the Equal Protection Clause by barring criminal defense attorneys from using race-based peremptory challenges (*Georgia v. McCollum*). The Court followed that decision by declaring that attorneys cannot exclude jurors based on their gender (*J. E. B. v. Alabama ex rel. T. B.*, 1994). The Court's flurry of decisions expanding equal protection rights for potential jurors was especially striking because it occurred during the Rehnquist Court era when the Court's dominant conservative majority tended to limit rather than expand constitutional rights related to both equal protection and criminal justice. In effect, the Court's decisions appeared to make a notably strong statement against racial discrimination in jury selection.

In 1995, the Court issued a decision that called into question its actual commitment to preventing racial discrimination in jury selection. The case raised the issue of what happens when a prosecutor appears to be excluding jurors based on race and, after the defense challenges the prosecutor's actions, the prosecutor provides a flimsy explanation for the exclusions. In other words, is it possible for an attorney to exclude jurors because of their race and gender through the use of peremptory challenges by using some other reason as a **pretext** for the exclusions? A pretext is a phony reason used to disguise someone's true motives. In *Purkett v. Elem* (1995), the Court examined a case in which a local prosecutor had been accused of systematically excluding African-

Americans from a jury in the case of an African-American defendant. When the trial judge asked the prosecutor to provide a nonracial reason for the exclusions, the prosecutor said the following:

> I struck [juror] number twenty-two because of his long hair. He had long curly hair. He had the longest hair of anybody on the panel by far. He appeared to not be a good juror for that fact, the fact that he had long hair hanging down shoulder length, curly, unkempt hair. Also, he had a mustache and a goatee type beard. Those are the only two people on the jury . . . with any facial hair. . . . And I don't like the way they looked, with the way the hair is cut, both of them. And the mustaches and the beards look suspicious to me.[15]

The trial judge accepted the prosecutor's reasons as permissible and rejected the defendant's claim that the justification merely masked improper racial discrimination. The U.S. Court of Appeals for the Eighth Circuit, however, reversed the trial court. According to the Court of Appeals, the prosecutor's reasons must somehow relate to the juror's ability to decide the case fairly and cannot be based merely on the prosecutor's preferences about the juror's choices regarding grooming or fashion. According to the appellate court,

> [W]here the prosecution strikes a prospective juror who is a member of the defendant's racial group, solely on the basis of factors which are facially irrelevant to the question of whether that person is qualified to serve as a juror in the particular case, the prosecution must at least articulate some plausible race-neutral reason for believing those factors will somehow affect the juror's ability to perform his or her duties as a juror. In the present case, the prosecutor's comments, "I don't like the way [he] look[s], with the way the hair is cut. . . . And the mustach[e] and the bear[d] look suspicious to me," do not constitute such legitimate race-neutral reasons for striking juror 22.[16]

When the case reached the Supreme Court, the high court reversed the decision by the Court of Appeals. The Court declared that the prosecutor provided a race-neutral justification that satisfies the requirements of the Equal Protection Clause. In its opinion, the Court also acknowledged that attorneys can put forward "implausible," "fantastic," "silly," and "superstitious" reasons for exclusions that appear to be based on race and the trial judge is permitted to accept such reasons as appropriate justifications that do not violate the right to equal protection. In dissent, Justice Stevens, joined by Justice Stephen Breyer, complained about the Court's acceptance of flimsy, irrational justifications for exclusions and argued that "It is not too much to ask that a prosecutor's explanation for his strikes be race neutral, reasonably specific, and trial related. Nothing less will serve to rebut the inference of race-based discrimination. . . ."

Summary

Is the equal protection right against race and gender discrimination in jury selection a substantive right or merely a symbolic slogan? The answer to that question depends on the actions of trial judges who must evaluate the use of

*peremptory challenges in each case. The Supreme Court made lofty state-
ments against discrimination in a series of cases concerning peremptory
challenges running from* Batson v. Kentucky *(1986) through* Georgia v.
McCollum *(1992) and* J. E. B. v. Alabama *ex rel.* T.B. *(1994). However,*
Purkett v. Elem *(1995) revealed that attorneys are permitted to discriminate
by race and gender in jury selection as long as they do not admit what they
are doing and they persuade the trial judge to accept their purportedly non-
racial- (or nongender-) based reason for systematic exclusion of members of
a particular demographic group. As one critic remarked, "*Batson *and [the
later peremptory challenge cases] have proven less an obstacle to discrimination than a road map to it. Parties now have a good idea of what they can
and cannot get away with in eliminating jurors and adjust their means to suit
their desired end."*[17] *Because the Supreme Court acknowledged that trial
judges are permitted to accept pretextual justifications that are implausible,
fantastic, silly, or superstitious, there is no guarantee that these judges will
prevent discrimination in jury selection, even when presented with the flim-
siest of excuses for race- and gender-based exclusions. In jury selection, the
right to equal protection rests entirely on the trial judge's skepticism about
excuses and determination to prevent discrimination from occurring. The
Supreme Court has done little to ensure that trial judges will actively guard
against discrimination and, in fact, has enabled them to turn a blind eye to
equal protection violations if they so choose.*

DUE PROCESS

Conventional Wisdom 35

*The right to due process guarantees that people will have access to the
courts in order to seek judicial protection of their constitutional rights.*

Constitutional rights mean very little if people have no way to seek protection of
those rights. Under the American system of government, judges bear a special
responsibility for interpreting the Constitution and protecting constitutional
rights. Although all public officials swear an oath to uphold the Constitution,
elected officials in the legislative and executive branches are not positioned to
bear primary responsibilities for the protection of rights. The democratic governing system is structured to encourage elected officials to respond to the
desires of the majority of voters. Presumably, legislators, governors, and presidents reflect the will of the majority in formulating legislation and public policy.
This is true both because the elected candidates' values and policy preferences
were apparently favored by the voters and because elected officials must please
the voters in order to gain reelection. The majoritarian pressures to which

elected officials respond are often incompatible with the protection of rights for people, such as criminal defendants and convicted offenders, who are despised by the majority of citizens. Similarly, political pressures and popular values often lead elected officials to be insensitive to other people who lack political power, such as small religious groups and racial minorities.

By contrast, judges are supposed to accept a special responsibility to uphold the Constitution, even if it requires making unpopular decisions. Early in the twentieth century, judicial decisions supporting equal protection for African-Americans were not necessarily popular with the majority of society, namely whites who accepted and benefited from racial discrimination that limited opportunities for and competition from African-Americans in employment, education, housing, and other sectors of American society. Similarly, judicial decisions supporting rights for criminal defendants are often unpopular when public sentiment favors being as tough as possible on those accused of being involved in crimes. The protection of constitutional rights can be difficult for some elected state judges because they must come up for reelection and risk being removed from office by the public if they make unpopular decisions, especially decisions supporting rights for criminal defendants. Fears about the ability of elected judges to be courageous and independent are enhanced when judges are removed from office because of decisions supporting constitutional rights. For example, a justice on the Tennessee Supreme Court was removed by voters for a single vote she cast in a death penalty case that ordered a new trial because of improper procedures during the original trial. Political opponents of the judge mounted a publicity campaign portraying the judge as favoring criminals and unsympathetic to crime victims. Justices on the California Supreme Court had previously lost their seats based on similar campaigns focused on their decisions in death penalty cases. Such events have the potential to deter state judges from taking a strong stand to protect rights in the criminal justice process.[18]

Unlike elected state judges, however, federal judges enjoy structural protections to permit them to make courageous, independent decisions in support of constitutional rights. After they have been appointed by the president and confirmed by a vote of the U.S. Senate, according to Article III of the Constitution, federal judges serve "during good Behaviour," which can effectively mean for life as long as they do not commit any crimes or serious violations of ethical rules that would warrant removal through impeachment. Impeachment is a long, cumbersome process that requires a trial and vote in Congress, so federal judges generally have secure tenure that permits them to make decisions that reflect their views about the proper course of action, even if that action is unpopular with elected officials and the public. Thus, in the criminal justice process, the *habeas corpus* process provides a potentially important vehicle for the protection of criminal defendants' constitutional rights because it permits people convicted in state courts to ask life-tenured federal judges to review alleged violations of the U.S. Constitution that occurred during the investigation and prosecution of their cases. If state trial and appellate judges, who are often elected to office and face periodic reelection campaigns, do not remedy violations of constitutional rights, then there is the possibility that federal judges can take remedial action in the *habeas corpus* process. Federal judges can play an additional role in protecting constitutional rights, because federal statutes permit people to file civil rights lawsuits against criminal justice officials in federal court when those officials' actions allegedly violate individuals' rights. None of these mechanisms for gaining judicial protection of rights mean much, however, if people lack opportunities to bring their constitutional claims to court. In other words, if the Supreme Court declares that a right exists but there is no procedure that permits people to have a judge examine alleged violations of that right, then the right is symbolic because it is unenforceable and can be readily ignored or violated by criminal justice officials.

The right to due process in the Fourteenth Amendment provides a mechanism to ensure that procedures exist to permit people to seek protection of and remedies for their constitutional rights. Historically, the right to due process has served as a "catch-all" right used by Supreme Court justices to provide a constitutional source for legal protections that are not evident in the words of the Bill of Rights. For example, early in the twentieth century, the Supreme Court used the right to due process to create a right to economic liberty that invalidated minimum wage and working condition laws in order to permit people to work for less money and in worse conditions than the minimum standards established by legislatures (*Lochner v. New York*, 1905). Although these early decisions about a right to economic liberty were subsequently overturned, the Supreme Court continued to use the Due Process Clause to create other kinds of rights. For example, the Court has also used the right to due process as the source of privacy-related rights, such as the right of competent adults to decline needed medical treatment (*Cruzan v. Missouri*, 1990). The use of the Due Process Clause to create these substantive rights is very controversial. However, there is a broad consensus that the right to due process appropriately guarantees a right to fair procedures before a person is deprived of rights or liberty. The Supreme Court interprets and applies the Due Process Clause, for example, when considering what procedures corrections officials must follow before imposing punishment on prisoners who violate institutional rules (*Wolff v. McDonnell*, 1974). Thus claimants and judges look to the right to due process when considering questions about the availability of proper procedures to protect constitutional rights.

Incarcerated offenders are in an especially vulnerable position with respect to the protection of their constitutional rights. These Americans possess limited rights, such as a limited right to practice their religions and the right to be free from cruel and unusual punishments, such as physical abuse or prison conditions that fall below humane standards for human habitability.

However, because these people are held within secure institutions in which their actions are closely controlled, it would be easy to cut them off from the outside world and violate their rights behind prison walls that block the view of the public and judges. Prisoners only have access to telephones, mail, and even paper and pencils because prison officials provide them with access. And prison officials provide this access, in part, because federal judges have ordered them to do so as a component of the right to due process. If prison officials decided to lock everyone in cells twenty-four hours each day and deny them food and medical care, the prisoners would have no ability to prevent that from happening without the assistance of people outside the prison. Moreover, while locked in their cells they would have no way to contact people outside the prison in order to make their situation known and seek help. Until the 1960s, prison officials could often do whatever they wanted to prisoners in the secrecy of the enclosed prison walls. In some prisons, this led to physical and psychological abuse.[19] However, judges began to take a greater interest in protecting the rights of prisoners, especially after the Supreme Court decided in 1964 that prisoners could file civil rights lawsuits in federal courts in order to protect their limited constitutional rights (*Cooper v. Pate*). If prisoners did not have the means to file such lawsuits, then judges would have no opportunity to scrutinize prison practices and conditions in order to ensure that constitutional rights are being respected. Thus the right to due process is especially important in the context of corrections.

Even before federal courts began to actively define the constitutional rights of prisoners in the 1960s and 1970s, the Supreme Court recognized that prisoners must have access to the courts in order to protect their rights. In *Ex parte Hull* (1941), the Supreme Court invalidated a Michigan regulation that permitted prison officials to review and reject prisoners' *habeas corpus* petitions and thereby prevent them from being mailed to the federal court. If corrections officials actually possessed such a power, then prisoners might have no opportunity to challenge alleged violations of constitutional rights that occurred in their trials. The Court's decision that prisoners possess the right to mail legal documents to the courthouse without interference from prison officials established prisoners' right of access to the courts. In its words, the Constitution does not provide any right of access to the courts. However, the justices see the existence of such a right as logical and necessary in light of the importance of protecting the other rights, such as the protection against cruel and unusual punishments, that are expressed in the Eighth Amendment and elsewhere. Even the Court's strongest opponent of the recognition of constitutional rights for prisoners, Justice Clarence Thomas, recognizes a right of access to the courts based on the Due Process Clause. According to Thomas, "In the end, I agree that the Constitution affords prisoners what can be termed a right of access to the courts. That right, rooted in the Due Process Clause and the principle articulated in *Ex parte Hull,* is a right to not be arbitrarily prevented from lodging a claimed violation of a federal right in a federal court" (*Lewis v. Casey*, 1996). Thomas sees the right of access for prisoners as limited to a right to not be prevented from mailing letters and documents to the federal courts. In other words, in Thomas's eyes, the right is fulfilled if there is a mail slot at the prison into which prisoners can place envelopes to be mailed to the court. By contrast, other justices see a broader right of access that obligates prison officials to provide paper, pencils, stamps, and law libraries or legal assistance to enable prisoners to prepare necessary documents for filing cases in court (*Bounds v. Smith*, 1977).

Convicted offenders primarily file three types of legal actions.[20] The first type of action is an **appeal.** Most appeals proceed through the higher levels of state court systems; only people convicted of crimes in federal courts can appeal to the U.S. courts of appeals. Appeals are used to challenge alleged errors, including violations of constitutional rights, that occurred during the prosecution and trial of a case. In most states, appeals are heard by elected judges or judges removable through retention election processes. Thus concerns about the judges' independence and willingness to make controversial decisions favoring the rights of criminal defendants loom largest in the state appeals process.

The second type of action is a *habeas corpus* petition, which, in the federal process, is used exclusively to seek examination of alleged violations of constitutional rights and which can move a state case into federal court for review by federal judges. States may have their own *habeas corpus* processes in state court that permit the presentation of a broader array of issues. The third type of action is a civil rights lawsuit seeking remedies for alleged violations of constitutional rights in the corrections system.

Despite their lack of training in law, offenders must attempt to prepare their own cases for most of these post-conviction actions. The Sixth Amendment provides a right to counsel only for the first appeal of right (*Douglas v. California*, 1963). A first appeal of right exists when a state statute provides an entitlement to appeal to the intermediate appellate court. All other post-conviction actions must be undertaken by the offender alone unless he or she has enough money to hire an attorney, an attorney volunteers to take the case, or state law provides an attorney—usually only for appeals rather than the other two types of actions.

An important point to remember is that there is no constitutional right to file any of the three types of post-conviction actions except for federal *habeas corpus* petitions, which are mentioned in the Constitution as a traditional legal action to challenge allegedly unlawful deprivations of liberty. Yet the procedures for *habeas corpus* are governed by statutes. If the statutory procedures are not followed, a *habeas* petition will be dismissed. There is not even a constitutional right to appeal. Appeals and civil rights lawsuits are governed by statutes. As the Supreme Court stated in *Abney v. United States* (1977), "The right to appeal, as we presently know it in criminal cases, is purely a creature of statute." If there were no state and federal statutes authorizing appeals, the government could bar any appeals and cases would become final at the conclusion of trials without any certain mechanisms for correcting errors other than constitutional rights violations that could be presented in a *habeas corpus* petition. The Constitution does not explicitly require any mechanism to correct trial judges' errors in evidentiary rulings, misapplications of criminal statutes, and other common mistakes. Most Americans do not realize that criminal cases could be terminated immediately and permanently after an error-filled trial without any constitutional requirement that further procedures be available to make sure that mistakes are not permitted to stand. Hypothetically, the Supreme Court could interpret the right to due process to provide such a requirement, but it has not done so.

People cannot make any assertions that they want in the three types of post-conviction actions. There are rules about what kinds of claims can be considered by courts for each type of action. If improper claims are presented, then the actions are dismissed. For example, what if a person is convicted of a crime and then files an unsuccessful appeal? Subsequently, new evidence is discovered that might demonstrate that the person is actually innocent of the crime for which he or she was convicted. A civil rights lawsuit is not useful for these purposes, because this action cannot be used to gain an offender's freedom. It can only be used to obtain money or a court order to correct prison conditions when a constitutional rights violation is proven. A *habeas corpus* action cannot be filed unless the prisoner can show that a constitutional right was violated during the trial of the case. If the newly discovered evidence was not hidden by the prosecutor or otherwise improperly kept out of the court, then there is no constitutional right violated. What if a new kind of DNA test has been developed that was not available at the time of trial? Should the right to due process guarantee that new evidence can be presented in court? Currently, the Supreme Court has not interpreted the Due Process Clause to provide such an entitlement. Instead, prosecutors can resist requests to retest old evidence and defense attorneys must beg judges to use their discretion to permit new tests and to consider the new evidence in court.

When Hollywood actor Harrison Ford starred in the hit film *The Fugitive*, legal commentators noted that the public does not realize that their assumptions about the justice process as portrayed in the film clash with the reality of post-conviction remedies—or the lack thereof. In the film, which was based on an old television series, a doctor is wrongly convicted for the murder of his wife. He escapes from custody and hunts for the real killers. In the film version, Ford finds the real killers and prevails in his battle with them. In real life, however, *habeas corpus* procedures would deny Ford any right to have a new trial, even after he found the real killers. His trial had reached a mistaken result, but there had been no procedural errors or rights violations that caused the erroneous verdict. A jury examined circumstantial evidence and rendered a guilty verdict. Thus his right to a fair trial was fulfilled. Because the real killers never confessed, Ford did not even have any compelling new evidence that might be the basis for asking a judge to re-open the case. Such evidence would not give him the right to have the case re-opened anyway. Although moviegoers came away from the film with the belief that an innocent man had triumphed over the legal system's errors to rid the world of his wife's killers, a real case with the same facts might lead the hero to be sent back to prison to serve his murder sentence *plus* face additional years of confinement for being charged with the crime of escaping from custody.[21]

In the *habeas corpus* process, convicted offenders face significant barriers to success in attempting to present claims about constitutional rights violations. Not only must prisoners attempt to prepare *habeas corpus* petitions themselves, despite their lack of training in law, they must also meet strict time limits and file all of their claims in one petition. The Supreme Court imposed limitations on prisoners' *habeas* petitions, such as the dismissal of subsequent petitions if all claims were not filed in the first petition, even if the second petition presents a newly discovered rights violation that was hidden from the defense at trial by prosecutor and the police (*McCleskey v. Zant*, 1991). The Court also ordered the dismissal of *habeas corpus* petitions if offenders' attorneys made mistakes during state appeals processes, such as filing an appeal late, that led the appeal to be dismissed (*Coleman v. Thompson*, 1991). The Court has also acknowledged that constitutional rights violations have occurred but refused to remedy them through the *habeas corpus* process because the justices did not believe that constitutional law was sufficiently clear at the time of the trial so that the trial judges should have known that the police or prosecutor actions violated the defendant's rights (*Butler v. McKellar*, 1990). The Court's focus is not on the question of whether a right was violated. Instead, the Court focuses on what judges should have known at the time of trial. Congress added further restrictions on the *habeas* process when it enacted the **Antiterrorism and Effective Death Penalty Act of 1996.** As a result of these developments, constitutional rights violations can exist and go unremedied because convicted offenders cannot make effective use of the *habeas corpus* process. Instead of treating procedural impediments in the *habeas corpus* process as a due process problem that interferes with the fulfillment of constitutional rights, the Supreme Court has been an active participant in the creation of new barriers to the protection of constitutional rights. Apparently, a majority of justices would rather reduce the number of *habeas* cases presented to federal courts than make sure that constitutional rights are protected in the criminal justice process.[22] If offenders in state courts do not have adequate access to the federal *habeas corpus* process, then the final decisions on the existence of federal constitutional rights violations are frequently made by elected judges in the *state* appeals process rather than by life-tenured, independent federal judges in the *habeas corpus* process.

As discussed in Chapter 8, convicted offenders' opportunities to use civil rights lawsuits to remedy violations of constitutional rights in corrections settings were limited by the enactment of the Prison Litigation Reform Act of 1996.[23] The congressional legislation limited the authority of federal judges to order remedies for constitutional violations in prison conditions. The act also barred prisoners from seeking waiver of filing fees after three previously filed claims had been dismissed as frivolous, malicious, or failing to state a cause of action. Because prisoners have no right to counsel for these cases and must prepare them on their own, it is easy for them to file petitions that fail to properly state a claim or that courts dismiss as frivolous, even when there is a legitimate issue that is simply being raised ineffectively by an uneducated prisoner. Indeed, federal judges and their assistants may dismiss poorly written prisoner filings without looking at them closely enough to determine whether a legitimate constitutional rights issue is detectable in the statement of the claim.[24] Such statutory barriers to the protection of prisoners' constitutional rights could plausibly deserve attention under the Supreme Court's authority to interpret the right to due process, yet the majority of justices accept the restrictions imposed by the Prison Litigation Reform Act.

Summary

Constitutional rights mean very little if adequate procedures are not available to remedy violations of those rights. Although the Supreme Court could apply the right to due process to ensure that such procedures are available, the Court has not done so. There is no constitutional right to appeal. Moreover, there is no constitutional right to have evidence newly discovered after a trial considered by a court. It is possible for innocent prisoners to languish in prison as prosecutors resist the testing and examination of new evidence and judges decline to reopen cases. Convicted offenders have a right of access to the courts, but the existence of this right is not likely to protect many of their other constitutional rights because, other than in first appeals by statutory right, they must attempt to prepare other appeals, habeas corpus petitions, and civil rights lawsuits on their own. In the habeas corpus process, the Supreme Court has joined with Congress to create barriers to the successful presentation of constitutional claims. The Court has placed a priority on limiting the number of habeas corpus petitions rather than seeking to ensure that all constitutional rights violations are identified and remedied. Similarly, the Court has accepted congressional legislation that limits convicted offenders' ability to file civil rights lawsuits and federal judges' authority to remedy violations found through such lawsuits. Thus constitutional rights violations can exist, yet the available post-conviction processes do not provide realistic opportunities to bring constitutional claims into court in order to seek remedies. This situation seems to demonstrate a lack of due process necessary for the vindication of constitutional rights, but the Supreme Court shows no inclination to interpret the Due Process Clause in ways that would increase the likelihood that constitutional rights in criminal justice will be protected.

CONCLUSION

The right to equal protection has been weakened considerably by the pervasive use of discretion by criminal justice officials. Racial profiling in police search and seizure practices, prosecutors' decisions about when to seek the death penalty, and other decision-making contexts can be affected by racial biases. The Supreme Court has ruled against formal policies that mandate racial discrimination, but the Court has made it very difficult for individuals to prove that discretionary decisions violate the right to equal protection. The Court's refusal to accept statistical evidence of racial discrimination in death penalty sentencing, even though such evidence is used in the less important context of employment discrimination, provides one of the clearest examples of the Court's failure to vigorously enforce equal protection, especially in light of Justice Scalia's memorandum that accepts racial discrimination in criminal justice as inevitable and incurable.

The Supreme Court made lofty statements prohibiting racial discrimination in jury selection in a series of cases in the 1980s and early 1990s. However, as demonstrated by the decision in *Purkett v. Elem* (1995), the majority of justices are actually willing to accept pretextual excuses that are silly and implausible when attorneys want to discriminate by using race or gender in peremptory challenges. If the attorney is willing to lie or provide flimsy excuses for the systematic exclusion of relevant demographic groups (i.e., racial groups, women, or men), trial judges are permitted to accept such excuses despite the adverse impact on the equal protection rights of potential jurors. The *Purkett* case revealed the Court's equal protection decisions on peremptory challenges to be less substantive than they initially appeared to be.

Americans who are drawn into the criminal justice system and convicted of crimes can have no confidence that available post-conviction procedures will correct errors that occurred in their trials and remedy violations of their constitutional rights. There is no constitutional right to appeal. Beyond the first appeal of statutory right, convicted offenders are not entitled to assistance from an attorney. Unless a state chooses to provide legal assistance for convicted offenders, the offenders must prepare legal actions for themselves, even if they have little understanding of law or the rules for filing appeals, *habeas corpus* petitions, and civil rights lawsuits. The Supreme Court contributed to the creation of barriers in the *habeas corpus* process rather than using its power to interpret the Due Process Clause to make sure that constitutional rights will be vindicated. Similarly, the Court has accepted legislative restrictions on prisoners' civil rights lawsuits that ensure that many constitutional rights violations will go unremedied. The Court has not interpreted the right to due process in ways that will enhance the justice system's ability to protect constitutional rights. Thus the criminal justice process provides fewer realistic possibilities for correcting errors and protecting rights than most people realize.

CONSTITUTIONAL RIGHTS AND THE WAR ON TERRORISM

chapter 10

Americans speak of the Constitution as the source and embodiment of fundamental principles that guide the government and define individuals' protected legal rights. When Americans debate the appropriate powers of various governmental branches or the meaning of the Bill of Rights' provisions, they do not purport to seek a redefinition of the governing system and its principles. People rarely say, "Let's write a new Constitution because we need to redesign our government." Instead, their debates present arguments about the Constitution's proper meaning. Nearly everyone agrees that the Constitution is an impressive and extremely important document. They merely disagree about how the individual provisions of the Constitution ought to be interpreted.

State judges, local prosecutors, legislators, presidential candidates, and other elected officials, no matter what their political party affiliation or policy positions, frequently campaign on a pledge to "defend the Constitution" and, indeed, they swear a formal oath to defend the Constitution if they are elected to office. A similar oath is taken by military personnel, law enforcement officers, lawyers, federal government employees, and others who make decisions about and implement governmental policies. Different people see alternate visions of congressional power, judicial authority, and legal rights within the nation's foundational document, but they all speak reverentially about their basic desire to see the Constitution interpreted and applied in accordance with its fundamental principles and purposes.

Americans' reverence for the Constitution is learned at an early age. Schoolchildren are taught to value the freedom and democracy provided by the constitutional governing system and to contrast their rights with the deprivations of liberty experienced by people in many other countries. The Declaration of Independence, the Constitution, and the Bill of Rights are identified as the sources of Americans' freedom. As they become older, people in the United States receive consistent messages from schooling, books, news reports, television shows, and government officials' statements that they have the "best" governing system in the world. As a result, Americans see the Constitution as an essential

193

element of their treasured "way of life" and they consistently express the desire to protect and defend their foundational document.

In the preceding chapters, we have seen many examples of situations in which provisions of the Constitution are arguably unfulfilled, misinterpreted, or misapplied. Why don't Americans mount angry protests against court decisions, governmental inaction, and other factors that diminish the fulfillment of constitutional rights? The answer is that sometimes they do—at least those of them who are sufficiently angry and who interpret the Constitution in a manner that leads them to identify the existence of an important failure to protect and implement rights. Protest marches concerning abortion, affirmative action, and other rights-related issues provide examples. Other people do not protest. Sometimes it is because they lack awareness about deficiencies in the fulfillment of constitutional principles. Alternatively, their recognition of flaws in the system may make them feel helpless or otherwise resigned to the necessity of tolerating imperfections and even injustice. Even if they are aware and concerned, they may not feel strongly enough about the issue to voice their concerns. An additional factor in the lack of political mobilization and backlash over rights issues is the fact that Americans do not share a consensus about the meaning of constitutional provisions. Thus the mobilized constituency for any specific rights deprivation includes only a segment of society. For example, some Americans believe that *Miranda* rights are an essential element of the Fifth Amendment but other Americans do not share that belief. A Supreme Court decision that changes the meaning of *Miranda* rights would clash with the constitutional vision of only one segment of American society. Similarly, some Americans believe that the Constitution should protect prisoners' constitutional rights, but others do not share this belief. Changes in prisoners' rights would be noticed by and objectionable to only a portion of society.

If we acknowledge and set aside a recognition of Americans' myriad disagreements about specific provisions of the Constitution, is it possible to identify any understandings or beliefs about the revered document that reflect a national consensus? Looking at the Constitution with a broader view, it is not difficult to express general statements that reflect views of Americans across the political spectrum. These statements reflect the shared understandings of and reverence for the Constitution that keep the country united, even during periods in which there are significant disagreements about constitutional interpretation and the most desirable policy options for the nation to pursue:

> "The Bill of Rights provides guaranteed rights for individuals" *[even if we disagree about the exact number, nature, and scope of those rights].*
>
> "The provisions of the Constitution are superior to and cannot be violated or nullified by other forms of law (e.g., legislatures' statutes) or by government officials' discretionary decisions" *[even if we disagree about the precise meaning of each constitutional provision].*

"One fundamental purpose of the Constitution is to limit the authority of governmental officials and prevent broad, uncontrolled assertions of governmental power" *[even if we disagree about exactly how much authority is properly possessed by each branch of government and each official within those branches].*

Times of national crisis can call into question whether these shared foundational principles always guide the country's actions. During World War II, for example, the government detained U.S. citizens of Japanese ancestry and moved them from the West Coast to barbed-wire-enclosed camps in Utah, Wyoming, Arizona, and other inland locations. The policy stemmed from fears that these Americans would engage in espionage or provide other wartime assistance to their ancestors' country of origin. Entire families were removed from their homes and they often lost their property, businesses, and careers in the process. Sometimes children were separated from their parents for long periods of time. In retrospect, this episode is viewed as an especially shameful violation of constitutional principles. Innocent people were deprived of their liberty and property without any proof of wrongdoing. Indeed, the harmful and improper nature of the government's actions was clearly acknowledged several decades later when Congress authorized compensation payments for people victimized by this policy. Despite widespread agreement that wartime fears led to the victimization of a specific ethnic group in violation of their constitutional rights, one can argue that this tragic episode did not reflect a complete rejection of the foundational principles that reflect Americans' shared understandings and beliefs about the Constitution. First, several Japanese-Americans were able to file legal actions challenging the basis of their confinement and, although the Supreme Court initially ruled against them, their ability to litigate reflected the existence of one element of rights: the right of access to the courts (at least for some detainees). Second, the Supreme Court's consideration of the constitutionality of the governmental policy indicated that other laws and policies are subordinate to and must not violate constitutional law. And, third, the threat that the judiciary would invalidate the executive branch's actions in detaining the Japanese-Americans reflected the constitutional principle of limitations on governmental authority and power. In sum, the Supreme Court's interpretation of the Constitution effectively reinforced the Japanese-Americans' victimization but the Court's actions in considering the cases demonstrated that the Constitution's underlying principles were still operating—albeit in a tragically flawed manner.

For contemporary Americans, airline hijackers' shocking suicidal attacks on the World Trade Center and the Pentagon on September 11, 2001, renewed questions about the fulfillment of constitutional principles during a period of national crisis. The government responded with actions to protect domestic security against terrorism as well as military initiatives in Afghanistan and elsewhere.

These actions have affected the nature and fulfillment of constitutional rights. Moreover, unlike the World War II–era example involving Japanese-Americans, the contemporary war on terrorism includes governmental actions that not only diminish rights and, for some individuals, deny their existence but also block access to judicial processes that are normally available to determine whether a excessive assertion of governmental power has deprived people of their rights.

RIGHTS WITHIN AMERICAN JURISDICTIONS

Conventional Wisdom 36

The Constitution embodies fundamental principles that apply to limit governmental authority and protect rights wherever the American government controls a jurisdiction and imposes the rules that govern people's behavior within that jurisdiction.

If the principles of the Constitution provide the fundamental rules for the operation of American government, shouldn't they guide the government in all of its actions? We take it for granted that the Constitution will apply to the government's operations and treatment of individuals in Maine, Mississippi, and the other states within the country's boundaries. But what about actions by the American government in other countries of the world? The Supreme Court has said that the Bill of Rights and other constitutional provisions affecting governmental authority and individual rights do not apply outside of the United States. In *United States v. Verdugo-Urquidez* (1990), American agents from the U.S. Drug Enforcement Agency, assisted by Mexican police, conducted warrantless searches of homes in Mexico owned by a Mexican citizen who had been arrested and turned over to U.S. officials a few days earlier. The U.S. Supreme Court said that Fourth Amendment protections, and presumably the protections of other provisions of the Bill of Rights, are reserved for the "class of persons who are part of [our] national community or who have otherwise developed sufficient connection with this community to be considered part of that community." The decision seemed to clearly limit the reach of constitutional rights and give American law enforcement officials significant flexible authority to undertake intrusive and coercive actions in foreign countries, especially when those activities affect people who are not U.S. citizens.[1]

After the hijackers' attacks on New York and Washington in 2001, the U.S. government sent military forces to fight the Taliban leaders who ruled Afghanistan and harbored top officials of the Al Qaeda organization that was responsible for the September 11th attacks. This military action effectively overthrew the government of Afghanistan and sent Al Qaeda members into hiding. During the military action, American troops captured Taliban and Al Qaeda fighters as well as other people mistakenly thought to be fighters from these groups. If the United States treated them as "prisoners of war," these detainees would have been entitled to specific rights under the **Geneva Conventions,** treaties concerning the conduct of war that the United States and most other countries agreed to obey. If the United States treated them as people who had committed "crimes" within Afghanistan, they would need to be placed in the custody of law enforcement officials in that country and dealt with through the laws of Afghanistan. If the United States treated them as people who had violated American criminal laws, then they would be entitled to constitutional rights during their prosecution in American courts. Thus the classification and location of the detainees served to define which laws applied to them and which rights they possessed.

In order to avoid providing selected prisoners with any rights at all, the United States labeled them as **unlawful combatants**—people fighting against the United States who are not members of a recognized country's armed forces (otherwise they would be "prisoners of war" and entitled to the protections of the Geneva Conventions).[2] Moreover, the government moved 640 prisoners, including citizens from forty-two different countries, to a U.S. Navy base at Guantanamo Bay, Cuba. Thus the prisoners were outside the national boundaries in which the Constitution applies, even though they were located in territory (i.e., a U.S. Navy base) completely controlled by the United States and its rules. In effect, the U.S. government moved the detainees and created a new classification in order to avoid any formal limitations on its power to detain indefinitely; to interrogate; and to deny contact with family members, lawyers, or officials from other governments. The classification and location were chosen in order to deny these individuals any legal rights under the U.S. Constitution or other sources of law.

In their restrictive confinement, the detainees are isolated in individual cells and permitted out of the cells only twice each week for fifteen minutes in order to shower and exercise. In the restrictive environment with no prospect for release or legal processing, there have been an extraordinarily high number of suicide attempts.[3] By its own choice, the United States permitted inspections by the International Red Cross to prove that the prisoners were being fed and housed in habitable conditions, but the government was not obligated to do so since it claimed that no laws or rules from the U.S. Constitution, the Geneva Conventions, the United Nations, or from international treaties governed its treatment of the prisoners. Because the prisoners include citizens from forty-two different countries, the United States faced criticism from a number of countries, including allies such as Great Britain and Australia, for taking actions calculated to deny the applicability of legal restraints on its actions and to prevent the individuals from having legal rights.

President George W. Bush issued an order in November 2001 specifying that non–U.S. citizens who are members of Al Qaeda or who threaten the United States may face trials before military tribunals. The definition of those

who threaten the United States is written quite broadly with the obvious intention of giving the government great flexibility in selecting people for prosecution in these tribunals. It includes noncitizens who have "engaged in, aided, or
abetted, or conspired to commit acts of international terrorism, or acts in
preparation therefor, that have caused, threaten to cause, or have as their aim
to cause injury to or adverse effects on the United States."[4] The rules for these
tribunals were developed by American military officials and include no opportunity to appeal to civilian courts. By contrast, under international law, captured soldiers should have the opportunity to appeal to American civilian
courts because American soldiers tried in military courts enjoy that right.[5]
However, because the United States refuses to treat these fighters captured in
battle as "soldiers," they do not benefit from any legal rights. If and when some
of these detainees are placed on trial in military tribunals, they will only benefit from limited procedural rights specifically designed and granted for them
by the American military.

Specific aspects of Americans' treatment of their foreign prisoners raised
concern and criticism at home and abroad. In 2003, military officials admitted
that several of the detainees at Guantanamo Bay are juveniles between the
ages of thirteen and fifteen. Although a U.S. Army spokesman said that they
were being held in separate facilities and given extra mental health counsel-
ing, they have not been allowed to speak with an attorney or been informed of
any charges against them. Like the other detainees, they face the possibility of
indefinite detention without ever being charged with a crime.[6] International
pressure and the discovery that some detainees had no involvement with terrorism led to the release of twenty-two individuals. At least one of the juveniles is expected to be released during 2003 on a similar basis.[7] The release of
prisoners who had spent many months in solitary cells at the naval base in
Cuba was based on discretionary decisions of the American government and
not attributable to any laws or legal rights.

American interrogation techniques applied to captives in Afghanistan and
elsewhere have also drawn criticism. According to a detailed report in the *New
York Times*,[8] prisoners held by American forces can be subjected to prolonged
questioning, extending day and night for weeks. Although international law
requires that they be permitted to sleep for eight hours each day, American
interrogators do not necessarily permit them to sleep for eight consecutive
hours. They can be kept bound and naked much of the time during these
interrogation periods. According to a report from Australian Broadcasting
Corporation News, if the United States cannot gain information from its
increasingly severe interrogation techniques, it hands suspects over to cooper-
ating countries that are known to use overt means of torture:

> After speaking to ten currently serving U.S. national security officials, the *Wash-
> ington Post* revealed the CIA's interrogation or "stress and duress" techniques.
> Blindfolded and manacled captives are kept standing or kneeling for hours.

> They're tied up in awkward, painful positions and they're deprived of sleep, held in tiny rooms for days at a time. Those rooms are flooded with light or painfully loud noise. Some are beaten when they're initially arrested, thrown into the walls while blindfolded. . . . After questioning, if they don't cooperate, they're handed over, "rendered," in official language, to foreign intelligence services in countries like Morocco, Jordan, and Egypt, countries where torture, including electrocution, has been documented.[9]

Such techniques constitute a clear violation of due process in criminal cases in the United States, as the U.S. Supreme Court made abundantly clear in *Brown v. Mississippi* (1936) when police officers routinely tortured African-American defendants into confessing to crimes. Physically torturous and otherwise coercive interrogation techniques are not merely inhumane; they also create grave risks that innocent people will be forced to confess to crimes.[10] Such treatment can tarnish the credibility of governmental actions, including actions by any judicial system that accepts the use of coerced statements in convicting and punishing defendants.

U.S. citizenship does not necessarily provide assurance that American interrogators will scrupulously avoid any conflicts with the protections purportedly provided by the Bill of Rights and the Supreme Court's interpretations of those provisions. John Walker Lindh, an American who was captured in Afghanistan fighting for the Taliban against their enemies, the Afghan fighters of the U.S.-supported Northern Alliance, was questioned by American military and Central Intelligence Agency (CIA) officials. On the day he was taken into custody, Lindh asked for an attorney, but he was not given access to an attorney nor told that his parents had hired an attorney to represent him.[11] An FBI agent who questioned Lindh nine days later informed him of his *Miranda* rights but also added to the warnings, "Of course, there are no lawyers here [in Afghanistan]," thus implying that there was no point in asserting a right to counsel.[12] Lindh was also detained under harsh conditions that were consistent with interrogators' strategies for encouraging cooperation and confessions:

> During this time, Lindh was sometimes kept blindfolded, naked, and bound to a stretcher with duct tape, according to a declassified account from a Navy physician. He was fed only a thousand calories a day, and was left cold and sleep-deprived in a pitch-dark steel shipping container. The physician described Lindh as "disoriented" and "suffering lack of nourishment," adding that "suicide is a concern."[13]

Unlike the foreign detainees at Guantanamo Bay and at American military bases in Afghanistan, Lindh faced criminal prosecution in the United States. He ultimately entered a guilty plea to the charge of violating a 1999 presidential executive order forbidding American citizens from assisting the Taliban.[14] The government dropped allegations that he conspired against the United States or bore legal responsibility for the death of a CIA officer who was killed by Taliban prisoners during an uprising at an Afghan prison.

Summary

The U.S. Supreme Court says that the provisions of the U.S. Constitution, including the Bill of Rights, do not apply to actions by the American government beyond its own borders. Thus American law enforcement officers operating in foreign countries can engage in activities, including coercive interrogations, that would violate Fourth and Fifth Amendment rights (and other rights) if those same actions were taken within the United States. These actions can be applied to American citizens who are taken into custody in foreign countries by American officials. In an effort to combat threats to the United States, the Bush administration has used the Supreme Court's interpretation of the Constitution in order to create a new category of prisoner who lacks any rights under the U.S. Constitution or international law. By choosing to call fighters captured in battle, including those fighting for the ruling government of Afghanistan, "unlawful combatants" rather than soldiers who would be "prisoners of war," the American government has asserted unlimited authority to hold, interrogate, and otherwise control and isolate these people for an indefinite period of time.

AMERICAN CITIZENS AS TERRORISM SUSPECTS

Conventional Wisdom 37

American citizens within the United States who are taken into custody because they are suspected of committing acts that violate American criminal laws are entitled to the protections of the Fourth Amendment, Fifth Amendment, Sixth Amendment, and other provisions of the Constitution.

Every day of every year, American law enforcement officials arrest people within the United States and charge them with crimes. Generally, they are informed of their *Miranda* rights before the processes of bail hearings, appointment of counsel, and the other elements of the constitutionally mandated procedures of criminal justice move forward. As indicated by the discussions in preceding chapters, the elements of rights provided to these criminal suspects do not necessarily embody the idealistic fulfillment of the underlying provisions of the Bill of Rights. For example, police officers may adapt their presentation of *Miranda* warnings in ways that confuse suspects or appointed counsel representing indigent defendants may fail to provide zealous advocacy that meets professional standards. Despite these potential deficiencies that can give rights a symbolic quality, elements of rights are evident in the procedures used to investigate and prosecute criminal cases. If criminal suspects suffered a complete deprivation of rights, the denial of constitutional protections would provide a basis for reversing any subsequent criminal conviction resulting from the lack of adherence to the Bill of Rights. Thus the conventional wisdom about the applicability of the Bill of Rights to Americans arrested within the United States is generally true—or at least it was true until the aftermath of the September 11, 2001, airline hijackings and attacks on New York and Washington.

On May 8, 2002, federal law enforcement officials in Chicago arrested Abdullah al Muhajir, an American citizen born in New York whose given name was Jose Padilla prior to his conversion to the religion of Islam. The warrant for his arrest specified that he was a "material witness" who was subpoenaed to testify before a grand jury about matters related to government investigations of groups suspected of terrorist activities. Al Muhajir had traveled to Pakistan and elsewhere, and he allegedly met with members of such groups. An attorney was appointed to represent al Muhajir, and he appeared with his attorney at two court hearings in the two-week period following his arrest. However, on June 9, 2002, the government informed the court that President Bush had designated al Muhajir as an **enemy combatant** and he had been moved to a military prison in South Carolina. According to public statements by Attorney General John Ashcroft, al Muhajir was involved in a plot to create a "dirty bomb" that would spread radioactive material when detonated as a terrorist act within an American city. No evidence was presented to the news media or to any court in support of this assertion.

As an "enemy combatant," al Muhajir's legal status and lack of rights paralleled those of the foreign detainees in Guantanamo Bay. He was not allowed to communicate with anyone, including his attorney. In the government's view, he could be held indefinitely in military custody without being granted any constitutional rights, despite the fact that he was an American citizen arrested on American soil in connection with a criminal investigation—an investigation of a conspiracy to plant bombs within the United States is, after all, the investigation of a crime.

The attorney representing al Muhajir filed a legal action seeking access to her client and challenging the basis of her client's detention and the denial of his constitutional rights. The attorney asserted that al Muhajir was entitled to legal hearings at which the government should be required to provide evidence to justify his detention. Moreover, the attorney argued that the government must proceed with criminal charges and proof to support those charges rather than hold her client indefinitely without any charges or evidence.

One of the issues in this case concerns the president's asserted authority to hold people designated as "enemy combatants" for the duration of an American "war." In this case, there was no formal declaration of war by Congress, although Congress did pass a joint resolution after September 11th granting President Bush the power to use necessary force to prevent future acts of terrorism against the United States. Even more problematic is the fact that the "war" against terrorism is fundamentally different than other American wars. In other wars, the United States fought against sovereign nations. The wars had a definite beginning point and a definite end point. By contrast, the war against terrorism could very well be a war without end. As long as there are organizations at home or abroad that seek to harm the United States and its citizens, a president could claim that the "war" against terrorism must continue. It is very likely that there will always be organizations of individuals that would like to use violence to oppose the United States and its policies. Thus, unlike in prior wars, the people labeled as "enemy combatants" in the "war" against terrorism could conceivably be held in isolation, without any contact with the outside world or access to legal proceedings and rights, for their entire lives.

The district judge who considered the claims presented by al Muhajir's attorney avoided addressing the implications of a possible war without end by deferring the question to some as-yet-unknown later date: "At some point in the future, when operations against Al Qaeda fighters end, . . . there may be occasion to debate the legality of continuing to hold prisoners based on their connection to Al Qaeda, assuming such prisoners continue to be held at that time" (*Padilla v. Bush*, 2002). A major problem with the judge's statement, however, is that there is no requirement that the government prove that an individual has a "connection to Al Qaeda" before holding the individual indefinitely in an isolated military prison. The president must merely declare that someone is an "enemy combatant," without providing any evidence, and the person loses all rights and any prospect for freedom in the foreseeable future. Overall, the district judge found that the president possesses the authority to designate American citizens as "enemy combatants" when arrested within the United States and to hold them indefinitely without constitutional rights based "both from the terms of the Joint Resolution [passed by Congress after September 11th], and from his constitutional authority as Commander in Chief."

Abdullah al Muhajir (referred to by his birth name Jose Padilla in court documents) is not the only American citizen being held within the United States as an "enemy combatant." Yaser Esam Hamdi was taken into custody by American military forces in Afghanistan and, when his American citizenship was discovered, moved to a military prison in the United States. Hamdi's family and an attorney filed an action challenging the legality of his detention and the deprivation of his rights. A district judge ordered the government to produce documents to support Hamdi's designation as an "enemy combatant," but the U.S. Court of Appeals for the Fourth Circuit overturned that order. The appellate court's opinion emphasized the need for the judiciary to show deference to the president during times of armed conflict. Moreover, the court implicitly considered Hamdi's case to be even weaker than al Muhajir's case because Hamdi was captured during an armed conflict in a foreign country: "We hold that no evidentiary hearing or factual inquiry on our part is necessary or proper, because it is undisputed that Hamdi was captured in a zone of active combat operations in a foreign country and because any inquiry must be circumscribed to avoid encroachment into the military affairs entrusted to the executive branch" (*Hamdi v. Rumsfeld,* 2003).

In order to assert the authority of the judiciary to protect constitutional rights and review the constitutionality of actions by other branches of government, the appellate court felt it necessary to emphasize that it was not endorsing unlimited power for the president:

> It is important to emphasize that we are not placing our imprimatur upon a new day of executive detentions. We earlier rejected the summary embrace of "a sweeping proposition—namely that, with no meaningful judicial review, any American citizen alleged to be an enemy combatant could be detained indefinitely without charges or counsel on the government's say-so."

Despite this lofty statement that implicitly promises judicial vigilance in the protection of rights, the statement is—as yet—entirely symbolic because the courts have, in fact, done nothing to limit the president's authority in this regard. Because the courts have not required the president to provide evidence to justify imposing the "enemy combatant" label on al Muhajir, who was arrested within the United States and not in a war zone, no limits have been defined on presidential power in this regard. Moreover, the government has pursued a strategy intended to diminish the likelihood that a court will limit the president's power. Specifically, the Justice Department has sought to place important terrorism suspects within the jurisdiction of the U.S. Court of Appeals for the Fourth Circuit, which oversees federal trial courts in Virginia, West Virginia, Maryland, North Carolina, and South Carolina. Thus Hamdi is held in a military prison in Virginia and al Muhajir is held in a similar facility in South Carolina. Lindh's prosecution occurred in a trial court in Virginia, which is the same location where the government brought its case against Zacarias Moussaoui, the alleged "20th hijacker" on September 11th, despite the fact that he was arrested prior to the hijackings at a flight school in Minnesota. By carefully placing these detainees and defendants in these states, the Justice Department apparently sought the benefit of appellate supervision from the federal court most likely to support governmental power and least likely to protect constitutional rights for individuals. As described by one analyst, "To admirers, the Fourth Circuit is a welcome corrective after years of soft, liberally activist benches, a brilliant court with a healthy respect for the concerns of prosecutors, business owners, of state officials—and of the Bush administration. . . ."[15] The appellate court is characterized as "bold and muscular in its conservatism" because it is "confident enough to strike down acts of Congress . . . and hardheaded enough to rule against nearly every death-row defendant who comes before it."[16]

Two major terrorism-related prosecutions proceeded in other federal courts, one in Detroit and the other in Buffalo, New York. The defendants in those cases resided in the communities in which they were prosecuted for aiding terrorist organizations. Although these defendants' cases were not in the Fourth Circuit's jurisdiction, the Justice Department demonstrated in the Buffalo case that it could draw from Fourth Circuit legal precedents in order to pressure defendants to confess. According to a report first published in the *Wall Street Journal*, the government confronted the Buffalo defendants with an agonizing choice: either plead guilty to the charges and accept a prison sentence or face the possibility that the government would drop the criminal charges, label the defendants as "enemy combatants," and hold them in isolation, potentially forever, in a military prison without any contact with the outside world and without any rights.[17] The Fourth Circuit's legitimizing of the "enemy combatant" label helped to make this strategy possible. Is there a risk that even an innocent person would plead guilty under such circumstances? Probably. By using the threat of "enemy combatant" status as a plea bargaining tool, the government can readily gain convictions and claim "victories" in the "war" against terrorism, even if it does not actually possess enough evidence to prove a defendant's guilt "beyond a reasonable doubt" at trial. In such a plea bargaining scenario, a trial is not an option. The choice is between a definite term of imprisonment and the possibility of disappearing into solitary confinement forever. If you were arrested amid allegations of terrorist activities, which option would you choose?

After September 11th, Attorney General John Ashcroft testified before the Senate Judiciary Committee by saying, "Our efforts have been crafted carefully to avoid infringing on constitutional rights, while saving American lives."[18] For Americans who suffer the consequences of the label "enemy combatant," Ashcroft's statement highlights the gap between the government's promised protection of the Constitution and the reality of their complete deprivation of constitutional rights.

Summary

In the aftermath of the tragic events of September 11, 2001, President Bush's administration asserted new powers to detain American citizens and deprive them of all constitutional rights, including access to attorneys or entitlement to any court proceedings in which the government would provide evidence of their wrongdoing. The Bush administration claims that it can label American citizens, including those arrested within the United States, as "enemy combatants" and thereby confine them indefinitely in military prisons without any constitutional rights. This presidential power was endorsed by the federal courts that had considered the issue by mid-2003. As a result, the "war" on terrorism facilitated the creation of a category of American citizens for whom the Constitution has no meaning. By virtue of a label applied to them by the president, they can be denied all contact with the outside world and all constitutional protections that would routinely be available to criminal defendants, including mass murderers and others whose harm to society is both severe and proven.

RIGHTS AND GOVERNMENTAL POWERS
WITHIN THE UNITED STATES

Conventional Wisdom 38

American citizens who have no connection with groups that seek to harm the United States continue to have their constitutional rights protected as they have always been protected in the past.

Legislation enacted by Congress after September 11th, especially the USA Patriot Act, as well as domestic security initiatives by the executive branch, can reduce the rights previously enjoyed by all Americans. For example, the USA Patriot Act expands federal law enforcement authority to undertake electronic surveillance of e-mail messages and telephone calls.[19] It also expands the government's authority to label domestic groups as "terrorist organizations" if they ever engaged in any violent activity in the past, thus potentially affecting environmental protection groups, anti-abortion groups, and animal rights organizations. People who innocently donate money to groups such as Operation Rescue (anti-abortion) or People for the Ethical Treatment of Animals without knowing that members of those groups had ever committed violent acts in the past might find themselves under investigation and, if noncitizens, subject to deportation if the government declares these groups to be "terrorist organizations."[20] Critics see these expansions of law enforcement power as eroding all Americans' rights related to searches, freedom of speech, and freedom of association.

Fears about the potential for overly broad use of the "terrorist organization" label are exacerbated because high officials use the terms *terrorist* and *support for enemies* very freely and loosely in condemning people who speak out against governmental policies. Attorney General John Ashcroft said in testimony before a Senate Committee that criticism by Americans of Bush administration security proposals "gives ammunition to America's enemies."[21] He also said, "To those who scare peace-loving people with phantoms of lost liberty, my message is this: your tactics only aid terrorists for they erode our national unity and diminish our resolve."[22] Richard Perle, a close advisor to President Bush, said in a Cable News Network (CNN) interview that an award-winning journalist at *The New Yorker Magazine* "is the closest thing American journalism has to a terrorist . . . [b]ecause he sets out to do damage and he will do it by whatever innuendo, whatever distortion he can."[23] In light of the broad definitions of "terrorist organizations" under post–9/11 laws, it is unknown how far government officials will extend the application of the label.

The Bush administration developed plans to encourage Americans to spy on each other and report suspicious activities of neighbors as well as to create a master database of electronic transactions and communications made by everyone in the United States. When these plans became public, members of both political parties in Congress immediately worked to stop what they perceived as unwarranted threats to the privacy of all Americans.[24]

Further expansions of governmental power are planned. In February 2003, a document was leaked to a nonpartisan group called the Center for Public Integrity that contained the Justice Department's plans for proposed legislation entitled the "Domestic Security Enhancement Act of 2003." The new legislation would revoke portions of the Freedom of Information Act to prevent citizens from seeking information about any friends or family members detained by the government. Citizens could also no longer seek information about threats to their health and community, such as toxic emissions. Ostensibly, this provision is designed to keep terrorists from gaining information about nuclear power plants, chemical factories, and other industrial sites, but it would also have the effect of keeping citizens in the dark about pollution and toxic wastes affecting their families.[25] The new legislation would also permit the government to revoke the citizenship of any Americans who "provide material support to . . . a terrorist organization," which, under the broad definition for such organizations under the USA Patriot Act, could conceivably mean loss of citizenship for an innocent donation to an environmental protection or animal advocacy group.[26] The proposed legislation would also expand governmental authority to conduct surveillance on domestic organizations, conduct secret searches, and require citizens to provide DNA samples. The collection of a DNA database may not seem threatening, but FBI officials admitted in April 2003 that its scientists had given false testimony and conducted faulty DNA tests that contributed to dozens of criminal convictions.[27] Can government officials always be trusted to test evidence properly and report honestly on results? Innocent citizens' fates are at stake when such issues are raised.

Although it remains to be seen whether the new legislation will be formally proposed and enacted, the existence of the draft bill demonstrates that the executive branch seeks to expand its powers at the expense of constitutional rights. This expansion of governmental power would undoubtedly impact citizens who have no connection to terrorism as law enforcement officials read e-mail messages and search homes without finding any evidence of wrongdoing. A reduction of constitutional rights can potentially affect anyone because it is difficult to predict what circumstances might lead an innocent citizen to come under surveillance merely by being a classmate, acquaintance, or neighbor of an individual whom the government suspects of wrongdoing.

Summary

The aftermath of September 11th brought expanded governmental authority to conduct electronic surveillance, seek search warrants, and otherwise watch and investigate people within the United States. The definitions of terrorist organizations and other terms within security laws and regulations tend to be so broad that government officials enjoy significant flexibility and discretion in deciding when and how to use their expanded powers. Moreover, proposals continue to emerge from the executive branch concerning an expansion of data gathering and surveillance that could affect many Americans who have no connection to terrorism.

CONCLUSION

The foregoing discussion need not be read as criticizing the Bush administration for its choices about policies designed to protect the United States from attacks by domestic and foreign organizations. Reasonable people may disagree about the desirability and importance of specific policies for investigating, detaining, and interrogating people who are suspected of activities related to terrorism. Instead, the issues highlighted in this chapter are intended to raise important questions about the nature of the Constitution and the applicability of constitutional rights. When the American government develops policies amid widespread fears of terrorism, should it just decide for itself which policies seem to provide the most protection or, alternatively, should the government's choices about policies be limited by the requirements of the Bill of Rights? At the heart of the debates about anti-terrorism laws and policies is the question of whether the Bill of Rights embodies fundamental principles that are essential elements of a democratic and free society. If anti-terrorism policies can ignore the Bill of Rights, does that mean that constitutional rights are "luxuries" that benefit people during times of peace but are set aside as nonessential legal concepts when there are perceived to be serious threats to the country's safety and security? History provides evidence that during wartime, in the words of Professor David Cole, "[Americans] place security above all, and they are quite willing to cede to the government extraordinary authority."[28] If rights are not essential, what will keep government officials from going "too far" in making discretionary decisions that unnecessarily limit individuals' freedom? Normally, Americans expect the judicial branch to make decisions that will keep the other branches of government from ignoring or violating the Constitution. The deference shown by judges to the executive branch in cases concerning American citizens labeled as "enemy combatants" and held indefinitely without rights merely continues American judges' tradition of avoiding conflicts with the president during times of war. Court cases during prior war eras typically show similar judicial support for presidential decisions that are justified on the grounds of national security.[29]

During the contemporary "war" on terrorism, the government has been aware that the Bill of Rights lurks as a potential limitation on decisions by the executive branch. Thus the Bush administration has used creative devices— the kinds of things that people often criticize as "legal technicalities"—in order to claim that judges have no basis for challenging executive decisions. The decision to hold foreign captives at the U.S. Navy base in Guantanamo Bay, Cuba, and label them as "unlawful combatants" rather than "prisoners of war" or "criminal defendants" demonstrates the creative use of labels as a means to avoid the possible impact of constitutional rights. In this case, the location in Cuba is labeled a foreign jurisdiction when, in reality, the U.S. Navy base where they are held is completely under the control of the United States and its laws. The decision to use the label "unlawful combatants" was made specifically to avoid triggering the obligation to provide legal rights under either international law (i.e., Geneva Conventions for prisoners of war) or the U.S. Constitution (i.e., Bill of Rights for criminal defendants). Similarly, the use of the label "enemy combatant" to justify holding American citizens indefinitely in military prisons is clearly intended to avoid any requirement that the government respect these individuals' constitutional rights. The language of law, as illustrated by the strategic use of these labels, can have a powerful impact on the existence—or lack thereof—of Americans' constitutional rights, especially during crisis periods in which judges are deferential to decisions by the executive branch.

What will happen when and if the U.S. Supreme Court addresses a case concerning the reduction of constitutional rights in an era characterized as a "war" against terrorism? It is impossible to predict with accuracy how the nine-member body will evaluate the actions of the executive and legislative branches. Several justices on the Rehnquist Court have already provided clues about their support for judicial deference. In a March 2003 speech in Cleveland, Justice Antonin Scalia said that during wartime "the protections [for individuals] will be ratcheted down to the constitutional minimum."[30] He implied that there were legitimate opportunities to reduce the constitutional rights enjoyed by Americans because, in his words, "most of the rights you enjoy go way beyond what the Constitution requires."[31] In the days following the hijackers' attacks on September 11, 2001, Justice Sandra Day O'Connor said that Americans must surrender some of their liberties in order to guard against terrorism.[32] In a previously published book entitled *All the Laws But One: Civil Liberties in Wartime,* Chief Justice William Rehnquist wrote with apparent approval about past presidents' actions in restricting constitutional rights. In Rehnquist's words, "In time of war, presidents may act in ways that push their legal authority to its outer limits, if not beyond."[33] There are no countervailing indications that other justices are inclined to place limits on assertions of presidential power in order to protect constitutional rights during the "war" on terrorism.

As demonstrated by the foregoing examples, the Bill of Rights can become merely a symbol of American democracy without any practical meaning for affected individuals during times of national crisis. The treatment of "enemy combatants," especially Abdullah al Muhajir (aka Jose Padilla), who was arrested in the United States, shows that constitutional rights are not necessarily treated as essential, core principles of the American governing system. Despite the fact that the framers of the Constitution believed that the provisions of the Bill of Rights were so important that they needed to be attached to the founding document as elements of the nation's fundamental law, American society has been willing to set them aside when there are serious fears about the nation's security. At the same time, the foregoing examples also raise an important question about whether there is any formal mechanism that can limit presidential actions when the Bill of Rights in placed on the shelf and judges avoid any confrontations with the executive branch. This issue is especially troubling during a "war" on terrorism that may never end because there could always be groups around the world that conspire to inflict harm on the United States and its citizens. In the face of risks that executive branch officials could engage in dictatorial actions, the governing system's protective response may rest in the hands of public opinion and elected members of Congress who represent American voters. This mechanism based on political pressure is not going to rescue the rights of individuals labeled as "enemy combatants." Moreover, it will lack any quick effectiveness, especially when presidential administrations are effective in controlling information released to the press and public. However, the American governing system's vitality as a democracy with a concern for the fate of individuals may ultimately rest on the mobilization of voters when a presidential administration has veered too far away from the expectations about rights and liberty possessed by the majority of Americans. Because continuing public fears can lead to popular support for continuing expansions of executive power and countervailing electoral pressure tends to develop gradually over a period of months or years after public fears subside, this political mechanism cannot substitute for judicial action as a means for directly protecting specific individuals' constitutional rights.

CONSTITUTIONAL RIGHTS IN CRIMINAL JUSTICE: ILLUSIONS AND COMPLEXITIES

Constitutional rights are important for the protection of liberty in American society. In the democratic governing system of the United States, rights help to define the limits of the government's authority. Without the rights contained in the Bill of Rights, the government could more easily create criminal laws that restrain people's freedom of speech, movement, and privacy. Individual government officials, including police officers, prosecutors, and corrections officers, could more easily stop, search, detain, prosecute, and punish people if not for the legal protections provided by the Fourth, Fifth, Sixth, Eighth, and Fourteenth Amendments. One can readily identify examples of other countries around the world where the lack of legal protections for individuals facilitates the exercise of sweeping powers by police officers, soldiers, and others employed by the government to maintain order, stifle dissent, and preserve a national leader's power.

Although constitutional rights play an important role in the American governing system, rights—by themselves as words on paper—have little impact on government officials who wish to conduct searches, make arrests, and hold people in jail. Legal rights are empty, illusory promises unless there are mechanisms to make them effective and real in the lives of a country's citizens. In the United States, we look to an authoritative judicial system as one important governing structure that can help to make rights real. American judges possess the authority to tell legislatures, governors, and even presidents that they must stop undertaking specific actions if those actions are unconstitutional. Many judges feel a special responsibility for upholding the Constitution and protecting citizens' rights. Thus judicial decisions regularly block actions by elected officials and employees of government agencies.

Under American law, we make many government officials vulnerable to citizens' lawsuits for violating the constitutional rights of citizens. This is another mechanism for enforcing rights. The president of the United States, judges, and prosecutors are generally immune from civil rights lawsuits. So, too, are legislators when undertaking their legislative duties. However, the government officials who have the most frequent and important daily contacts with citizens, including police officers, probation officers, and corrections officers, are susceptible to lawsuits if they undertake illegal searches; use excessive force; and otherwise cause injuries, damage property, or improperly deprive people of liberty in the course of violating constitutional rights. These lawsuits can lead to judicial orders that force government agencies to change their policies and procedures. Lawsuits can also produce monetary awards for citizens whose rights were violated. These awards are often paid by the state, city, or county that employs the officials who caused the rights violations, but individual police and corrections officers are sometimes forced to compensate citizens out of their own bank accounts.

Despite the existence of mechanisms within the American governing system for the enforcement of constitutional rights, the discussions in the foregoing chapters of this book demonstrate the complex nature of rights in the criminal justice system. Someone who reads the Constitution's words will gain one picture of their constitutional rights. Someone else who reads court decisions interpreting those words will gain a slightly different picture. And someone who observes how criminal justice officials implement, or fail to implement, those rights will gain a third perspective on how legal protections affect people who come into contact with the justice system. For any individual who is stopped or arrested by the police, there is no absolute certainty about which constitutional rights will actually provide protections against actions by government officials. All rights are susceptible to being violated, and only some of those violations will be remedied effectively. Indeed, the actual protection provided by some constitutional rights bears little resemblance to the protections that the public would expect from reading the words of the Constitution, analyzing legal opinions, or recalling the lofty portrayal of our constitutional democracy presented in American schools. The illusory or symbolic nature of many rights is evident upon close examination. The symbolic nature of these rights, which is produced by several factors, presents specific lessons for those who examine closely how law affects individuals in the criminal justice system.

THE DEFINITION OF RIGHTS

Lesson 1

The definition and meaning of specific rights differ from the portrayal of those rights by the words of the Constitution.

The discussion of the nature of rights in Chapter 1 emphasized that people's everyday use of the term *rights* tends to be too broad. People often use the word *rights* to refer to their perceptions of legally protected interests that they possess, even when no such legal protections exist, especially in disputes with other private citizens. Chapter 1 emphasized the need for people to look closely at the words of the Constitution in order to recognize exactly what rights are provided by the Bill of Rights and how those rights focus on the relationship between individuals and government. Thus many people are surprised to see that the First Amendment's enunciation of rights to freedom of speech, press, religion, and assembly refers specifically to prohibiting infringements produced through laws enacted by Congress.

Obviously, the Constitution's words, by themselves, do not define the rights possessed by people. Those words are subject to interpretation by judges, and judges sometimes create interpretations that seem contrary to the most obvious and natural meaning of the words. For example, the Sixth Amendment says, "In *all* criminal prosecutions, the accused shall enjoy the right to a speedy and public trial, by an impartial jury. . . ." (emphasis supplied). In *Lewis v. United States* (1996), however, the Supreme Court emphasized that there is no right to trial by jury in criminal prosecutions for petty offenses that are each punishable by sentences of six months in jail or less. In fact, according to the Court, the right to trial by jury does not exist even when someone is sentenced to many years of incarceration based on convictions for multiple petty charges that lead to individual six-month sentences that must be served consecutively (i.e., one served after another) rather than concurrently (i.e., all served simultaneously). For example, a defendant who, like the defendant in *Lewis v. Casey,* stole letters from the U.S. Postal Service could face individual criminal charges worth six months each for every letter stolen. If the defendant were convicted of thirty counts for stealing thirty letters and had to serve the sentences consecutively, that could produce a fifteen-year sentence without the benefit of the right to trial by jury. The Sixth Amendment's words "in all prosecutions" could not be clearer, yet the Supreme Court's concerns about administrative efficiency and the cost of jury trials apparently led the majority of justices to define the jury right in a manner contrary to the Constitution's words. To those who read its words, the Sixth Amendment provides symbolic reassurance about the importance of jury trials and the role of common people in deciding the fates of their fellow citizens. For the defendant who is denied a jury trial when charged with a petty criminal offense, the words of the Sixth Amendment are an empty promise.

Unlike the Sixth Amendment's words "in all prosecutions," which are presented in such a definitive, clear manner that they do not invite interpretation, other words in the Constitution must necessarily be interpreted by the Court. Some of these words and phrases, however, end up being defined in ways that appear to conflict with any reasonable or logical meaning of the term in question. For example, the Sixth Amendment includes "the right to a speedy and public trial." The word "speedy" is ambiguous and requires definition. However, one cannot help but wonder how trials that are delayed anywhere from five to seven years can in any way be regarded as "speedy." In light of the average life expectancy of contemporary Americans, the Court's decisions indicate that people could spend nearly one-tenth of their lives under the threatening cloud of a single prosecution without any violation of the right to a speedy trial.

Is the right to a speedy trial a substantive right or is it largely symbolic? In some cases, the courts have dismissed charges when prosecutors have delayed too long in moving forward with a case. Thus the right can have substantive content, provided that the delay has reached the judges' threshold for an extreme and unreasonable delay. For many defendants, however, the right will seem symbolic because the Supreme Court's four-part balancing test from *Barker v. Wingo* (1972) can permit very lengthy delays when judges believe that the combination of factors weigh against holding the prosecution primarily responsible for a burdensome delay. In *Barker,* the prosecution was responsible for requesting repeated continuances that produced the five-year delay. Yet the Court did not hold the prosecution primarily responsible because the balancing test permitted the justices to impose partial blame on the defendant who did not demand an immediate trial. The Sixth Amendment does *not* say that there is a right to a speedy trial except when a defendant fails to complain about delays and a long delay will not adversely affect a defendant's case. The Supreme Court has moved the actual meaning of the right toward that formulation nonetheless.

Lesson 2

Rights are not necessarily enduring because their definitions can change quickly whenever five members of the U.S. Supreme Court interpret the Constitution in a new way.

Constitutional rights are often presumed to be more powerful and enduring than other forms of law. Statutes can be rewritten at the whim of legislatures, and executive agencies can readily change the regulations that they issue. By contrast, constitutional rights are written into the nation's enduring legal document that supposedly can only change if a sufficient political super-majority in the country pushes amendments through the long and difficult amendment process. Moreover, the rights contained in the Bill of Rights are presumptively of supreme importance because they were enshrined in the foundational legal document by the country's founders. Therefore it was expected that they would endure as guiding principles even as legislatures change and adjust various kinds of statutory laws.

In reality, however, constitutional rights are not enduring. A five-member majority of the nine-justice Supreme Court can change the definition of constitutional rights unexpectedly in a single day simply by issuing a new interpretation of a particular amendment in the Bill of Rights. The justices can create a right that did not exist the day before or remove a right that has existed for decades. There are political influences that constrain the justices from becoming excessively dictatorial and attempting to make wholesale changes in the Bill of Rights that clash with public expectations. Among these limiting influences are the justices' concerns about maintaining the Court's image of legitimacy, the fact that justices are drawn from the mainstream of the American political spectrum, and the prospect of strong political counter-reactions from other branches of the government and the public.[1] Despite these limitations, the Court frequently exercises its authority to redefine constitutional rights.

Changes in the definition of constitutional rights often occur slowly through a series of incremental adjustments in constitutional law. The development of the right to counsel can be traced over a period of forty years as the Court began with the limited recognition of a due process right to representation for poor defendants facing capital charges in state courts (*Powell v. Alabama*, 1932). Gradually, the Court identified a right to representation for indigents facing serious charges in federal courts (*Johnson v. Zerbst*, 1938); a right to representation in state court for defendants lacking the capacity to present their own version of the facts in a case (*Betts v. Brady*, 1942); and, finally, a right to representation in state court for all indigents facing serious charges (*Gideon v. Wainwright*, 1963). Later, the Court demonstrated that it had halted the incremental expansion of the right to counsel by identifying the circumstances in which it was not willing to recognize a right to representation, including discretionary appeals (*Ross v. Moffitt*, 1974) and trials of defendants facing only a minor fine as punishment (*Scott v. Illinois*, 1979). Similarly, the definition of the Fourth Amendment right to exclusion of evidence as a remedy for violations of the prohibition on unreasonable searches and seizures developed slowly in an incremental fashion. The Court began with the exclusion of evidence for Fourth Amendment violations in federal cases (*Weeks v. United States*, 1914) and later incorporated the Fourth Amendment without the exclusionary rule (*Wolf v. Colorado*, 1949) before applying the exclusionary rule to the states in *Mapp v. Ohio* (1961). Although these examples show that the Supreme Court does not always make dramatic, instantaneous changes in the definition of constitutional rights, the justices are not precluded from making such immediate changes.

When the Supreme Court issued its decision in *Miranda v. Arizona* (1966), the Court, in effect, created a new legal protection for criminal suspects by requiring police officers to inform them of their rights before beginning custodial questioning. This sudden expansion of rights sought to have an immediate impact on police practices and produced a notable outcry from many police chiefs and elected officials. Over time, *Miranda* proved to have less impact on law enforcement practices and effectiveness than many chiefs initially feared, but the ruling was a sudden change in the meaning of constitutional rights nonetheless. By contrast, the Supreme Court's decision in *Payne v. Tennessee* (1991) represented a quick redefinition of constitutional rights that reduced legal protections for individuals. The decision diminished the scope of protections for capital defendants by permitting prosecutors to present Victim Impact Testimony in capital sentencing hearings. The change produced in *Payne* was all the more dramatic because it overturned two Supreme Court precedents that were two and four years old, respectively, which had produced rulings directly opposed to the one announced in *Payne*. It is indeed possible to have a constitutional right one day and have that right disappear at 10 A.M. the next morning when the Supreme Court announces its next set of rulings. Obviously, no constitutional right is enduring unless the majority of justices on the Supreme Court continue to support its existence through their interpretations of the Bill of Rights.

Ironically, despite the image of constitutional rights as especially powerful and enduring elements of law, statutory legal entitlements can, in fact, be stronger and more enduring than constitutional rights. Consider, for example, the issue of private ownership of firearms. Some people claim that gun ownership is a constitutionally protected right, and they point to the Second Amendment as the source of that right. Unfortunately, many of these advocates of private gun ownership quote the words of the Second Amendment by beginning with its final clause: ". . . the right of the people to keep and bear arms shall not be infringed." This use of a selective quotation is deceptive because the Second Amendment is actually more complex. The amendment really says, in its entirety:

> A well-regulated Militia, being necessary for the security of a free State, the right of the people to keep and bear arms shall not be infringed.

The Second Amendment is a single sentence with connected clauses. The first section cannot stand alone in order to treat the last clause as if it presents an independent idea. Any honest interpretation of the amendment would require the interpreter to grapple with the entire sentence. Thus people argue about whether the word "Militia" is meant to refer to all Americans or whether it refers only to the organized militia of each state, the National Guard. Other people argue that the amendment should be regarded as providing a right to gun ownership because the framers of the Constitution intended for it to have that meaning. One three-judge panel in the U.S. Court of Appeals for the Fifth Circuit has endorsed this conclusion (*United States v. Emerson*, 2001), but a different panel of judges on the U.S. Court of Appeals for the Ninth Circuit came to a completely contrary conclusion (*Silveira v. Lockyer,* 2002). The original intent argument, if it is factually accurate, ignores the fact that only two justices on the Supreme Court, Antonin Scalia and Clarence Thomas, argue that rights should be defined according to the original intentions of the framers and even they sometimes deviate from their purported adherence to originalist interpretation. Other justices do not rely on the underlying history of amendments to determine the meaning of the provisions of the Bill of Rights. As a result, the inescapable reality is that the Supreme Court has never interpreted the Second Amendment as providing a constitutional right to private gun ownership. States can regulate and even ban private gun ownership without interference by the Second Amendment, unless they have their own state constitutional provisions that prevent them from taking such actions.

Although gun ownership is not recognized as a constitutional right, it is arguably a more strongly protected and enduring legal entitlement than constitutionally based entitlements defined as rights through the Supreme Court's interpretations of the Bill of Rights. Private gun ownership is not protected through lawsuits and appeals that seek judicial decisions protecting such ownership as a legal entitlement. Instead, private gun ownership is a secure, **politically protected privilege.** Hypothetically, the government could enact legislation to take away people's privilege of owning guns, but, in reality, it cannot happen. There are millions of guns in homes, cars, pockets, and purses throughout the country. Any legislation against gun ownership would be extremely ineffective because of the reality of pervasive firearms ownership. In addition, political interest groups favoring private gun ownership are well financed, well organized, and influential. The National Rifle Association and its allies have been very effective in protecting the privilege of gun ownership. They do not win every battle that they fight. These battles revolve around marginal issues: How will firearms be sold? Which firearms will be available to the public? Can people carry firearms as concealed weapons? With respect to the fundamental issue of private gun ownership, the NRA has already won the war. Congress and state legislatures never even propose legislation that would threaten the basic legal privilege of owning firearms, except with respect to small categories of citizens, such as ex-convicts and children, whom the NRA does not choose to defend. Interestingly, the Second Amendment's words contain no exception for convicted offenders, children, or anyone else, yet even the amendment's most ardent defenders who complain about judges' failure to follow the amendment's words (i.e., ". . . the right of the people to keep and bear arms will not be infringed") never complain about the adverse impact of statutory restrictions on "the right of the people" who happen to be either young or convicted felons.

Another example of a secure legal protection that is stronger and more enduring than a constitutional right is the mortgage interest deduction under federal tax laws. Homeowners are allowed to deduct the interest payments from their home loans when reporting their income for annual tax purposes. This law permits homeowners, but not renters, to save money on their taxes. The tax savings for an individual homeowner typically amount to something within a range from several hundred dollars to several thousand dollars each year. This tax policy encourages private homeownership but also reduces government tax revenues and gives homeowners financial benefits that are not enjoyed by renters, many of whom have low incomes and are in more desperate need of financial help from the government than are homeowners. Because homeowners, as a subset of the American population, account for a huge proportion of active voters and people who contribute to political campaigns, it would be political suicide for any politician to propose repealing this financial benefit that primarily helps middle-class and more affluent people, even if the proposal was made on the claim that we need to treat all Americans, homeowners and renters, the same for purposes of taxation. Middle-class and affluent Americans regard the mortgage interest deduction as a sacred entitlement, and they possess the political power to ensure that they continue to receive the benefit. The same is likely true of Social Security payments for retirees. Despite widespread speculation that the Social Security system will be bankrupt before the middle of the twenty-first century, public expectations about receiving such payments during retirement are likely to be so powerful that politicians will make sure that this statutory entitlement is preserved, albeit perhaps with some modifications.

In sum, constitutional rights are susceptible to change and even elimination through the interpretive decisions of judges. Thus constitutional rights are not necessarily powerful and enduring. Indeed, other legal entitlements based on statutes are arguably more powerful and enduring than constitutional rights if those entitlements enjoy the protection of widespread or otherwise powerful political support.

THE ROLE OF VAGUE STANDARDS

Lesson 3

The Supreme Court can create or enhance the symbolic nature of rights through vague standards for the definition of rights and rights violations.

The foregoing example of the *Barker v. Wingo* (1972) four-part balancing test for the right to a speedy trial demonstrates the impact of a vague standard as well as a definition of a right that can clash with a reasonable understanding of a specific word (i.e., "speedy"). The balancing test does not tell judges how to evaluate speedy trial claims as much as it provides judges with possible justifications for deciding such claims either for or against the defendant depending on the judge's preferences, priorities, and sense of justice. As commentators have noted, judges may be inclined to dismiss minor charges, perhaps in order to remind prosecutors that they must move forward with cases. When serious charges are involved, however, judges may be much less likely to find that the balance of factors, no matter what they may be, weigh in favor of the defendant's claim.[2] Quite understandably, a judge may be willing to tolerate significant delays by the prosecution rather than permit a murder defendant to go free without trial. In effect, the Court's vague and flexible test permits the substance of the right to a speedy trial to be defined by the judge's assessment of society's interests in community safety and law enforcement. The words of the Constitution focus on legally protected entitlements for individuals. But the development of constitutional interpretation and judicial power within the American legal system has permitted consideration of interests other than those of the individual suspect or defendant to define the nature of rights in criminal justice.

The standards for defining ineffective assistance of counsel are similarly vague. Defendants who claim that they were denied their Sixth Amendment right to counsel because their attorneys performed poorly face the difficult challenge of identifying specific errors by their attorneys that demonstrate that the attorneys did not meet professional standards and that the attorneys' failures affected the outcome of the case. These are exceptionally difficult elements to prove, especially when judges are so reluctant to second-guess attorneys' tactics and strategic inaction. Lurking beneath this vague standard is a realistic fear that the courts will be inundated with ineffective assistance of counsel claims and numerous orders for new trials if the standards of proof can be easily met. While the Supreme Court has an understandable concern about administrative efficiency and the court system's limited resources, the justices must sacrifice the liberty interests and Sixth Amendment rights of many poorly represented defendants when establishing a standard that will shield the court system from numerous claims.

In addition to protecting the courts at the expense of defendants, the Supreme Court's standard also protects the American legal profession's interests in permitting any licensed attorney, no matter how inexperienced or lacking in expertise, to handle any kind of case. If the legal profession emulated the medical profession by having a system in which attorneys undertake special training and licensing exams for certification of expertise in specific areas of law, the Court could create stricter, more meaningful performance standards because only certified experts would handle criminal cases. However, attorneys' interests in autonomy are too great, criminal cases are too numerous, and resources devoted to criminal defense are too scarce to reassure the Supreme Court's justices that the system can handle meaningful standards. As a result, the right to counsel is largely symbolic for many defendants whose attorneys are disinterested, self-interested, lacking in appropriate expertise, or otherwise unwilling or unable to be effective, zealous advocates for their clients.

In the issue of ineffective assistance of counsel, the vague standard fails to supply a clear threshold for recognizing when the protections of the right to counsel are triggered. Similar problems exist with respect to vague threshold standards for other rights. The Supreme Court has never defined which fines are unconstitutional under the Eighth Amendment's prohibition on "excessive fines." In the lone case in which the Supreme Court identified a violation, a cash-sniffing police dog at a Los Angeles airport was being walked past luggage in an effort to identify whether any drug traffickers or others engaged in illegal activity were attempting to take large sums of cash out of the country. Under federal law, people must file a report when they are taking $10,000 or more in cash out of the country. There is no law against carrying the cash. The law simply requires that the amount be reported. The dog indicated to its handlers that a large amount of cash was contained in one traveler's luggage. The traveler admitted that he had several thousand dollars in cash but he denied that the amount exceeded $10,000. The dog's reaction indicated otherwise so law enforcement officials searched the luggage. Inside, they found $357,000. The man would have faced only a $5,000 fine and a possible short jail sentence for violating the law upon his return to the United States if the government had discovered his failure to file the required papers after he took the cash out of the country. Because the police caught him as he was transporting the cash, however, the government made him forfeit the entire amount he was carrying. Instead of a $5,000 fine and a short jail sentence, he lost the entire $357,000. In a narrow 5-to-4 decision, Justice Clarence Thomas deserted his usual conservative colleagues in order to provide the deciding vote for the Court's more liberal justices. Thomas even wrote the majority opinion declaring that the man's Eighth Amendment right against excessive fines had been violated. The Court's opinion does not give clear guidance about how to determine when the government has violated the Eighth Amendment right. Instead, this one case with its glaring gap between the amount seized and the usual statutorily defined fine serves as the lone example of a violation. With such a lack of clarity about the definition of the right, is the right substantive or symbolic for people who believe that courts have imposed excessive fines or seized an excessive valuation of assets through forfeiture? This is difficult to answer. One thing is clear, however. In the entire history of courts using fines and asset forfeiture in the United States, only one man has clearly received the protection of the Eighth Amendment right in the Supreme Court's decisions.

Vague standards established by the Supreme Court can also nullify the substance of rights by granting greater discretionary authority to individual decision makers who help to determine the fates of people drawn into the criminal justice system. In 1982, a slim majority of justices declared that the Eighth Amendment prohibition on cruel and unusual punishments was violated when Florida sentenced a getaway car driver to death for murders committed by his companions who walked up to a house and sought to steal money from an elderly couple (*Enmund v. Florida*). Justice Byron White's majority opinion said a death sentence was a disproportionate punishment in violation of the Eighth Amendment when imposed on a felony-murder accomplice who did not participate in the actual killing. Five years later, the four *Enmund* dissenters managed to persuade White to provide the decisive fifth vote in joining them to adjust the rule established in *Enmund*. The new majority established a different rule that permitted juries to impose the death penalty on felony-murder accomplices who did not participate in an actual killing as long as those accomplices demonstrated "reckless disregard for human life" (*Tison v. Arizona*, 1987). The Court claimed that it was leaving the *Enmund* rule intact but merely adding a new element to the rule. In reality, the *Tison* rule obliterated the *Enmund* rule by permitting juries to sentence to death nearly any murder accomplice whom they wished to label as showing "reckless disregard." The Eighth Amendment right against disproportionate sentences for accomplices may appear to be intact, but the Court's vague, new standard effectively gave juries the discretionary authority to impose death sentences on felony-murder accomplices whenever they felt it was appropriate to do so.[3] For those accomplices sentenced to death, especially those whose involvement was no greater than accomplices in other cases who were not given capital punishment, the Eighth Amendment right as enunciated in *Enmund* is hollow and symbolic.

The creation of vague standards has also affected the right to exclusion of evidence under the Fourth and Fifth Amendments as the Supreme Court's decisions expanded the discretionary authority of police officers. For example, how broad is the "public safety" exception to *Miranda* and the exclusionary rule? The Court has said that officers may dispense with *Miranda* warnings in order to undertake immediate questioning of suspects as well as warrantless searches when such quick actions are required by threats to "public safety" or by other "exigent circumstances." Thus officers can make a determination that a public safety or exigent circumstance situation exists and thereby move ahead with investigatory actions that would otherwise be limited by the Fifth Amendment *Miranda* requirement or the warrant clause of the Fourth Amendment. There is a risk that a judge may later exclude the evidence by disagreeing with the officers' justification for ignoring constitutional rights and taking quick actions. However, the officer has the opportunity to portray the situation as urgent in describing the scene when giving after-the-fact testimony at a preliminary hearing concerning the possible exclusion of evidence. Moreover, many judges have great reluctance to second-guess police officers who must make snap decisions, often in circumstances in which they believe that their lives may become endangered. Thus officers' discretionary authority is expanded by the vague standards at the expense of the protection of individuals' constitutional rights. Because these exceptions to *Miranda* (public safety exception) and the Fourth Amendment exclusionary rule (exigent circumstances) are so vague, it is very difficult to tell how much of the constitutional right can be swallowed up by the exceptions to the Supreme Court's previously established, rights-defining rules. For the individual suspects whose cases are affected by these exceptions, the constitutional rights at issue no longer provide their promised substantive protections.

RIGHTS WITHOUT REMEDIES

Lesson 4

For many suspects, defendants, and convicted offenders, specific constitutional rights are entirely symbolic because there is no remedy available when violations occur.

Can a constitutional right honestly be said to exist if there is no remedy for its violation? People could be told, "You actually have this constitutional right, but you simply do not enjoy its protections," but that is really just another way of saying that the right is symbolic rather than substantive. Yet, that is precisely the situation faced by many people as a result of both Supreme Court decisions and legislative enactments by Congress.

The Supreme Court's decisions that tolerate rights violations when police officers act in "good faith" effectively deprive individuals of remedies for the violations of their legal interests that are supposed to be protected by the Constitution. In *United States v. Leon* (1984), the Court permitted the prosecution to use incriminating evidence seized in an improper search because the police officers involved had acted in good faith when they applied for a search warrant but the judicial officer had made a mistake in issuing the warrant without sufficient evidence to support probable cause. The issuance of the warrant and resulting search violated the defendant's Fourth Amendment rights, yet the Supreme Court would not apply the usual remedy of excluding the improperly obtained evidence from use in court. The Court conceded that the defendant's rights were violated but took no action to remedy that violation.

Similarly, in *Illinois v. Rodriguez* (1990), the Supreme Court permitted an improper search to generate incriminating evidence when officers mistakenly believed that the apartment resident's girlfriend lived in the apartment and possessed the authority to consent to a search. In *Arizona v. Evans* (1995), the Court supported a search incident to an *unlawful* arrest when police received information from the central computer that erroneously informed them that there was a warrant for the arrest of the man they had stopped for a traffic violation. In both instances, the Supreme Court tolerated violations of constitutional rights because they regarded the rights violations as stemming from mistakes that were not the fault of the police. When the Court examines rights violations by asking "Did the police do anything wrong?" rather than "Were any constitutional rights violated?," then the individuals affected by those rights violations do not receive the protection of the rights that the Supreme Court's rights-defining decisions say they should possess.

Are there remedies for these rights violations other than the exclusionary rule that the Supreme Court refuses to impose when the justices view officers as acting in good faith? In a decision concerning the Fourth Amendment in 1949, Justice Felix Frankfurter declared that the exclusionary rule need not apply in state and local cases because alternative remedies were available for violations of Fourth Amendment rights (*Wolf v. Colorado*). Frankfurter indicated that individuals could file lawsuits against the police or police administrators could discipline officers when rights violations occur. Frankfurter never supported the incorporation of the exclusionary rule in *Mapp v. Ohio* (1961), yet even he admitted that his 1949 opinion was not entirely correct and that there were some cases in which exclusion of evidence was the only realistic way to remedy Fourth Amendment rights violations. Despite the fact that he never endorsed a blanket exclusionary rule, in *Rochin v. California* (1952) Frankfurter insisted on the exclusion of incriminating evidence when police officers entered a home without a warrant and attempted to forcibly extract from a man's throat some pills that he had just swallowed. The dissenters in *Wolf* argued that it was unrealistic to expect police officials to punish their officers for using improper means to catch actual lawbreakers or to rely on jurors to force police officers to pay money to lawbreakers whom they caught through improper means. The Warren Court ultimately decided in *Mapp v. Ohio* that alternative remedies do not work; and thus they imposed a categorical rule, without exceptions, demanding that improperly obtained evidence be excluded from use in court. By contrast, since the 1970s, the Supreme Court under the leadership of Chief Justices Warren Burger and William Rehnquist has demonstrated a lack of concern about whether any remedies are needed in certain situations in which police officers violate constitutional rights while undertaking searches. The Supreme Court's unwillingness to enforce constitutional rights in these good-faith cases does not preclude the use of other mechanisms for enforcing rights. However, in the real world of civil rights lawsuits for rights violations in criminal justice, jurors are only likely to award money damages in cases in which police actions caused personal injuries, property damage, egregious home invasions, or improper deprivations of liberty. In cases in which police officers took good-faith actions that resulted in the acquisition of incriminating evidence through an improper search, civil rights lawsuits are usually not a realistic mechanism for protecting rights. Internal discipline within the police department is also likely to be ineffective, especially when the search resulted in a conviction, except in those cases in which the police officers' actions placed their employing agency at risk of liability through civil litigation

Remedies for rights violations are also unavailable to many convicted offenders because of court decisions and legislation that produced impediments to effective access to the legal processes for seeking post-conviction remedies. The Supreme Court's interpretations of the right to counsel have meant that indigent criminal offenders must fend for themselves in preparing discretionary appeals, *habeas corpus* petitions, and civil rights lawsuits. The inability of untrained criminal offenders to follow technical court procedures and effectively present their claims diminishes the likelihood that even valid claims about rights violations can be raised in a manner that produces remedial action by a court. The Supreme Court's decisions on *habeas corpus* procedures, including those limiting successive petitions (*McCleskey v. Zant*, 1991) and mandating forfeiture of *habeas* claims if a claim has been previously dismissed for violating a state appellate procedure (*Coleman v. Thompson*, 1991), make it even more difficult for unrepresented offenders to understand and comply with the multitude of court procedures that must be followed in order to raise a claim concerning constitutional rights violations. The Court's decision that limits lower court judges' ability to order legal assistance for prisoners poses further difficulties for offenders who may wish to raise claims concerning rights violations (*Lewis v. Casey*, 1996). Congress imposed additional impediments through the Antiterrorism and Effective Death Penalty Act, which imposed stricter limits on *habeas corpus,* and the Prison Litigation Reform Act, which limited the authority of federal judges to formulate remedies for rights violations and made it more difficult for prisoners to file lawsuits alleging violations of their constitutional rights. Thus rights violations can go unremedied because the victims of those violations lack the effective means to make use of the court procedures that are intended to provide remedies.

The Supreme Court's decisions and the legislation enacted by Congress seem to show greater concern for alleviating the federal courts' burden of cases filed by prisoners than for ensuring that constitutional rights are remedied. According to Professor Larry Yackle, the development of impediments to the vindication of convicted offenders' rights does not really involve a debate about administrative issues. The impediments created by the Supreme Court and Congress are a pretext for seeking to diminish the constitutional rights granted to suspects, defendants, and offenders in the criminal justice process by earlier Supreme Court decisions. In Yackle's words,

> The battle over *habeas* is driven, in the main, not by relatively sterile concerns for federalism and congested federal dockets, but by an ideological resistance to the Warren Court's innovative interpretations of substantive federal rights.[4]

In effect, the impediments to effective utilization of post-conviction processes for remedying rights violations permit the justice system to claim that the constitutional rights exist, yet many individuals drawn into the criminal justice system have no realistic possibility of actually gaining a remedy for any rights violations. For those who have truly endured a violation of their constitutional rights, yet remain incapable of pursuing a remedy by following technical aspects of law and detailed court procedures on their own, such rights are merely illusory and symbolic.

GOVERNMENT OFFICIALS' CONTROL OF RIGHTS

Lesson 5

Americans cannot rely on the U.S. Supreme Court to protect their constitutional rights. Instead, the protection of several rights rests largely in the hands of officials within the criminal justice system.

The composition of the Supreme Court changes over time. The Court's membership is determined by the quirks of the fateful timing that produces resignations, retirements, and deaths among the justices while particular presidents reside in the White House and control the nomination process. Since the end of the 1960s, the timing of retirements gave conservative Republican presidents the opportunity to install a dominant conservative majority on the Court. The decisions by these justices have generally reduced the scope of rights in criminal justice, created exceptions and vague standards that contribute to the symbolic nature of rights, and supported impediments to vindication of rights in post-conviction processes. The Court's composition will change in the future, but Americans cannot count on the Court to elevate the protection of constitutional rights over policy preferences for permitting police officers to take good-faith actions and for reducing the number of post-conviction claims filed in the courts.

Even if the Court's composition changed in a way that made the protection of constitutional rights into a paramount priority, the justices handle a limited caseload each year and thus they cannot remedy all of the rights violations that may occur in a large country. Since 1995, the Supreme Court has decided between twenty-two and thirty-six criminal justice–related cases each year out of the seventy-five to eighty-five total cases given complete consideration and full opinions annually. Only about half of those criminal justice cases concern constitutional rights. The rest of the criminal justice cases involve interpretations of federal criminal statutes, sentencing guidelines, and court procedures.[5] Because the Court typically handles fewer than two dozen cases concerning constitutional rights in criminal justice each year, there is no way that it can supervise the protection of rights in the thousands of criminal cases in which rights issues arise. Hopefully, judges in lower courts throughout the country will do their jobs in protecting constitutional rights. Those judges in state courts who are elected officials may, however, lack the job security and structural protections from political pressure necessary to make unpopular decisions in support of the protection of rights for criminal suspects, defendants, and convicted offenders. If lower courts fail to remedy rights violations, there is no guarantee that courts of last resort, either state supreme courts or the U.S. Supreme Court, will act to make corrections. Chief Justice William Rehnquist summarized his view of the Supreme Court's responsibilities by saying, "The Supreme

Court of the United States should be reserved . . . for important and disputed questions of law, not for individual injustices that might be corrected and should be corrected in other courts."[6] Such views leave open the question of what happens if the lower courts do not remedy rights violations and correct injustices. If the Supreme Court will not remedy such uncorrected injustices, then those injustices are likely to remain unremedied.

Because appellate courts can handle only a limited number of cases and not all judges are inclined to remedy rights violations, the protection of many constitutional rights actually rests in the hands of decision makers in the criminal justice system who determine the fates of suspects, defendants, and offenders. As discussed in Chapter 5 and Chapter 6, police officers exercise significant discretionary authority in conducting searches, making arrests, and undertaking questioning of suspects. By using their inherent power as armed police officers whose presence can intimidate many citizens, they have opportunities to take actions that exceed their authority and violate the rights of citizens. If police officers insist on searching people or vehicles, even without proper legal justifications, there is little that the citizen can do to stop such searches from occurring. Officers may also engage in improper questioning without fear of sanction if there are no witnesses to their actions that ignore the substance and intent of *Miranda* rights. The Supreme Court has granted police officers significant flexibility in undertaking searches, arrests, and questioning by creating exceptions to the Fourth Amendment warrant requirement, the exclusionary rule, and *Miranda* warnings. Moreover, these exceptions provide officers with the opportunity to manufacture after-the-fact justifications and rationalizations for improper actions that occurred during a search or arrest. When called to the witness stand in court, officers can creatively describe and even mischaracterize events to convince the judge that the officers' actions fit within the "public safety" exception, exigent circumstances, or some other available exception to constitutional protections for individuals' rights. Prosecutors, corrections officers, probation officers, and parole officers also possess flexible authority and discretion for undertaking searches and questioning, filing charges, and other activities that, if done improperly, can violate people's constitutional rights.

Criminal justice officials have tens of thousands of interactions with people every day throughout the United States. These interactions, in the form of such encounters as traffic stops, street corner questioning, and patdown searches, are all supposed to be governed by the constitutional rights contained in the Fourth and Fifth Amendments. Yet, there is no supervisory authority that can effectively monitor how criminal justice officials behave during these interactions. Officers are mobile, relatively independent actors who decide which people and situations to investigate and how to conduct those investigations. Thus, if Fourth and Fifth Amendment rights are to be substantive rather than symbolic, individual criminal justice officials must conduct themselves as ethical, trained professionals who respect and emphasize the importance of the Bill of Rights. Officers must not view constitutional rights as impediments to law enforcement that are to be ignored, avoided, or minimized whenever possible. Instead, officers must recognize and take seriously the reality that they hold the Constitution in their hands every time they stop a vehicle or consider questioning and searching a person on the streets. If individual criminal justice officials do not emphasize the protection of constitutional rights, even when it diminishes the ease and likelihood of discovering criminal activity, then Fourth and Fifth Amendment rights may be merely illusory, symbolic entitlements rather than substantive, meaningful legal protections.

The Reduction of Rights During a National Crisis

Lesson 6

During times of perceived national crisis, constitutional rights can shrink and, for some individuals, disappear as judges defer to decisions of executive branch officials about the policies that are necessary for the safety and security of the nation.

Although the Bill of Rights is portrayed as a core element of American law, the contemporary war on terrorism demonstrates how constitutional rights can shrink and disappear when the president asserts authority to take actions in the name of national security. The Bush administration's actions demonstrate how the creative use of legal terms can help government officials to avoid obeying the requirements of the U.S. Constitution. By sending detainees to a naval base in Cuba, government officials can claim that these prisoners are in a foreign jurisdiction beyond the reach of the U.S. Constitution despite the fact that they are incarcerated on territory that is completely under the control of Americans and American law. By asserting that American citizens can be labeled as "enemy combatants" who will be held indefinitely without any evidence of wrongdoing, access to the courts, or constitutional rights, the government has demonstrated that the Bill of Rights does not comprise a fundamental set of principles that are superior to the discretionary decisions of government officials. As long as judges defer to the executive branch, as they normally do during times of war, there is no legal limitation on the government's authority to deny people the rights promised by the Constitution. Moreover, there is no foreseeable end point to these deprivations of rights because the war on terrorism is different than prior American wars. Other wars were fought against sovereign nations with definite beginning points and end points. The war on terrorism may never end because the United States is likely to be the focus of hostility from various organizations around the world that use violence as a means to pursue a vision of social order that differs dramatically from the values evident in American society. Because judges generally avoid conflicts with the executive branch during times of national crisis, any limitations on the executive branch's ability to reduce or ignore constitutional rights may have to come from opposing efforts originating in Congress or popular opposition from the American public. Politics rather than law may determine the existence of rights during the war on terrorism.

CITIZENS AND THE PROTECTION OF RIGHTS

Lesson 7

Individual citizens can play a role in working to make constitutional rights substantive rather than symbolic.

A recognition that constitutional rights are not self-enforcing and may not fulfill citizens' beliefs and expectations about their nature and power can lead to a fatalistic cynicism about the criminal justice system. For some people, a close examination of constitutional rights and the gap between stated definitions and the actual impact, or lack thereof, of rights on people's lives may lead to such sentiments as "I always knew the system was hopelessly corrupt and now I see that there's nothing that can be done about it." Although there is no magic wand that can miraculously unify a system with pervasive discretion and interpretive judicial authority, a democratic governing system provides opportunities for individuals to exert their power to push law and policy in preferred directions. For example, during state judicial elections in which people campaigning for judgeships try to outdo each other by claiming to be "tough on crime," voters can look closely to see which candidates also recognize that our constitutional democracy emphasizes the protection of rights as well as crime control. Voters can similarly incorporate concerns about the protection of constitutional rights into their consideration of candidates for county prosecutor, county sheriff, state legislature, U.S. Senate, and president of the United States. These officials establish policy and provide leadership for the street-level officials who affect the implementation of rights on a daily basis. Moreover, senators and the president control the selection of federal judges, including justices on the U.S. Supreme Court. If these officials are preoccupied with the rhetoric of crime control without also demonstrating concern about the protection of constitutional rights, they are likely to exacerbate the problem of symbolic rights.

Individuals can also assert their political power in ways other than voting to enhance the substance of constitutional rights. For example, the Supreme Court and other courts have not used their powers of constitutional interpretation to deter, reduce, or supervise the use of race in profiling by law enforcement officers that leads members of racial minority groups to be subjected disproportionately to stops and searches. However, public outcry about racial profiling and civil lawsuits filed by the American Civil Liberties Union have generated attention from the news media that, in turn, pushed politicians and police administrators to take action on the issue. As a result, police agencies feel increasing pressure to be careful about using race in determining whom to stop and search in order to avoid producing disparities in the treatment of drivers and pedestrians. As described by one news magazine,

> The response of politicians to the outcry over racial profiling amounts to a lawmaking jamboree. Congress is considering the End Racial Profiling Act, which would force local police to record the race of everyone subjected to a traffic or pedestrian stop and to punish officers who rely on race when deciding whether to stop someone. Thirteen states and hundreds of localities have enacted legislation designed to reduce or at least study racial profiling. Bills are pending in at least 12 other states.[7]

The elected officials who feel pushed to react against racial profiling are not merely political liberals who have been waiting for an opportunity to expand individuals' rights and reduce the authority of police officers. Conservative politicians, such as New York City's former tough-on-crime mayor, Rudolph Giuliani, have felt compelled to take action, too.[8] According to news reports, "[E]veryone from Attorney General John Ashcroft, long a conservative on race issues, to Senator Hillary Rodham Clinton, long a liberal, has denounced racial profiling. Declared President [George W.] Bush in February [2001]: 'It is wrong, and we must end it.'"[9] As indicated by the example of the racial profiling issue, political mobilization by the public can apply pressure to restrain criminal justice policies and procedures and thereby provide corresponding benefits for the effective rights of individuals.

Individuals also serve on juries. In criminal cases, concerned and knowledgeable jurors can listen closely and skeptically to the testimony of police officers, just as they listen critically to testimony by witnesses and defendants. The knowledge that some officers might be less than completely truthful when characterizing the events surrounding a search, arrest, or interrogation should lead jurors to avoid both automatically believing whatever an officer says and reflexively assuming that the officer is truthful when there is a disagreement between testimony by an officer and testimony by witnesses and defendants. When jurors can send a message to police officers that they are detecting untruthful statements or that they are concerned about the possibility that rights violations affected the reliability of evidence, such as in the case of an improperly obtained confession, unethical officers have less incentive to violate constitutional rights unless they wish to risk the possibility that their questionable actions will adversely affect the prosecution's case. In civil rights lawsuits against criminal justice officials, jurors who are open-minded about the claimant's case, even when the claimant is a lawbreaker, may find the police liable for violations and thereby encourage police agencies to create better training, policies, and procedures that diminish the risk of constitutional rights violations.[10]

Individuals may also advance the substance of rights by becoming knowledgeable about the Bill of Rights and the Supreme Court's interpretations. Research shows that people who challenge a police officer's authority are more likely to be arrested than people who are contrite and cooperative. Yet, there may be some benefits to be gained from monitoring police officers' actions and letting the officers know that the individual citizen has an awareness of whether those actions comply with constitutional requirements established by the Supreme Court and other courts. If a police officer begins to undertake an improper search and the person being searched politely reminds the officer that the search does not have a proper legal basis, there is a risk that the officer will be angry and continue anyway—or worse, create some reason to make an arrest. On the other hand, such a comment, if delivered politely, may also cause the officer to pause and consider whether there is a risk that searching this individual outside of the rules may lead to adverse consequences for the officer if this is a citizen who might file a complaint. Although many citizens who have filed complaints with police departments concerning the actions of specific officers believe that police supervisors will always protect their fellow officers, there may be benefits from complaining. If complaints become numerous, police supervisors cannot avoid worrying that issues will attract the attention of the news media and elected officials, just as occurred with racial profiling. Complaints are most effective when they come from informed citizens who have a basis for claiming that officers violated their rights. Thus individuals' knowledge about constitutional rights may, under the right circumstances, translate into the necessary power to push for remedial action.

Obviously, one particular group of individuals can have an enormous impact on giving substantive content to constitutional rights if they make the protection of rights one of their primary priorities. Those individuals are students who plan to work within the criminal justice system as police officers, probation officers, prosecutors, corrections officers, and other officials. On a daily basis, these individuals will find themselves in the position to determine whether specific rights will be substantive or symbolic for the citizens whom they encounter while on the job. In addition, these individuals will influence the behavior of their colleagues, either by example or through the training and socialization that they provide when new officers join their agencies. In reality, a single individual can have a powerful impact on the fulfillment of constitutional rights if that individual is dedicated to the idea of carrying out job responsibilities in accordance with the highest ethical and legal standards of his or her profession. That one individual may, by example, set a standard for performance for other colleagues to emulate. That one individual may deter misconduct and questionable actions by other officers who will fear, with good reason, that their ethical colleague will not cover for them if their actions that violate constitutional rights are revealed. That one individual may eventually influence the training and supervision of new officers and thereby help to ensure that respect for constitutional rights is an important element of a criminal justice agency's prevailing norms and culture.

CONCLUSION

In the United States, symbolic rights are the inevitable product of many factors. American judges possess the authority to make definitive interpretations of constitutional rights, even when those interpretations clash with the Constitution's words or imply the existence of rights that the Constitution does not mention. Thus the definition of rights develops in unpredictable ways. Moreover, the definition of rights changes as the composition of courts changes over time. In addition, the United States is a vast country that lacks a single, unified governing system. Thus policy-making authority and administrative control for most criminal justice practices rest in the hands of state and local government officials. This fragmented governing structure inevitably produces differences in the training, practices, and procedures employed by the many street-level officials who must implement constitutional rights. Individual criminal justice officials possess significant discretionary authority to make decisions and take actions. Because those decisions are made and those actions are taken in situations that cannot be observed and supervised by administrative officials, significant differences in the implementation of rights can exist within a single city or a single criminal justice agency.

Gaps between the purported substance of rights and their actual symbolic content also develop because Americans do not share a consensus about how rights should be defined. The definition and protection of rights often become part of policy debates and political battles involving interest groups, election campaigns, and political parties. In the realm of criminal justice, the protection and implementation of constitutional rights are affected by public reactions to and fears about crime. Even after a decade of steady decreases in the rate and occurrence of violent crimes, politicians in the early twenty-first century still use the issue of crime as means to arouse voters' fears and provide reassurances that specific candidates can protect them. For example, candidates in the 2001 mayoral race in New York City ran graphic television commercials about the threat of crime, despite steady decreases in crime for the preceding decade.[11] This time-tested technique for capturing the voters' attention by feeding their fears is especially prevalent when politicians discuss crime and punishment.[12] These political battles help to shape presidential and other elections and, in turn, determine who will be selected to serve on the Supreme Court. Because conservative Republicans held the White House for most of the final years of the twentieth century in which Supreme Court justices retired and were replaced, the Court's composition tilted away from an emphasis on broad rights. As indicated in the chapters of this book, many rights are defined by the Supreme Court in ways that permit those rights to be diminished when the justices place an emphasis on giving criminal justice officials greater flexibility and authority for controlling crime.

One might ask why the Supreme Court's decisions maintain rights that are highly symbolic. The Court could abolish *Miranda* warnings, the exclusionary rule, and other protections that do not flow directly from the words of the Constitution. In so doing, the Court could reduce the public's expectations about rights and thereby close the gaps between the formal definitions of rights and the implementation of those rights. Yet, as indicated by the justices' decision concerning the continuation of *Miranda* warnings in *United States v. Dickerson* (2000), a case discussed in Chapter 6, the Supreme Court may play its own role in providing reassurance to the public that we are blessed with the protection of many constitutional rights, even when those rights are less protective than the Court is willing to admit. Chief Justice Rehnquist's opinion justified the continuation of *Miranda* warnings, in part, by noting that the warnings had become part of our national "culture." In other words, people have come to expect and accept the notion that suspects are entitled to be informed of their rights before questioning. If the Court abolished *Miranda*, the justices might arouse the public in ways that needlessly tarnish the Court's legitimacy. An easier and safer course of action is to keep *Miranda* alive, at least in spirit, while creating exceptions and flexible standards that permit police officers to advance the Supreme Court majority's policy preference for crime control. Perhaps such results fit perfectly well with the preferences of the American public, if Americans like the idea of rights in the abstract, but express a diminished desire for rights when those rights will specifically benefit a criminal suspect, defendant, convicted offender, or suspected terrorist.

Americans' mixed feelings about criminal justice rights may represent one of the difficulties that will always impede our ability to address the issue of symbolic rights. People know that Fourth Amendment rights and other rights apply to protect the innocent as well as the guilty. But as long as law-abiding citizens do not personally encounter overly aggressive police officers who threaten *their* liberty, privacy, and expectations about legal protections, it is difficult for them to become concerned about the reduction of rights for the benefit of lawbreakers whom they fear and read about in the newspaper. Periodically, news stories emerge about middle-class people who are shocked to find themselves drawn into the criminal justice system. They may be arrested through mistaken identity or the unexpectedly aggressive enforcement of minor offenses, such as arrests for failing to wear seatbelts (*Atwater v. City of Lago Vista*, 2001). These eye-opening experiences can change those individuals' views about the importance of rights and trustworthiness of criminal justice officials.[13] For other Americans, however, who feel personally untouched by a specific need for criminal justice rights, it is undoubtedly more difficult to think about how or why they should incorporate such concerns into their thoughts and actions as voters, jurors, campaign contributors, or other roles that may, even in small ways, affect the fulfillment of constitutional rights.

Notes

Chapter 1

1. David G. Savage, "With Conservative Edge, High Court Cuts a Wide Swath," *Los Angeles Times,* July 1, 2001 (www.latimes.com); Linda Greenhouse, "Supreme Court Term, Beyond *Bush v. Gore,*" *New York Times,* July 2, 2001 (www.nytimes.com).
2. Francie Latour and Thomas Farragher, "Sexual Abuse in Suffolk Prison," *Boston Globe,* May 23, 2001 (www.bostonglobe.com); Sean P. Murphy and Michael Rezendes, "Rouse Often an Absentee Sheriff," *Boston Globe,* May 25, 2001 (www.bostonglobe.com).
3. April Witt, "Allegations of Abuse Mar Murder Cases," *Washington Post,* June 3, 2001, A1; April Witt, "Police Bend, Suspend Rule," *Washington Post,* June 5, 2001, A1; April Witt, "Police Tactics Taint Court Rulings, Victims' Lives," *Washington Post,* June 6, 2001, A1.
4. Jim Dwyer, "Ex-Officer Off Tough Beat Seeks to Free the Innocent," *New York Times,* June 10, 2001 (www.nytimes.com).
5. Craig Whitlock and David S. Fallis, "Officers Killed with Impunity: In Every Case, Officials Ruled Firing Was Justified," *Washington Post,* July 1, 2001, A1.
6. Crystal Nix Hines, "Lack of Lawyers Blocking Appeals in Capital Cases," *New York Times,* July 5, 2001 (www.nytimes.com).
7. Stuart A. Scheingold, *The Politics of Rights: Lawyers, Public Policy, and Political Change,* New Haven, Conn.: Yale University Press, 1974, 13.
8. David E. Kyvig, *Explicit and Authentic Acts: Amending the U.S. Constitution, 1776–1995,* Lawrence, Kan.: University Press of Kansas, 1996, 393.
9. Dean Jaros and Robert Roper, "The U.S. Supreme Court: Myth, Diffuse Support, Specific Support, and Legitimacy," *American Politics Quarterly* 8 (1980): 95.
10. Ibid.
11. John M. Scheb II and William Lyons, "Public Holds U.S. Supreme Court in High Regard," *Judicature* 77 (1994): 273–274.
12. Gallup Poll News Service, "Public Opinion of the Supreme Court," December 1, 2000 (www.gallup.com).
13. See, for example, David Barstow and Don Van Atta Jr., "How Bush Took Florida," *New York Times,* July 15, 2001 (www.nytimes.com).
14. Gallup Poll News Service, "Hispanics, Whites Rate Bush Positively, While Blacks Are Much More Negative," June 21, 2001 (www.gallup.com).

15. David Adams, "Top Court Disbars Outspoken Akron Attorney Spittal," *Akron Beacon Journal*, May 31, 1990, A5.
16. Ibid.
17. *Baker v. Carr*, 369 U.S. 186, 267 (1962) (Frankfurter, J., dissenting).
18. *Mistretta v. United States*, 488 U.S. 361, 407 (1989).
19. Joseph Burke, "The Cherokee Cases: A Study in Law, Politics, and Morality," *Stanford Law Review* 21 (1971): 500–547.
20. *Planned Parenthood v. Casey*, 505 U.S. 833 (1992).
21. Christopher E. Smith, *Courts, Politics, and the Judicial Process*, 2nd ed., Chicago: Nelson-Hall, 1997, 151–192.
22. See Philip L. DuBois, *From Ballot to Bench: Judicial Elections and the Quest for Accountability*, Austin, Tex.: University of Texas Press, 1980.
23. See Richard A. Watson and Rondal G. Downing, *The Politics of Bench and Bar*, New York: John Wiley, 1969.
24. See, for example, Sheldon Goldman, "Reagan's Judicial Legacy: Completing the Puzzle and Summing Up," *Judicature* 72 (1989): 318–330; Neil Lewis, "Bush Travels Reagan's Course in Naming Judges," *New York Times*, April 10, 1990, A1; Sheldon Goldman and Elliot Slotnick, "Clinton's Second Term Judiciary: Picking Judges Under Fire," *Judicature* 82 (1999): 265–284.
25. See, for example, Christopher E. Smith, "Polarization and Change in the Federal Courts: *En Banc* Decisions in the U.S. Courts of Appeals," *Judicature* 74 (1990): 133–137; Jeffrey A. Segal and Harold J. Spaeth, *The Supreme Court and the Attitudinal Model*, New York: Cambridge University Press, 1993; Ronald Stidham, Robert A. Carp, and Donald R. Songer, "The Voting Behavior of President Clinton's Judicial Appointees," *Judicature* 80 (1996): 17–20.
26. *South Carolina v. Gathers*, 490 U.S. 805, 824 (1989) (Scalia, J., dissenting).
27. *Payne v. Tennessee*, 501 U.S. 808, 844 (1991) (Marshall, J., dissenting).
28. *Payne v. Tennessee*, 501 U.S. 808, 867 (1991) (Stevens, J., dissenting).
29. Ibid., 856.
30. William H. Rehnquist, *The Supreme Court: How It Was, How It Is*, New York: William Morrow, 1987, 291.
31. Christopher E. Smith and Joyce A. Baugh, *The Real Clarence Thomas: Confirmation Veracity Meets Performance Reality*, New York: Peter Lang, 2000; David A. Schultz and Christopher E. Smith, *The Jurisprudential Vision of Justice Antonin Scalia*, Lanham, Md.: Rowman & Littlefield, 1996.

Chapter 2

1. See George Anastaplo, *The Amendments to the Constitution: A Commentary*, Baltimore: Johns Hopkins University Press, 1995; Robert Allen Rutland, *The Birth of the Bill of Rights, 1776–1791*, Chapel Hill, N.C.: University of North Carolina Press, 1955.
2. See David J. Bodenhamer, *Fair Trial: Rights of the Accused in American History*, New York: Oxford University Press, 1992.
3. See Michael Kent Curtis, *No State Shall Abridge: The Fourteenth Amendment and the Bill of Rights*, Durham, N.C.: Duke University Press, 1986.
4. Christopher E. Smith, "Bright-Line Rules and the Supreme Court: The Tension Between Clarity in Legal Doctrine and Justices' Policy Preferences," *Ohio Northern University Law Review* 16 (1989): 119–137.
5. See Christopher E. Smith and Joyce A. Baugh, *The Real Clarence Thomas: Confirmation Veracity Meets Performance Reality*, New York: Peter Lang, 2000;

David A. Schultz and Christopher E. Smith, *The Jurisprudential Vision of Justice Antonin Scalia*, Lanham, Md.: Rowman & Littlefield, 1996.

6. Archibald Cox, *The Supreme Court and the Constitution*, Boston: Houghton Mifflin, 1987.

7. Miriam Bensimhon, "The Advocates," *Life Magazine* 14 (Fall Special 1991): 98.

8. Lee Epstein and Joseph Kobylka, *The Supreme Court and Legal Change: Abortion and the Death Penalty*, Chapel Hill, N.C.: University of North Carolina Press, 1992.

Chapter 3

1. Charles A. Johnson and Bradley Canon, *Judicial Policies: Implementation and Impact*, 2nd ed.,Washington, D.C.: Congressional Quarterly Press, 1999.

2. Christopher E. Smith and John Hurst, "The Forms of Judicial Policymaking: Civil Liability and Criminal Justice Policy," *The Justice System Journal* 19 (1997): 341–354.

3. Amy Franklin, "Law Officers Briefed on New Weapons Law," *Lansing State Journal*, July 18, 2001, B1.

4. Neal A. Milner, *The Court and Local Law Enforcement: The Impact of Miranda*, Beverly Hills, Calif.: Sage, 1971.

5. See, for example, Victor I. Vieth, "Interviewing the Child Molester: Ten Tips for Eliciting Incriminating Statements," *American Prosecutors Research Institute Update* 11 (1998): 1–2.

6. Milner, 229.

7. April Witt, "Allegations of Abuses Mar Murder Cases," *Washington Post*, June 3, 2001, A1.

8. Adam Liptak, "County Says It's Too Poor to Defend the Poor," *New York Times*, April 15, 2003. Available at www.nytimes.com

Chapter 4

1. Thomas R. Hensley, Christopher E. Smith, and Joyce A. Baugh, *The Changing Supreme Court: Constitutional Rights and Liberties*, St. Paul, Minn.: West/Wadsworth, 1997, 222.

2. *See* dissenting opinion of Justice Harry Blackmun, Employment Division of Oregon v. Smith, 494 U.S. 872 (1990).

3. "Man Recovering from Snake Bite at Church Service," *Lexington Herald*, July 4, 2000. Available at Appalachian Focus Cultural News, www.appalachianfocus.org/_culture/0000000f.htm

4. Information on litigation available at www.rluipa.com, a Web site maintained by the Becket Fund for Religious Liberty.

5. "Student Pleads Guilty in Harassment Incident," *Lansing State Journal*, March 1, 2003, 3B.

6. "U.S. Lawyer Arrested for Wearing a 'Peace' T-Shirt," Reuters News Service, March 4, 2003.

7. Philip Shenon, "Some Secret Documents in Terror Case Can Be Unsealed," *New York Times*, April 22, 2003. Available at www.nytimes.com

8. Hensley et al., 355.

9. Adam Liptak, "Traces of Terror: Immigration: A Court Backs Open Hearings on Deportation," *New York Times*, August 27, 2002, A1.

10. Philip Shenon, "Some Secret Documents in Terror Case Can Be Unsealed," *New York Times*, April 22, 2003. Available at www.nytimes.com

11. Henry J. Abraham, *Freedom and the Court*, 5th ed., New York: Oxford University Press, 1988, 221.

12. George Lardner Jr., "Bill Aimed at Reversing Bush Order on Records," *New York Times,* April 12, 2002, A8.

13. Timothy W. Maier, "Bush Team Thumbs Its Nose at FOIA," Insightmag.com, April 8, 2002. Available at the Web site of The Freedom of Information Center, http://foi.missouri.edu

14. Laura Parker, Kevin Johnson, and Toni Locy, "Secure Often Means Secret Post-9/11, Government Stingy with Information," *USA Today,* May 16, 2002, 1A.

15. Leslie Eaton, "A Flashback to the 60s for an Antiwar Protester," *New York Times,* April 27, 2003. Available at www.nytimes.com

16. Ibid.

17. Kary L. Moss, "Drum-Majors for Justice Should Begin Pounding," *ACLU Michigan Civil Liberties Newsletter,* March 2003, 8.

Chapter 5

1. Kim Curtis, "California Court: Students Can Be Searched," Associated Press Wire Service, August 14, 2001.

2. Jim Irwin, "Critics Assail Arrest Numbers in Detroit Murder Investigations," Associated Press Wire Service, March 23, 2001.

3. "Homicide Investigators Reassigned After Locking Up Witness," Associated Press Wire Service, March 30, 2001.

4. "Report: Suspects Hurt in Police Rides," *Lansing State Journal,* June 3, 2001, 10A.

5. Charles H. Whitebread and Christopher Slobogin, *Criminal Procedure: An Analysis of Cases and Concepts,* 4th ed., New York: Foundation Press, 2000, 150.

6. Jennifer Loven, "Black Women Searched More Often," Associated Press Wire Service, April 10, 2000; General Accounting Office, *U.S. Customs Service: Better Targeting of Airline Passengers for Personal Searches Could Produce Better Results,* Washington, D.C.: Government Printing Office, 2000.

7. David W. Neubauer, *Criminal Justice in Middle America,* Morristown, N.J.: General Learning Press, 1974, 182.

8. Ibid.

9. Christopher E. Smith, "Criminal Justice and the 1998–99 United States Supreme Court Term," *Widener Journal of Public Law,* 1999, 51–52.

10. Christopher E. Smith, "Criminal Justice and the 1996–97 U.S. Supreme Court Term," *University of Dayton Law Review* 23, 1997, 41–42.

Chapter 6

1. Seth Mydans, "The Police Verdict: Los Angeles Policeman Acquitted in Taped Beating," *New York Times,* April 30, 1992, A1.

2. See Ronald Allen, Bard Ferrell, and John Ratnaswamy, "The Double Jeopardy Clause, Constitutional Interpretation, and the Limits of Formal Logic," *Valparaiso University Law Review* 26, 1991, 281–306.

3. See Richard Seeburger and R. Stanton Wettick, "*Miranda* in Pittsburgh: A Statistical Study," *University of Pittsburgh Law Review* 29, 1967, 1–26.

4. See, for example, Richard A. Leo, "*Miranda's* Revenge: Police Interrogation as a Confidence Game," *Law and Society Review* 30, 1996, 259–288.

5. Ibid., 272–273.

6. Victor I. Vieth, "Interviewing the Child Molester: Ten Tips for Eliciting Incriminating Statements," *American Prosecutors Research Institute Update* 11, 1998, 1–2.

7. Paul G. Cassell and Richard Fowles, "Handcuffing the Cops? A Thirty-Year Perspective on *Miranda*'s Harmful Effects on Law Enforcement," *Stanford Law Review* 50, 1998, 1055–1145.

8. See Joseph D. Grano, *Confessions, Truth, and the Law*, Ann Arbor, Mich.: University of Michigan Press, 1993.

9. April Witt, "Allegations of Abuse Mar Murder Cases," *Washington Post*, June 3, 2001, A1.

10. Ibid.

11. Raymond Bonner, "Argument Escalates on Executing Retarded," *New York Times*, July 23, 2001 (www.nytimes.com).

12. Charles H. Whitebread and Christopher Slobogin, *Criminal Procedure: An Analysis of Cases and Concepts*, New York: Foundation Press, 2000, 387–390.

13. George F. Cole and Christopher E. Smith, *Criminal Justice in America*, 3rd ed., Belmont, Calif.: Wadsworth, 2001, 66.

Chapter 7

1. Charles H. Whitebread and Christopher Slobogin, *Criminal Procedure: An Analysis of Cases and Concepts*, New York: Foundation Press, 2000, 655.

2. Ibid.

3. Anthony Lewis, *Gideon's Trumpet*, New York: Random House, 1963, 132–133.

4. Ibid., 237–238.

5. Jim Dwyner, "Testimony of Priest and Lawyer Frees Man Jailed in '87 Murder," *New York Times*, July 25, 2001 (www.nytimes.com).

6. Christopher E. Smith, "Examining the Boundaries of *Bounds*: Prison Law Libraries and Access to the Courts," *Howard Law Journal* 30, 1987, 34–35.

7. See, for example, *Prison Legal News* 12, July 2001, 1–35.

8. Adam Liptak, "County Says It's Too Poor to Defend the Poor," *New York Times*, April 15, 2003. Available at www.nytimes.com

9. See Abraham Blumberg, *Criminal Justice*, Chicago: Quadrangle Books, 1967.

10. R. J. Uphoff, "The Criminal Defense Lawyer: Zealous Advocate, Double Agent, or Beleaguered Dealer?," *Criminal Law Bulletin* 28, 1992, 419–456.

11. James Eisenstein, Roy B. Flemming, and Peter F. Nardulli, *The Contours of Justice: Communities and Their Courts*, Boston: Little, Brown, 1984, 146–147.

12. David Firestone, "Defense System in Georgia Needs Overhaul, Lawyers Say," *New York Times*, July 21, 2001 (www.nytimes.com).

13. "Quality of Representation Is Goal of Defender Services Committee," *The Third Branch* 33, July 2001, 11.

14. Ibid., 10.

15. Stephen B. Bright, "Counsel for the Poor: The Death Sentence Not for the Worst Crime but for the Worst Lawyer," *Yale Law Journal* 103, 1994, 1835–1883; Richard Lacayo, "You Don't Always Get Perry Mason," *Time*, June 1, 1992, 38.

16. Paul M. Barrett, "Lawyer's Fast Work on Death Cases Raises Doubts About System," *Wall Street Journal*, September 7, 1994, 1.

17. Bennett L. Gershman, "Themes of Injustice: Wrongful Conviction, Racial Prejudice, and Lawyer Incompetence," *Criminal Law Bulletin* 29, 1993, 502–515.

Chapter 8

1. Stack v. Boyle, 342 U.S. 1, 5–6 (1951).

2. Talley v. Stephens, 247 F.Supp. 683 (E.D. Ark. 1965).

3. Jackson v. Bishop, 404 F.2d 371 (8th Cir. 1968).
4. Christopher E. Smith, *Law and Contemporary Corrections,* Belmont, Calif.: Wadsworth, 2000, 166–169.
5. Whitley v. Albers, 475 U.S. 312 (1986).
6. Ingraham v. Wright, 430 U.S. 651 (1977).
7. Ibid.
8. Ibid.
9. Ibid.
10. *See* "District Gives 1,326 Paddlings in '92–'93," *Akron Beacon Journal,* May 11, 1994, D2; Christopher E. Smith, "The Use of Research in Local Policy Making: A Case Study of Corporal Punishment in Public Education," *Educational Policy* 10, 1996, 502–517.
11. Pugh v. Locke, 406 F.Supp. 318 (M.D. Ala. 1976).
12. "Jail Fire Victims Were Held on Minor Infractions," Associated Press, May 5, 2002. Available at www.foxnews.com/story/0,2933,51965,00.html
13. *See* Malcolm Feeley and Edward Rubin, *Judicial Policy Making and the Modern State. How the Courts Reformed America's Prisons,* New York: Cambridge University Press, 1998.
14. Wilson v. Seiter, 501 U.S. 294 (1991).
15. Rhodes v. Chapman, 452 U.S. 337 (1981).
16. Falzerano v. Collier, 535 F.Supp. 800,03 (D. N.J. 1982).
17. After three dismissals of "frivolous" cases, prisoners could only seek to have court fees waived for subsequent cases if those cases concerned their immediate health and safety.
18. 28 U.S.C. section 1915.
19. 18 U.S.C. section 3626.
20. Paige M. Harrison and Allen J. Beck, "Prisoners in 2001," *Bureau of Justice Statistics Bulletin,* July 2002, 1.
21. John Scalia, "Prisoner Petitions Filed in U.S. District Courts, 2000, with Trends 1980–2000," *Bureau of Justice Statistics Bulletin,* January 2002, 1.
22. *See* Larry W. Yackle, "The Habeas Hagioscope," *Southern California Law Review* 66, 1993, 2349–2357.
23. *See* www.deathpenaltyinfo.org
24. Ibid.
25. Gomez v. Fierro, 77 F.3d 301 (9th Cir. 1996).
26. Ibid.
27. *See* John C. Tucker, *May God Have Mercy,* New York: Dell, 1998; www.deathpenaltyinfo.org
28. Oral argument in *State* ex. rel. *Amrine v. Luebbers,* Missouri Supreme Court, February 4, 2003. Audio playback available via the Internet at www.missourinet.com
29. *The Case for Innocence,* 2000, PBS film, "Frontline" series. *See* "The Case for Innocence: Update" at www.pbs.org/wgbh/pages/frontline/shows/case/ etc/update.html
30. Gomez v. Fierro, 519 U.S. 918 (1996).
31. *See* Larry C. Berkson, *The Concept of Cruel and Unusual Punishment,* Lexington, Mass.: Lexington Books, 1975.

Chapter 9

1. "Stop the Killing Machine," *The Progressive,* August 2001, 10.
2. Ibid.
3. Pam Belluck, "Nebraska Is Said to Use Death Penalty Unequally," *New York Times,* August 2, 2001 (www.nytimes.com).

4. See Bob Herbert, "Texas Travesty," *New York Times*, August 2, 2001 (www.nytimes.com).

5. Christopher E. Smith, "The Supreme Court and Ethnicity," *Oregon Law Review* 69, 1990, 830.

6. Dennis Dorin, "Far Right of the Mainstream: Racism, Rights, and Remedies from the Perspective of Justice Antonin Scalia's *McCleskey* Memorandum," *Mercer Law Review* 45, 1994, 1077.

7. *Ibid.*, 1077.

8. U.S. v. Armstrong, 116 S.Ct. 1480 (1996) (Stevens, J., dissenting).

9. Michael Tonry, *Malign Neglect: Race, Crime, and Punishment in America*, New York: Oxford University Press, 1995, 94.

10. Stuart Eskenazi, "Minorities Get Searched More Often by Patrol," *Seattle Times*, January 17, 2001 (www.seattletimes.com).

11. John Cloud, "What's Race Got to Do with It," *Time*, July 22, 2001 (www.time.com).

12. *Driving While Black: Racial Profiling on Our Nation's Highways*, An American Civil Liberties Union Special Report, June 1999.

13. General Accounting Office, *U.S. Customs Service: Better Targeting of Airline Passengers for Personal Searches Could Produce Better Results*, Washington, D.C.: Government Printing Office, 2000, 2.

14. See Valerie Han and Neil Vidmar, *Judging the Jury*, New York: Plenum Press, 1986.

15. Purkett v. Elem, 115 S.Ct. 1769, 1770 (1995).

16. Purkett v. Elem, 25 F.3d 679, 683 (1994).

17. Karen Bray, "Reaching the Final Chapter in the Story of Peremptory Challenges," *U.C.L.A. Law Review* 40, 1992, 554–555.

18. See Penny J. White, "An American Without Judicial Independence," *Judicature* 80, 1997, 174–177.

19. See Pugh v. Locke, 406 F.Supp. 318 (M.D. Ala. 1976).

20. See Christopher E. Smith, *Law and Contemporary Corrections*, Belmont, Calif.: West/Wadsworth, 2000, 29–51.

21. Clarence Page, "In Real Life, 'Fugitive' Would Have Been Toast," *Akron Beacon Journal*, September 14, 1993, A9.

22. Christopher E. Smith, "Judicial Policy Making and *Habeas Corpus* Reform," *Criminal Justice Policy Review* 7, 1995, 91–114.

23. Ricardo Solano Jr., "Is Congress Handcuffing Our Courts?," *Seton Hall Law Review* 28, 1997, 282–311.

24. Christopher E. Smith, "United States Magistrates and the Processing of Prisoner Litigation," *Federal Probation* 52, December 1988, 13–18.

Chapter 10

1. Charles H. Whitebread and Christopher Slobogin, *Criminal Procedure: An Analysis of Cases and Concepts*, 4th ed., New York: Foundation Press, 2000, 110.

2. Neil A. Lewis, "Tribunals Nearly Ready for Afghanistan Prisoners," *New York Times*, April 8, 2003. Available at www.nytimes.com

3. Dan Van Atta Jr., "Questioning Terror Suspects in a Dark and Surreal World," *New York Times*, March 9, 2003. Available at www.nytimes.com

4. Ibid.

5. Ibid.

6. Richard A. Serrano, "About 6 Juveniles Found in Guantanamo Camp," *Boston Globe,* April 23, 2003, A2.
7. Neil A. Lewis, "More Prisoners to Be Released from Guantanamo," *New York Times,* May 5, 2003. Available at www.nytimes.com
8. Van Atta, "Questioning Terror Suspects." www.nytimes.com
9. Rafael Espstein, "Detention and Interrogation Methods in the War on Terror," ABC Local Radio-Australia. Available at www.abc.net.au/am/s796322.htm
10. Christopher E. Smith, *Criminal Procedure,* Belmont, Calif.: Wadsworth, 2003, 211.
11. Jane Mayer, "Lost in the Jihad," *The New Yorker,* March 10, 2003, 57.
12. Ibid.
13. Ibid.
14. Ibid., 50.
15. Deborah Sontag, "The Power of the Fourth," *New York Times,* March 9, 2003. Available at www.nytimes.com
16. Ibid.
17. "Shuffled Off in Buffalo," *Christian Science Monitor,* April 7, 2003, 10.
18. "Ashcroft: Critics of New Terror Measures Undermine Effort," Cable News Network, December 7, 2001. Available at http://www.cnn.com/2001/US/12/06/inv.ashcroft.hearing/index.html
19. Henry F. Tepker, "The USA Patriot Act," *Extensions: A Journal of the Carl Albert Congressional Research and Studies Center,* Fall 2002, 11.
20. Kary Moss, "Drum-Majors for Justice Should Begin Pounding," *Civil Liberties Newsletter* 7 (March 2003): 8, "How the USA Patriot Act Allows for the Detention and Deportation of People Engaging in Innocent Associational Activity." Available at http://archive.aclu.org/congress/l102301h.html
21. Neil A. Lewis, "Ashcroft Defends Antiterror Plans and Says Criticism May Aid Foes," *New York Times,* December 7, 2001. Available at www.nytimes.com
22. Ibid.
23. Perle's comments came in response to the journalist's article that criticized Perle for a conflict of interest for chairing the government's most important defense advisory board while also receiving a six-figure consulting fee from business interests for lobbying on their behalf to the Defense Department. CNN Late Edition with Wolf Blitzer, March 9, 2003. Available at www.reclaimdemocracy.org
24. "Justice Denied," *The Washington Spectator,* 29 [5], March 1, 2003, 3.
25. "Orange Alert for Civil Liberties." Available at www.reclaimdemocracy.org
26. Ibid.
27. John Solomon, "New Allegations Target DNA, Bullet Analysis at FBI Lab," (Associated Press) *Lansing State Journal,* April 16, 2003, 3A.
28. Robin Toner, "Despite Some Concerns, Civil Liberties Are Taking a Back Seat," *New York Times,* November 18, 2001. Available at www.nytimes.com
29. Ibid.
30. Nat Hentoff, "Vanishing Liberties," *The Village Voice,* April 11, 2003. Available at www.villagevoice.com
31. Ibid.
32. Ibid.
33. Ibid., quoting William H. Rehnquist, *All the Laws But One: Civil Liberties in Wartime,* New York: Knopf/Vintage, 1998.

Chapter 11

1. Christopher E. Smith, *Courts, Politics, and Judicial Process,* 2nd ed., Chicago: Nelson-Hall, 1997, 293–301.
2. Charles H. Whitebread and Christopher Slobogin, *Criminal Procedure: An Analysis of Cases and Concepts,* New York: Foundation Press, 2000, 655.
3. Christopher E. Smith, "Bright-Line Rules and the Supreme Court: The Tension Between Clarity in Judicial Doctrine and Justices' Policy Preferences," *Ohio Northern University Law Review* 16, 1989, 119–137.
4. Larry W. Yackle, "The Habeas Hagioscope," *Southern California Law Review* 66, 1993, 2331.
5. Christopher E. Smith, "Criminal Justice and the U.S. Supreme Court's 1999–2000 Term," *North Dakota Law Review* 77, 2001, 1–26.
6. Interview with Chief Justice William Rehnquist in documentary film *This Honorable Court* (PBS Television Broadcast, September 12, 1989).
7. John Cloud, "What's Race Got to Do with It," *Time,* July 22, 2001 (www.time.com).
8. Richard Lezin Jones, "Mayor Backs Bill to Make Police Report Race in Frisks," *New York Times,* July 26, 2001 (www.nytimes.com).
9. Cloud, "What's Race Got to Do with It."
10. Christopher E. Smith and John Hurst, "The Forms of Judicial Policy Making: Civil Liability and Criminal Justice Policy," *The Justice System Journal* 19, 1997, 341–354.
11. Michael Cooper, "Your Vote or Your Life: Ads Focus on Old Crime Fears," *New York Times,* August 19, 2001 (www.nytimes.com).
12. See Murray Edelman, *The Symbolic Uses of Politics,* Urbana, Ill.: University of Illinois Press, 1964.
13. See, for example, Chris Kridler, "Sergeant Friday, Where Are You?," *Newsweek,* May 17, 1989, 14; Byronn Bain, "Walking While Black: The Bill of Rights for Black Men," *Village Voice,* April 26–May 2, 2000 (www.villagevoice.com/issues/0017/bain.php).

Table of Cases

Glossary

adversarial legal process The legal process model employed in the United States in which the truth is presumed to emerge from the clash of opposing advocates in the courtroom, and therefore the attorney's performance is a key factor in determining the fate of individuals drawn into the court system.

advisory opinions An opinion interpreting a statute, regulation, or other law based on a hypothetical situation rather than an actual case. Such opinions are sometimes issued by state attorneys general to give guidance to government officials about the meaning of a law, but the U.S. Supreme Court will not issue such opinions, even if asked to do so by Congress or the president.

affidavit Written statement of fact, supported by oath or affirmation, that police officers may submit to judicial officers to fulfill the requirements of "probable cause" for obtaining a warrant.

American ideology Dominant values and beliefs concerning government and society in the United States, including an emphasis on such elements as individualism, personal liberty, limited government, and equality in the eyes of the law.

anecdotal evidence Isolated examples of a phenomenon; contrasts with the systematic collection of data that produces statistical evidence about phenomena.

Antiterrorism and Effective Death Penalty Act of 1996 Congressional legislation that made it more difficult for convicted offenders to file *habeas corpus* petitions.

appeal Challenge to the result of a trial court decision that is raised before a higher court with the authority to overrule the previous court decision. Appeals must be based on specific allegations of errors in law and procedure, such as the admission of improper evidence or incorrect jury instruction. Generally, determinations of guilt and the severity of sentences are not appealable.

appointed counsel Private practice attorney who accepts appointments from the court to represent indigent criminal defendants for modest hourly wages.

acquittal The result of a criminal trial when a defendant is found by the judge or jury to be "not guilty" of the crime.

Article III, U.S. Constitution Provision of the U.S. Constitution that defines the role and powers of federal courts and judges.

authority   Range and extent of decision making and action by government officials that is permitted under law.

Bail Reform Act of 1984   Federal statute that explicitly empowers federal judges to deny bail to defendants who, after the presentation of evidence at a bail hearing, are found to be likely to flee or to pose a danger to community.

bench trial   A trial conducted in front of a judge with no jury present.

Bill of Rights   The first ten amendments to the U.S. Constitution that define the relationship between individuals and government by giving individuals specific protections under law.

case or controversy   The actual conflict between individuals, businesses, or government actors that must exist in order for the courts to accept an issue for hearing.

challenge for cause   The authority of prosecutors and defense attorneys to request the exclusion of any jurors whose responses to questions from the attorneys and judge indicate the existence of a bias that could interfere with the individual jurors' capacity to be neutral decision makers in the trial at hand.

change of venue   An order moving the location of a trial from the jurisdiction where the crime occurred to a different city where the citizens who will serve as jurors have heard less information about the case.

civil rights lawsuits   Civil lawsuits, usually seeking financial awards, filed by individuals against government officials for alleged violations of the individuals' constitutional rights.

collegial court   A court comprised of multiple judges, such as an American appellate court, in which the judges must interact and work together in order to reach a decision.

concurrent sentences   The sentences for multiple offenses served simultaneously.

consecutive sentences   The sentences for multiple offenses served back to back, with the sentence for the second crime beginning after completion of the sentence for the first crime.

constitution   The fundamental laws contained in state or federal documents that outline the design of the government and the basic rights for individuals.

continuance   A delay in court proceedings requested by one side in the case and approved by the trial judge.

contract counsel   Private practice attorney who bids on a year-long contract to handle representation of indigent criminal defendants in a specific county or city.

contracts   Legally enforceable agreements between individuals, businesses, and government agencies that create entitlements and obligations for each party to the agreement.

courts of last resort   The highest courts in the hierarchy of American judicial systems. In the United States, this term refers to the U.S. Supreme Court in the federal system and state supreme courts within state judicial systems.

defamation   Civil law cause of action that permits individuals to sue news media, publishers, and other individuals for publishing statements that are false and harmful. Slander actions concern defamatory words that are spoken, and libel actions concern defamatory statements that are written.

dicta   Discussion in a judicial opinion, other than the statement of the rule of the case, which does not create a precedent for other courts to follow.

enemy combatant   Designation created by the U.S. government and applied to selected American citizens as part of the "war" against terrorism in order to deny those Americans any constitutional rights.

exclusionary rule   Legal principle that evidence obtained in violation of a person's constitutional rights cannot be used against the person in a criminal prosecution.

Ex Post Facto Clause   Constitutional protection against *ex post facto* laws whereby the government defines crimes or increases punishments after the newly prohibited act or crime has already been committed.

forfeiture   Government seizure of property under statutory authority, especially when that property may have been used in or acquired from criminal enterprises.

Fourteenth Amendment   Provision added to the Constitution after the Civil War to provide individuals with constitutional rights against actions by state and local governments. These rights include "due process of law" and "equal protection of the laws."

Geneva Conventions   International meetings that produced agreements signed by most of the world's countries concerning the rules of war and the treatment of prisoners of war.

good-faith exception   Exception to the exclusionary rule that permits the use of improperly obtained evidence when police officers acted in honest reliance on a warrant improperly issued by a magistrate, defective statute, or a consent to search by someone who lacked the authority to give such permission.

habeas corpus   A traditional legal action filed by an offender who has been unsuccessful in the appellate process but who wishes to allege that his or her federal constitutional rights were violated during the investigation and prosecution of a criminal case. This petition permits a federal judge to review prior actions and decisions in state criminal cases.

harmless error   Legal concept applied by appellate courts to trial court errors that are not believed to have affected the verdict and therefore do not justify overturning a conviction.

holding   The statement of the legal rule in a judicial opinion that will serve as a precedent for later cases.

hung jury   A deadlocked jury that is unable to reach a conclusion and therefore leads to the declaration of a mistrial by the judge. In a criminal trial, the prosecutor must decide whether to conduct an entirely new trial in front of a new jury or to dismiss the charges against the defendant.

impeach testimony   To show through witness testimony or other evidence presented in court that a witness testified in an untruthful manner or should be regarded as an unreliable source of information.

implementation   The process of carrying out a law so that it affects people's lives. In effect, implementation translates the law into policies, which do not necessarily fulfill the lawmakers' intentions if there are problems with cooperation, communication, and resources for the people, such as lower court judges and police officers, who must interpret and apply laws in order to implement them.

incommunicado interrogation   Questioning of an individual by government officials in a private setting in which there are no witnesses present nor attorneys to represent the individual. Such interrogation raises the risk of abusive techniques employed to coerce confessions without providing the individual with any opportunity to prove that improper pressure was applied.

incorporation   The process by which the U.S. Supreme Court applies provisions of the Bill of Rights to state and local governments by including those provisions in the Due Process Clause of the Fourteenth Amendment.

indigent defendants   Criminal defendants who are too poor to hire their own attorneys and therefore are entitled to have attorneys supplied for them by the state when they face the possibility of incarceration.

ineffective assistance of counsel   A difficult-to-prove rights violation claim asserted by convicted offenders who claim that their attorneys' performances were so inadequate that they failed to fulfill the requirements of the Sixth Amendment.

inevitable discovery exception   Exception to the exclusionary rule that permits the use of improperly obtained evidence when it would have been discovered eventually anyway through legal investigatory processes that were already in progress.

legitimacy   The image of governmental institutions, especially courts, in the eyes of the public that affect the public's respect for and obedience to decisions by those institutions.

natural rights theory   The philosophy of rights underlying the U.S. Constitution and based on the idea that all human beings, whether good or bad, are entitled to protections against improper government actions.

obscenity   Depictions of sexual activity and other matters that, due to their extreme nature, are not included under the protections for free expression in the First Amendment. Many materials with sexual content, such as a variety of books, paintings, photographs, and films, are protected. The Supreme Court asserts that certain depictions can be regulated because they are "obscene," yet it has struggled to develop a workable definition of obscenity that will permit observers to identify which films, photographs, and other materials can be banned.

originalism   An approach to constitutional interpretation, also known as "original intent jurisprudence," that seeks to interpret constitutional provisions according to the intentions of the people who wrote those provisions.

peremptory challenge   The authority of prosecutors and defense attorneys to exclude a limited number of potential jurors without giving any reason as long as the exclusion is not admitted to be based on the potential juror's race or gender.

petty offense   A crime for which the maximum punishment is six months or less of incarceration or nonincarcerative punishments.

plain view doctrine   Doctrine that permits police officers to identify criminal evidence that is openly visible from a vantage point of a location where they are legally permitted to be and to seize such items on public property or on private property where they are lawfully located.

plurality opinion   Judicial opinion supported by the largest number of justices or judges on an appellate court when there is no opinion supported by a majority of justices or judges. Plurality opinions can determine the outcome of a case, but they do not establish precedent.

politically protected privileges   Privileges protected by legislative and executive officials because of the power of pressure from voters or the influence of wealthy and persuasive interest groups. Such privileges are potentially more secure and enduring than constitutional rights that can be changed instantly through a judicial decision reinterpreting the Constitution.

power   Decision making and action undertaken by government officials and others, especially that which forces other individuals to engage in involuntary actions, including such decisions and actions that are not permitted by law.

prejudice   A legal term for a disadvantage imposed on one party in a case. If a judge dismisses criminal charges "with prejudice," it typically imposes a disadvantage on the prosecutor by barring the refiling of those charges. In evaluating possible violations of the right to speedy trial, the courts must examine whether the delay in the case caused prejudice or disadvantage to the preparation and presentation of the defendant's case.

presumption of innocence   Legal concept underlying American criminal justice system that requires the prosecution to prove a criminal defendant's guilt because no inferences about culpability are to be drawn from the fact that police chose to investigate and arrest a specific individual.

pretext   Decision or action taken under the claim of a specific justification that is actually undertaken for a different reason, such as police officers stopping a motorist based on racial profiling but claiming that the stop was for a traffic violation.

Prison Litigation Reform Act   Congressional legislation that made it more difficult for prisoners to file civil rights lawsuits and limited the authority of federal judges to order remedies and supervise correctional authorities in the aftermath of such lawsuits.

privileges   Unlike rights, which are protected by the Constitution, privileges are entitlements granted by an authority, such as the government, that are also subject to regulation and removal by that same authority.

procedural criminal law   Statutes and judicial decisions that mandate the steps in the criminal justice process and provide legal protections for criminal suspects, defendants, and convicted offenders.

profiling   Police practice of targeting for observation, investigation, and searches certain groups of people based on physical and behavioral characteristics. Such activities can produce illegal discrimination if profiling is based on race, gender, or ethnicity.

public defender   Criminal defense attorney who works exclusively for indigent defendants as a salaried government employee.

public safety exception   Exception to *Miranda* requirements that permits police to immediately question a suspect in custody without providing any warnings when public safety would be jeopardized by taking the time to supply the warnings.

regulations   Legal rules created by government agencies based on authority delegated to them by legislatures, governors, or presidents.

Religious Freedom Restoration Act   The congressional statute designed to counteract Justice Scalia's opinion in *Employment Division of Oregon v. Smith* by imposing a higher burden of justification upon government actions colliding with free exercise of religion, including actions in the corrections setting. The statute was declared unconstitutional by the U.S. Supreme Court in *City of Boerne v. Flores* (1997).

Religious Land Use and Institutionalized Persons Act   The congressional statute designed to require judges to apply the strict scrutiny standard in free exercise of religion cases affecting land use and those concerning institutionalized persons after the Supreme Court struck down the Religious Freedom Restoration Act.

rights   Individuals' legally protected entitlements, especially those found in the provisions of the Bill of Rights in the U.S. Constitution.

serious offense A crime for which the punishment is six months or more of incarceration.

social contract philosophy A philosophy of rights based on the idea that people lose their claim to society's benefits if they violate society's rules.

stare decisis Reliance on case precedents in making judicial decisions.

statutes Law created by the people's elected representatives in legislatures.

strict scrutiny test The usual test for the constitutionality of laws, regulations, and government officials' actions affecting fundamental rights. The test requires that the government bear the burden of showing a compelling reason for its regulation and that the regulation take the least restrictive approach.

substantive criminal law Laws that define which behaviors will be subject to punishment by government.

symbolic right A right that has not been implemented according to the words of a constitution, statute, or judicial decision and thus provides less protection than people expect.

testimonial evidence The type of evidence covered under the privilege against compelled self-incrimination because it consists of statements by the suspect that might otherwise be used against him or her in court.

unlawful combatants Designation used by the U.S. government for foreign fighters captured in Afghanistan during the American military action there in the aftermath of the tragic attacks on New York and Washington on September 11, 2001. The designation was created and used in order to avoid giving the captives the rights to which they would be entitled if they were designated as "prisoners of war" and thereby covered by the Geneva Conventions.

voir dire The process of selecting jurors in which potential jurors are asked questions by attorneys and the judge.

Index